P9-EMK-276

DISCARD
HIALEAH GARDENS
MEDIA CENTER 7191

Early Civilizations in the Americas
Almanac

Early Civilizations in the Americas Almanac

Volume 1

Sonia Benson

Deborah J. Baker, Project Editor

U.X.L
A part of Gale, Cengage Learning

GALE
CENGAGE Learning™

Detroit • New York • San Francisco • New Haven, Conn • Waterville, Maine • London

GALE
CENGAGE Learning·

Early Civilizations in the Americas: Almanac
Sonia Benson

Project Editor
Deborah J. Baker

Editorial
Michael D. Lesniak, Sarah Hermsen, Mary Bonk, Allison McNeill, Ralph Zerbonia

Rights Acquisitions and Management
Shalice Shah-Caldwell, William Sampson

Imaging and Multimedia
Kelly A. Quin, Lezlie Light, Dan Newell

Product Design
Jennifer Wahi, Pamela Galbreath

Composition and Electronic Prepress
Evi Seoud

Manufacturing
Rita Wimberley

©2005 Gale, a part of Cengage Learning

For more information, contact:
Gale
27500 Drake Rd.
Farmington Hills, MI 48331-3535
Or you can visit our Internet site at gale.cengage.com

ALL RIGHTS RESERVED
No part of this work covered by the copyright hereon may be reproduced or used in any form or by any means—graphic, electronic, or mechanical, including photocopying, recording, taping, Web distribution, or information storage retrieval systems—without the written permission of the publisher.

For permission to use material from this product, submit your request via Web at http://www.gale-edit.com/permissions, or you may download our Permissions Request form and submit your request by fax or mail to:

Permissions Department
Gale
27500 Drake Rd.
Farmington Hills, MI 48331-3535
Permissions Hotline:
248-699-8006 or 800-877-4253, ext. 8006
Fax: 248-699-8074 or 800-762-4058

While every effort has been made to ensure the reliability of the information presented in this publication, Gale, a part of Cengage Learning does not guarantee the accuracy of data contained herein. Gale accepts no payment for listing; and inclusion in the publication of any organization, agency, institution, publication, service, or individual does not imply endorsement by the editors or publisher. Errors brought to the attention of the publisher and verified to the satisfaction of the publisher will be corrected in future editions.

LIBRARY OF CONGRESS CATALOGING-IN-PUBLICATION DATA

Benson, Sonia.

Early civilizations in the Americas. Almanac / Sonia G. Benson ; Deborah J. Baker, project editor.

p. cm. – (Early civilizations in the Americas reference library)

Includes bibliographical references and indexes.

ISBN 0-7876-9252-2 (set : hardcover : alk. paper) – ISBN 0-7876-7679-9 (v. 1) – ISBN—0-7876-7681-0 (v. 2) – ISBN 0-7876-9395-2 (e-book)

1. Indians–Antiquities–Juvenile literature. 2. America–Antiquities–Juvenile—literature. I. Baker, Deborah J. II. Title. III. Series.

E77.4.B46 2005

980'.012–dc22

2004020163

This title is also available as an e-book.
ISBN 0-7876-9395-2 (set).
Contact your Gale representative for ordering information.

Printed in the United States of America
3 4 5 6 7 8 14 13 12 11 10 09 08

Contents

Reader's Guide ix
Timeline of Events xiii
Words to Know xxi
Research and Activity Ideas xxxvii

Volume 1
Chapter 1: Introduction to Early American Civilizations . . 1
    The World's First Civilizations (box) 5
    Steps to Civilization: Worldwide Firsts (box). . . . 6
    Sumer, Mesopotamia: The Cradle of
    Civilization (box) 9

Chapter 2: Before the Rise of Civilization:
The First Americans 19
    Native American Graves Protection and
    Repatriation Act (box) 30

Chapter 3: Early Andeans: From Nomads to City Folk . . 35
    The First Mummies (box) 41
    New World Camelids (box) 42

Chapter 4: Chavín Culture 59
    Oracles (box) 68

Chapter 5: Nazca Society 75
    An Alternative Idea about the
    Nazca Lines (box) 83

Chapter 6: Moche Culture 87
    Finding the Lord of Sipán (box) 94

Chapter 7: Tiwanaku Culture 105
    The Tiwanaku Ruins (box) 113
    A Little Help from the Ancients (box) 117

Chapter 8: Wari Culture 121
    Chicha and the Reciprocity Ceremony (box) . . 131

Chapter 9: Kingdom of Chimor 137

Chapter 10: The Rise of the Incas 155
    The Chroniclers of the Inca Empire (box) 168
    The Inca Rulers (box) 171

Chapter 11: Inca Government and Economy 179
    The Administrative Hierarchy (box) 187

Chapter 12: Inca Religion, Arts, and Sciences 199
    Inca State Ceremonies (box) 209
    Runasimi: The Quechua Language (box) 214
    Inca Medicine (box) 218

Chapter 13: Daily Life in the Inca Empire 221
    The History of the Potato (box) 234

Chapter 14: The Conquest of the Incas **241**
    The Smallpox Epidemic (box) 244
    The Last Words of the Last Conquistador (box) . 255

Where to Learn More . . . . **xlv**
Index . . . . **xlix**

Volume 2

Chapter 15: Early Mesoamerican Peoples **261**
    Timeline of Early Mesoamerica (box) 268

Chapter 16: Olmec Culture **275**

Chapter 17: Zapotecs and Monte Albán **299**
    The First Mesoamerican Calendar
    Systems (box) 306

Chapter 18: Teotihuacán **315**
    Teotihuacán and the Aztec Legend of
    the Fifth Sun (box) 324

Chapter 19: Mystery of the Maya **333**
    A Note about Rain Forests (box) 340

Chapter 20: The Rise and Fall of Maya Cities **347**
    San Bartolo (box) 352

Chapter 21: Maya Religion and Government **371**
    The Epic Tale of the Hero Twins (box) 376

Chapter 22: Maya Arts and Sciences **391**
    Deciphering the Work of Scribes (box) 394
    The Bonampak Murals (box) 404

Chapter 23: Maya Economy and Daily Life **415**
    Xocolatl: The Drink of the Gods (box) 430

In the Eye of the Beholder (box) 432
The Lacandón Maya (box) 435

Chapter 24: Toltec Culture **437**
Two Early Societies of the United States (box) . . 452

Chapter 25: The Rise of the Aztecs **457**
Two Spanish Sources: Sahagún and Díaz (box). . 468
The Man behind the Emperors (box) 472

Chapter 26: Aztec Government and Economy **477**
The Aztec Kings and Emperors,
1376 to 1521 (box) 484

Chapter 27: Aztec Religion, Culture, and Daily Life . . . **501**

Chapter 28: The Conquest of the Aztecs **529**
The Conquistadores (box) 534
The Toll of Epidemics on the Native
Populations of Mexico (box) 542

Where to Learn More . . . . **xlv**
Index . . . . **xlix**

Reader's Guide

Many American history books begin with the year 1492 and the discovery of the Caribbean Islands by Spanish explorer Christopher Columbus (1451–1506). For the great civilizations of Mesoamerica and South America, though, 1492 proved to be the beginning of the end of their civilization. The products of thousands of years of history—the great cities, the architecture, markets, governments, economic systems, legal systems, schools, books, holy shrines—even the daily prayers of the people—were about to be willfully eliminated by the conquering European nations. The rupture would prove so deep that many aspects of pre-Hispanic American culture and tradition were forever deleted from the human memory. Fortunately, some of the important history of the early civilizations has survived and more is being recovered every day.

The three-volume Early Civilizations in the Americas Reference Library provides a comprehensive overview of the history of the regions of the American continents in which two of the world's first civilizations developed: Mesoamerica (the name for the lands in which ancient civilizations arose in Central America and Mexico) and the Andes Mountains region of South America (in present-day Peru and parts of Bolivia, northern Argentina, and Ecuador). In both regions, the history of civilization goes back thousands of years. Recent studies show that the first cities in the Americas may have arisen as early as 2600 B.C.E. in the river valleys of present-day Peru. The earliest evidence of civilization in Mesoamerica dates back to about 2000 B.C.E.

When the Spanish conquistadores (conquerors) arrived in Mesoamerica and the Andes in 1521 and 1531, respectively, they found many native societies, but they were most amazed by two great empires–the Aztecs and the Incas. In the early sixteenth century the Aztecs and the Incas had spectacular cities that could rival those of Europe in size, art and architecture, organization, and engineering. These capital cities ruled over vast empires—the Aztecs with a population of more than 15 million and the Incas with a population of about 12 million—with remarkable efficiency.

The Spaniards at that time could not have understood how many civilizations had preceded those of the Aztecs and the Incas, each one bringing its own advances to the empires they witnessed. In the Andes, many of the key ingredients of civilization were in place by 2600 B.C.E. in early urban centers. From that time forward, the Andean culture was adopted, developed, and slowly transformed by the societies of the Chavín, the Moche, the Nazca, the Wari, the Tiwanaku, and the Chimú, among many others, before the Incas rose to power. Mesoamerican civilization apparently had its roots in the early societies of the Olmecs and Zapotecs, whose ancestors were living in present-day central Mexico by 2000 B.C.E. The Mayas skillfully adopted the calendars, glyph-writing, art and architecture, astronomy, and many other aspects of these earlier civilizations, adding greatly to the mix. The people of the great city of Teotihuacán and later the Toltecs created vast empires that unified the Mesoamerican culture. Later the Aztecs created a government that encompassed all of these early civilizations.

Early Civilizations of the Americas: Almanac presents the story of this development—the dates, locations, sites, history, arts and sciences, religions, economies, governments, and eventual declines of the great ancient American civilizations. Volume 1 features an overview of ancient civilization in general and a brief summary of modern theories about the earliest immigrants and early life in the Americas. The remainder of the volume focuses on the rise of the Andean civilization from the early urban centers to the Inca empire. Volume 2 focuses on the rise of the Mesoamerican civilizations from the Olmecs through the Aztecs.

A note about the use of the word "civilization" in these volumes. The word "civilization" is used here to convey the type of organization and the size of a society, and certainly not to make a quality judgment about whether the society was sophisticated or refined. Besides the civilizations that arose in Mesoamerica and the Andean region, there were thousands of indigenous (native) societies throughout the two American continents with varying levels of the kind of organization experts call "civilization." The civilizations featured in Early Civilizations in the Americas Reference Library are the New World civilizations that developed around the same time and with some patterns similar to the first civilizations of the Old World: Mesopotamia, Egypt, the Indus Valley, and China. Their history has been little known until the last century; indeed, only recent studies have included the Americas in the list of the world's first civilizations.

Features

Early Civilizations in the Americas: Almanac contains numerous sidebar boxes that highlight people and events of special interest, and each chapter offers a list of additional sources that students can consult for more information. The material is illustrated by 192 black-and-white photographs and illustrations. Each volume begins with a timeline of important events in the history of the early American civilizations, a "Words to Know" section that introduces students to difficult or unfamiliar terms, and a "Research and Activity Ideas" section. The volumes conclude with a general bibliography and a subject index so students can easily find the people, places, and events discussed throughout *Early Civilizations in the Americas: Almanac.*

Early Civilizations in the Americas Reference Library

The two-volume *Early Civilizations in the Americas: Almanac* is one of two components of the three-volume U•X•L

Early Civilizations in the Americas Reference Library. The other title in the set is:

- ***Early Civilizations in the Americas: Biographies and Primary Sources*** (one volume) presents a collection of biographies and primary sources—both text and photographs of artifacts—that provide detailed and focused views of the people of the early American civilizations, the artifacts they left behind, and the sources upon which the history of the early American civilizations are based. The volume is divided into three chapters: the Incas, the Mayas and their Ancestors, and the Aztec Empire. Each chapter is arranged loosely by topic and chronology. The biographies include Inca emperor Pachacutec, Maya king Pacal, and Aztec emperor Montezuma II. The primary sources feature artifacts such as the Inca *quipu,* or knotted counting cords, the Maya sacred calendar, and the Aztec Sun Stone. Also included are excerpts from the memoirs and histories compiled by indigenous writers and Spanish missionaries and conquerors in the decades following the conquest.

- A cumulative index of both titles in the U•X•L Early Civilizations in the Americas Reference Library is also available.

Comments and Suggestions

We welcome your comments on *Early Civilizations in the Americas: Almanac* as well as suggestions for other topics to consider. Please write to: Editor, *Early Civilizations in the Americas: Almanac,* U•X•L, 27500 Drake Road, Farmington Hills, Michigan, 48331-3535; call toll-free: 800-877-4253; fax to 248-699-8097; or send e-mail via http://www.gale.com.

Timeline of Events

40,000–15,000 B.C.E. The earliest people to settle in the Americas begin their migrations to the North and South American continents.

c. 15,000–12,000 B.C.E. People leave behind traces of their life at a camp now called Meadowcroft Rockshelter in present-day Pennsylvania.

c. 11,000 B.C.E. People regularly camp at a tiny settlement now called Monte Verde in south-central Chile.

c. 9000 B.C.E. A group of hunter-gatherers called the Clovis culture becomes widespread throughout the present-day United States and Mexico.

c. 25,000 B.C.E.
Homo sapiens use small pits lined with hot embers to cook food

c. 10,000 B.C.E.
Humans populated most of the major landmasses on Earth

20,000 B.C.E.   10,000 B.C.E.

c. 7000 B.C.E. Worldwide climate change alters the environments of the Americas.

c. 7000–3000 B.C.E. Formerly nomadic people in the Andes Mountain region of South America begin to settle into rough homes, gradually forming tiny villages.

c. 6000–4000 B.C.E. People begin to farm and raise animals in the Andean region.

c. 5000 B.C.E. Simple farming begins in Mesoamerica.

c. 3000 B.C.E. The Andean people in a number of different areas begin building very large ceremonial complexes (large, urban centers where people come to practice their religion) and make advances in art, religion, politics, and trade.

c. 2600 B.C.E. The city of Caral arises in the Supe Valley of Peru. It has thousands of permanent residents, complex architecture, and trade, and small urban centers surround it. Caral may have been the first city of the Americas.

c. 2500–1600 B.C.E. Mesoamericans in some regions form tiny villages.

c. 2500 B.C.E. An engraving of an Andean god known as the Staff God is carved on a bowl made from a gourd in Peru. It is the oldest known religious artifact in the Andean region.

c. 2200 B.C.E. Pottery appears in Mesoamerica.

c. 1800 B.C.E. Andean societies begin to organize themselves by the river valleys in which they live.

c. 1600 B.C.E.–150 C.E. Large permanent settlements begin to form in Mesoamerica; in the Oaxaca (pronounced wah-HAH-kah) Valley and the Valley of Mexico.

---

c. 7000 B.C.E.
The first human settlements were developed in Mesopotamia

c. 3500 B.C.E.
Beginnings of Sumerian civilization

c. 2680–2526 B.C.E.
Building of the Great Pyramids near Giza, Egypt

c. 1792–1750 B.C.E.
Hammurabi creates empire of Babylonia

| 7000 B.C.E. | 4000 B.C.E. | 3000 B.C.E. | 2000 B.C.E. |

c. 1500–1200 B.C.E. The earliest distinct Olmec culture emerges in San Lorenzo, along the Gulf of Mexico, south of Veracruz.

c. 800 B.C.E. The Chavín people in the northern highlands of Peru begin to build their ceremonial center, Chavín de Huántar (pronounced cha-VEEN deh WAHN-tar). Their religion and culture spreads through a vast area, unifying many communities of the Andes.

650 B.C.E. The first known example of writing from the Americas is carved by an Olmec artist onto a ceramic stamp bearing what appears to be a royal seal.

600 B.C.E. Another early example of Mesoamerican writing—a glyph, or a figure representing a calendar date was found at a Zapotec site—dates back to this time.

500 B.C.E. Building begins on the Zapotec city of Monte Albán in the Oaxaca Valley.

c. 400 B.C.E. The Olmec city La Venta experiences upheaval and never recovers. The ancient civilization begins a rapid decline.

c. 200 B.C.E. The Chavín culture in the Andean region collapses.

c. 200 B.C.E.–200 C.E. The Zapotec city of Monte Albán rules over the Oaxaca Valley.

c. 150 B.C.E. The Maya cities of Cival and El Mirador arise in the present-day Guatemalan state of Petén.

c. 100 B.C.E.–700 C.E. The Nazca people make large-scale drawings in the desert sands of present-day Peru.

c. 1 C.E. The communities of the Andes mountain valleys create armies for defense; military actions become widespread in some parts of the region.

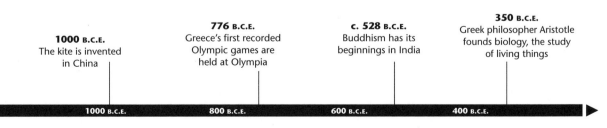

1000 B.C.E.
The kite is invented in China

776 B.C.E.
Greece's first recorded Olympic games are held at Olympia

c. 528 B.C.E.
Buddhism has its beginnings in India

350 B.C.E.
Greek philosopher Aristotle founds biology, the study of living things

1000 B.C.E.   800 B.C.E.   600 B.C.E.   400 B.C.E.

c. 1 C.E. The Moche people begin to build their state, ruling from Cerro Grande in the southern Andean region and from various northern cities.

c. 200 City of Tiwanaku arises on Lake Titicaca in present-day Bolivia with a population of about 50,000 and advanced arts and religion.

c. 250 The classic Maya era begins, in which the cities of Tikal, Palenque, and Copán flourish in the southern highlands of the Maya world.

400–700 The city of Teotihuacán in the Valley of Mexico rules over a vast economic empire that includes much of the southern two-thirds of Mexico, most of Guatemala and Belize, and some parts of Honduras and El Salvador. The city reaches its height around 500 C.E. with a population between 100,000 and 200,000 people. It is the sixth largest city in the world at this time.

c. 500–600 The city of Wari arises in the south-central area of present-day Peru and begins to spread its rule and influence to surrounding regions.

615 Maya king Pacal begins his rule of Palenque; the city builds its greatest architecture during his long reign.

695 18 Rabbit begins his rule of Copán, bringing about a new age of art and writing in the city.

c. 700–900 The cities of Tiwanaku and Wari both hold influence over large, but separate, areas of the Central Andes in what may have been the first empire-building era in the Americas.

c. 750 The powerful city of Teotihuacán in the Valley of Mexico is destroyed and abandoned.

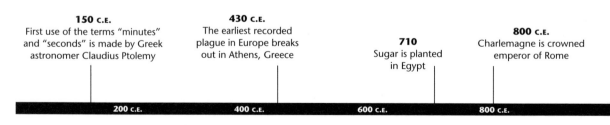

150 C.E.
First use of the terms "minutes" and "seconds" is made by Greek astronomer Claudius Ptolemy

430 C.E.
The earliest recorded plague in Europe breaks out in Athens, Greece

710
Sugar is planted in Egypt

800 C.E.
Charlemagne is crowned emperor of Rome

200 C.E.   400 C.E.   600 C.E.   800 C.E.

850 The Chimú begin to build their capital city of Chan Chan in northern coastal Peru. It will thrive for more than six centuries, with a peak population of 50,000 to 70,000 people.

c. 900 The classic Maya era ends when the dominant cities of the southern highlands, including Tikal, Palenque, and Copán, are abandoned. The Mayas scatter, but Maya cities in the present-day Mexican state of Yucatán, particularly Chichén Itzá (pronounced chee-CHEN eet-SAH) become powerful in the Maya world.

c. 968 Toltec ruler Topiltzin-Quetzalcoatl (pronounced toe-PEEL-tzin kates-ahl-koh-AH-tul) establishes the Toltec capital at Tula in the Valley of Mexico.

1000 A profound Toltec influence takes over Chichén Itzá.

1064 After upheaval in the Toltec capital of Tula, most Toltecs abandon the city.

c. 1100 The Tiwanaku and the Wari abandon their cities.

1150 The Chimú begin to expand their empire. By the fifteenth century, it is the largest pre-Inca empire of the Andean region.

c. 1200 Mayas in the present-day Mexican state of Yucatán shift their capital to the city of Mayapán. Chichén Itzá begins to decline.

1200 The Incas rise to prominence in Cuzco, in the highlands of southeast Peru.

1325 The Aztecs establish their city of Tenochtitlán (pronounced tay-notch-teet-LAHN) on an island in Lake Texcoco in the Valley of Mexico.

1016
Viking Canute I, the Great begins rule as king of England, Denmark, and Norway

1200
Famine ravages England and Ireland throughout this century

1337
A Hundred Years' War between England and France begins

1421
Mohammed I dies

1000 C.E.   1200 C.E.   1300 C.E.   1400 C.E.

c. 1350 The Incas begin a series of military campaigns, rapidly conquering the communities around them.

1376 The Aztecs select Acamapichtli (pronounced ah-cahm-ah-PEECH-tlee) as their first *huey tlatoani* (ruler).

1428 The Aztecs are the most powerful group in Mesoamerica. They form the Triple Alliance with Texcoco and Tlacopan and rapidly build a vast empire of an estimated 15 million people.

1433 King Nezahualcoyotl (pronounced neza-hwahl-coy-OH-tul) takes the throne in Texcoco in the Valley of Mexico, beginning an era of artistic, educational, and cultural development in that city.

1438 Inca Pachacutec successfully fights the invading Chanca army at Cuzco and becomes the supreme Inca leader, or Sapa Inca, starting the one hundred-year Inca empire.

1440 Montezuma I becomes the ruler of the Aztecs; the empire expands and Tenochtitlán grows more prosperous.

1470 The Incas take control of the Chimú.

1471–1493 Pachacutec's son Tupac Inca Yupanqui rules an ever-expanding Inca empire.

1493–1525 Huayna Capac (pronounced WHY-nah CAH-pahk) rules the Inca empire, but takes up residence in Quito (Ecuador), dividing the Incas.

1502 Montezuma II takes the throne of the Aztec empire.

1517 Mayas successfully fight off the forces of Spanish explorer Francisco Fernández de Córdoba. Soon epidemics of small pox and the measles break out among the Mayas, eventually killing as many as 90 percent of the people.

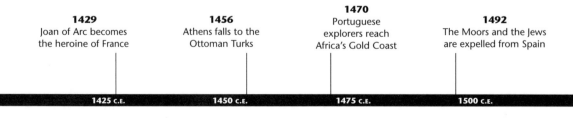

1429
Joan of Arc becomes the heroine of France

1456
Athens falls to the Ottoman Turks

1470
Portuguese explorers reach Africa's Gold Coast

1492
The Moors and the Jews are expelled from Spain

1425 C.E.   1450 C.E.   1475 C.E.   1500 C.E.

March 1519 Spanish conquistador Hernán Cortés receives a "gift" from the Mayas of a young woman called Malinche. She becomes his interpreter and mistress during the Spanish conquest of Tenochtitlán.

September 1519 Cortés enlists the help of the Tlaxcala, who will be his allies against the Aztecs.

November 1519 Cortés' expedition arrives at Tenochtitlán. Within a few weeks the Spanish imprison the Aztec ruler, Montezuma II.

June 1520 Montezuma II is killed during an uprising against the Spaniards. The Spaniards flee from Tenochtitlán.

July 1520 Epidemics of smallpox and measles strike the Aztecs at Tenochtitlán and elsewhere. In the twenty years that follow, the Aztec population will be reduced to one-half its former size.

May 1521 The Cortés forces attack Tenochtitlán.

August 1521 The Aztecs surrender to the Spanish. Spanish conquistadores finish destroying the city of Tenochtitlán and begin building their own capital city, Mexico City, on top of the ruins.

1522 Spanish missionaries begin their efforts to convert the native people of Mesoamerica to Christianity. They destroy thousands of Aztec codices, or painted books, and prohibit all religious practice, hoping to break the people's connections to their religion. Hundreds of thousands of Mesoamericans convert to Catholicism.

1525 Huáscar becomes the Sapa Inca, but his brother Atahuallpa continues to rule the armies in Quito.

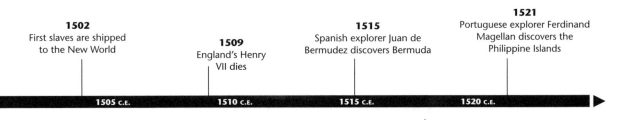

1502 First slaves are shipped to the New World

1509 England's Henry VII dies

1515 Spanish explorer Juan de Bermudez discovers Bermuda

1521 Portuguese explorer Ferdinand Magellan discovers the Philippine Islands

1505 C.E. 1510 C.E. 1515 C.E. 1520 C.E.

1525 A deadly smallpox epidemic strikes the Inca empire. It will eventually kill an estimated 75 percent of the population of the Inca empire.

1526 Another Spanish attack on the Mayas is repelled; once again, the Spanish flee.

1529 Civil war breaks out among the Incas, with the forces of Huáscar fighting the forces of Atahuallpa.

1531 Spanish forces take over the Maya city of Chichén Itzá, but the Mayas rise against them and force them to flee.

1532 Atahuallpa captures Huáscar and becomes the Sapa Inca.

1532 Spanish conquistador Francisco Pizarro and his expedition arrive at Atahuallpa's camp at Cajamarca. The next day they slaughter about six thousand unarmed Incas and capture Atahuallpa.

1532 Spanish priests establish missions in the Maya world and begin strenuous efforts to convert the Maya to Christianity.

1533 Spaniards kill Sapa Inca Atahuallpa and take over the rule of Cuzco and the Inca empire.

1536–1572 The Incas operate a rebel capital in Vilcabamba, a region northwest of Cuzco.

1542 The Spanish set up a capital at Mérida in the present-day Mexican state of Yucatán. Over the next five years they take control of much of the Maya world.

1562 Spanish missionary Diego de Landa begins a book-burning campaign, destroying thousands of Maya codices in his efforts to eliminate the Maya religion. Only three known Maya codices survive.

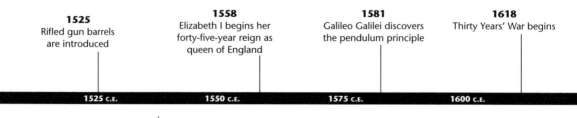

1525
Rifled gun barrels
are introduced

1558
Elizabeth I begins her
forty-five-year reign as
queen of England

1581
Galileo Galilei discovers
the pendulum principle

1618
Thirty Years' War begins

1525 c.e.   1550 c.e.   1575 c.e.   1600 c.e.

Words to Know

A

aboriginal: Native to the land; having existed in a region from the earliest times.

aclla: A young woman chosen by the Incas to live in isolation from daily Inca life while learning how to weave and how to make *chicha* and foods for festivals; some *acllas* were eventually married to nobles, and others became religious workers.

acllahuaci: A house where young women chosen by the Incas were isolated from daily Inca life; these women were trained in the arts of weaving fine cloth and making *chicha* and foods for festivals, and some went on to become religious workers.

administration: The management and work (rather than the policy making or public relations) of running a public, religious, or business operation.

administrative center: The place in a region or state in which the day-to-day operations of business, government, and religion are carried out.

administrator: A person who manages or supervises the day-to-day operations of business, government, and religious organizations.

adobe: Sun-dried earthen brick used for building.

agriculture: The science, art, and business of cultivating the soil, producing useful crops, and raising livestock; farming.

alliances: Connections between states or other political units based on mutual interests, intermarriage of families, or other relations.

alpaca: A member of the camelid family; a domesticated mammal related to the llama that originated in Peru and is probably descended from the guanaco. The Andeans used the long silky wool of the alpaca in their textiles.

altiplano: A high plateau; also referred to as a puna. In the central Andes Mountains of South America, where early Andean civilizations arose, the altiplano is about 12,000 to 16,500 feet (3,658 to 5,029 meters) high.

Amerindian: An indigenous, or native, person from North or South America.

anthropology: The study of human beings in terms of their social structures, culture, populations, origins, race, and physical characteristics.

aqueducts: Human-made channels that deliver water from a remote source, usually relying on the pull of gravity to transport the water.

archaeological excavation: The scientific process of digging up and examining artifacts, remains, and monuments of past human life by experts in the field.

archaeology: The scientific study of digging up and examining artifacts, remains, and monuments of past human life.

architecture: The art or practice of designing and constructing buildings or other large structures.

Arctic: The areas centered on the North Pole consisting of the Arctic Ocean and the lands in and around it.

artifact: Any item made or used by humans, such as a tool or weapon, that may be found by archaeologists or others who seek clues to the past.

astronomer: A person who studies the planets, sun, moon, and stars and all other celestial bodies.

astronomical observatory: A place designed to help people observe the stars and planets and all celestial phenomena.

astronomy: The science that deals with the study of the planets, sun, moon, and stars and all other celestial bodies.

atlantes: Large stone statues of warriors, often used as columns to support the roofs of Toltec buildings.

atlatls: Spearthrowers.

authoritarian government: Strict rule by the elite; in this type of government, leaders are not constitutionally responsible to the people, and the people have little or no power.

ayllu: A group of extended families who live in the same area, share their land and work, and arrange for marriages and religious rituals as a group; the basic social unit of the Andean peoples.

B

bajo: The Spanish word for "under," referring to lowlands or swampy depressions in the earth's surface. In a rain forest, *bajos* are generally wetlands from July to November and dry the rest of the year.

baptism: A Christian ritual celebrating an individual joining a church, in which sprinkling holy water or dunking signifies his or her spiritual cleansing and rebirth.

barbarian: A word used to describe people from another land; it often has a negative meaning, however, suggesting the people described are inferior to others.

basalt: A fine-grained, dark gray rock used for building.

bas-relief: A carved, three-dimensional picture, usually in stone, wood, or plaster, in which the image is raised above the background.

bioglyph: A symbolic animal or plant figure etched into the earth.

burial offerings: Gifts to the gods that are placed with the body of a deceased person.

C

cacao beans: Beans that grow on an evergreen tree from which cocoa, chocolate, and cocoa butter are made.

callanca: An Inca word meaning "great hall"; a place where people gathered for ceremonies and other events.

calpulli: (The word means "big house"; the plural form is *calpultin*.) Social units consisting of groups of families who were either related in some way or had lived among each other over the generations. *Calpultin* formed the basic social unit for farmers, craftspeople, and merchants. The precise way they worked is not known.

camelid: A family of mammals that, in the Americas, includes the llama, the alpaca, the vicuña, and the guanaco.

cenote: Underground reservoirs or rivers that become accessible from above ground when cave ceilings collapse or erode.

ceque: A Quechua word meaning "border"; *ceques* were imaginary lines that divided Cuzco into sections, creating distinct districts that determined a person's social, economic, and religious duties.

ceremonial centers: Citylike centers usually run by priests and rulers, in which people from surrounding areas gather to practice the ceremonies of their religion, often at large temples and plazas built specifically for this purpose.

chacmool: A stone statue of a man in a reclining position, leaning to one side with his head up in a slightly awkward position; the statue's stomach area forms a kind of platform on which the Toltecs placed a bowl or plate for offerings to the gods—sometimes incense or small animals, but often human hearts.

chasqui: A messenger who was trained to memorize and relay messages. *Chasqui* posts stood about a mile apart along the road system of the Inca empire. When a message was given to a *chasqui,* he would run to the next post and convey the message to the *chasqui* there, who would then run to the next post, and so on.

chicha: A kind of beer that Andean peoples made from maize or other grains.

chiefdom: A social unit larger and more structured than a tribe but smaller and less structured than a state, which is mainly governed by one powerful ruler. Though there are not distinct classes in a chiefdom, people are ranked by how closely they are related to the chief; the closer one is to the chief, the more prestige, wealth, and power one is likely to have.

chinampa: A floating garden in a farming system in which large reed rafts floating on a lake or marshes are covered in mud and used for planting crops.

chronicler: A person who writes down a record of historical events, arranged in order of occurrence.

city-state: An independent self-governing community consisting of a single city and the surrounding area.

codex: (plural: codices) A handmade book written on a long strip of bark paper and folded into accordion-like pages.

colca: Storehouse for food and goods.

colony: A group of people living as a community in a land away from their home that is ruled by their distant home government.

conquistador: (plural: conquistadores) The Spanish word for "conqueror"; in English, the word usually refers to the leaders of the Spanish conquests of Mesoamerica and Peru in the sixteenth century.

controversial: Tending to evoke opposing views; not accepted by everyone.

coya: The Sapa Inca's sister/wife, also known as his principal wife, and queen of the Inca empire.

creole: A person of European descent who is born in the Americas; in this book, a Spaniard who is born in Mexico.

cult: A group that follows a living religious leader (or leaders) who promote new doctrines and practices.

cultural group: A group of people who share customs, history, beliefs, and other traits, such as a racial, ethnic, religious, or social group.

culture: The arts, language, beliefs, customs, institutions and other products of human work and thought shared by a group of people at a particular time.

curaca: A local leader of a region conquered by the Incas; after the conquest, *curacas* were trained to serve their regions as representatives of the Inca government.

D

decipher: To figure out the meaning of something in code or in an ancient language.

deify: Place in a godlike position; treat as a god.

deity: A god or goddess, or a supreme being.

drought: A long period of little or no rainfall.

E

egalitarian: A society or government in which everyone has an equal say in political, social, and economic decisions and no individual or group is considered the leader.

El Niño: An occasional phenomenon in which the waters of the Pacific Ocean along the coast of Ecuador and Peru warm up, usually around late December, sometimes bringing about drastic weather changes like flooding or drought.

elite: A group of people within a society who are in a socially superior position and have more power and privileges than others.

empire: A vast, complex political unit extending across political boundaries and dominated by one central power, which generally takes control of the economy, government, and culture in communities throughout its territory.

encomienda: A grant to Spanish conquistadores giving them privilege to collect tribute from Amerindians in a particular region. The *encomendero* (grant holder) had the responsibility to train Amerindians in Christianity and Spanish, and to protect them from invasion. Most *encomenderos,* however, treated the Amerindians under their grants like slaves, forcing them into inhuman labor conditions often resulting in the collapse or death of the workers.

epidemic: A sudden spreading of a contagious disease among a population, a community, or a region.

evolution: A process of gradual change, from a simple or earlier state to a more complex or more developed state.

excavation: The process of carefully digging out or uncovering artifacts or human remains left behind by past human societies so that they can be viewed and studied.

export: To send or transport goods produced or grown in one's home region to another region in order to trade or sell them there.

F

feline: A member of the cat family; or resembling a member of the cat family.

fertility: The capacity of land to produce crops or, among people, the capacity to reproduce or bear children.

frieze: A band of decoration running around the top part of a wall, often a temple wall.

G

geoglyph: A symbolic figure or character etched into the earth.

glyph: A figure (often carved into stone or wood) used as a symbol to represent words, ideas, or sounds.

government: A political organization, usually consisting of a body of people who exercise authority over a political unit as a whole and carry out many of its social functions, such as law enforcement, collection of taxes, and public affairs.

guanaco: A member of the camelid family; a South American mammal with a soft, thick, fawn-colored coat, related to and resembling the llama.

H

hallucinogenic drug: A mind- and sense-altering drug that may create visions of things not physically present.

heartland: The central region of a cultural group where their traditional values and customs are practiced.

hierarchy: The ranking of a group of people according to their social, economic, or political position.

highlands: A region at high elevation.

huaca: A sacred place, usually used for a temple, pyramid, or shrine.

human sacrifice: Killing a person as an offering to the gods.

I

iconography: A method of relaying meaning through pictures and symbols.

idol: A likeness or image of an object of worship.

import: To bring goods from another region into one's home region, where they can be acquired by trade or purchase.

Inca: The word Inca originally meant "ruler" and referred to the king or leader. It is also used to mean the original group of Inca family clans that arose to prominence in the city of Cuzco. As the empire arose, the supreme ruler was called the "Sapa Inca" and members of the noble class were called "Incas."

indigenous: Native to an area.

L

legend: A legend is a story handed down from earlier times, often believed to be historically true.

llama: A member of the camelid family; a South American mammal that originated in Peru and probably descended from the guanaco. Llamas were used for their soft, fleecy wool, for their meat, and for carrying loads.

logogram: A glyph expressing a whole word or concept.

logosyllabic: A mixed system of writing in which some symbols represent whole words or ideas, while other symbols represent the syllables or units of sound which make up words.

lowlands: An area of land that is low in relation to the surrounding country.

M

mammoth: An extinct massive elephant-like mammal with thick, long hair and long curved tusks.

mass human sacrifices: Large-scale killing of people—or many people being killed at one time—as offerings to the gods.

mercenary soldiers: Warriors who fight wars for another state or nation's army for pay.

Mesoamerica: A term used for the area in the northern part of Central America, including Guatemala, Honduras, El Salvador, and Belize, and the southern and central parts of present-day Mexico, where many ancient civilizations arose.

mestizo: A person having mixed ancestry, specifically European and Amerindian.

missionary: A person, usually working for a religious organization, who tries to convert people, usually in a foreign land, to his or her religion.

mit'a: A tax imposed on the common people by the Inca government; the tax was a labor requirement rather than a monetary sum—the head of every household was obliged to work on public projects (building monuments, repairing roads or bridges, transporting goods) for a set period each year.

mitima: An Inca resettlement policy that required potential rebels in newly conquered regions to leave their villages and settle in distant regions where the majority of people were loyal to the Inca empire; this policy helped the Incas prevent many uprisings.

monogamy: Marriage to one partner only.

monumental architecture: Buildings, usually very large, such as pyramids or temple mounds, that are used for religious or political ceremonies.

mummification: Preservation of a body through a complex procedure that involves taking out the organs, filling the body cavity with preservative substances, and then drying out the body to prevent decay; mummification can also occur naturally when environmental conditions, such as extreme cold or dryness preserve the body.

mummy: A body that has been preserved, either by human technique or unusual environmental conditions, such as extreme cold or dryness.

myth: A traditional, often imaginary story dealing with ancestors, heroes, or supernatural beings, and usually making an attempt to explain a belief, practice, or natural phenomenon.

N

Nahuatl: The language spoken by the Aztecs and many other groups in the Valley of Mexico.

New World: The Western Hemisphere, including North and South America.

nomadic: Roaming from place to place without a fixed home.

O

observatory: A building created for the purpose of observing the stars and planets.

obsidian: Dark, solid glass formed by volcanoes used to make blades, knives, and other tools.

offerings: Gifts for the gods.

oral tradition: History and legend passed from generation to generation through spoken accounts.

outpost: A remote settlement or headquarters through which a central government manages outlying areas.

P

Paleoamerican: A member of a theoretical first population group in the Americas; scholars use this term to make a distinction between this group and the Paleo-Indians, a later group, who are generally considered to be the ancestors of modern Amerindians.

Paleo-Indian: A member of the group of people who migrated to the United States from Asia during the last part of the Great Ice Age, which ended about ten thousand years ago; Paleo-Indians are thought to be the ancestors of modern Amerindians.

pampa: The partly grassy, partly arid plains in the Andean region.

pantheon: All of the gods that a particular group of people worship.

Patagonia: A vast barren flat-land spreading through Argentina and into Chile between the Andes Mountains and the Atlantic Ocean.

Peninsulares: People living in Mexico who were born in Spain.

pilgrim: A person who travels to a holy place to show reverence.

pilgrimage: A journey to a holy place to show faith and reverence.

plateau: A large, elevated level area of land.

polygamy: Marriage in which spouses can have more than one partner; in Inca society, some men had multiple wives, but women could not take multiple husbands.

pre-Columbian American: A person living in the Americas before the arrival of Spanish explorer Christopher Columbus in 1492.

prehistory: The period of time in any given region, beginning with the appearance of the first human beings there and ending with the occurrence of the first written records. All human history that occurred before there was writing to record it is considered prehistoric.

primogeniture: A system in which the oldest son inherits his father's position or possessions.

Q

Quechua: The Inca language, still spoken by Andean people today.

quetzal: A Central American bird with bright green feathers.

quinoa: A high-protein grain grown in the Andes.

quipu: Also *khipu.* A set of multicolored cotton cords knotted at intervals, used for counting and record keeping.

R

radiocarbon dating: A method of testing organic (once living) material to see how old it is. Radiocarbon dating measures the amount of carbon 14 found in a sample. All plant and animal matter has a set amount of carbon 14. When an organism dies, the carbon 14 begins to decay at a specific rate. After measuring the extent of the decay, scientists can apply a series of mathematical formulas to determine the date of the organism's death—and consequently the age of the organic matter that remains.

rain forest: Dense, tropical woodlands that receive a great quantity of rain throughout the year.

religious rites: Established ceremonial practices.

remains: Ancient ruins or fossils, or human corpses or bones.

ritual: A formal act performed the same way each time, usually used as a means of religious worship by a particular group.

S

sacrifice: To make an offering to the gods, through personal possessions like cloth or jewels, or by killing an animal or human as the ultimate gift.

sacrifice rituals: Ceremonies during which something precious is offered to the gods; in early civilizations, sacrifice rituals often involved killing an animal or sometimes even a human being—the life that was taken was offered as a gift to the gods.

Sapa Inca: Supreme ruler of the Incas.

sarcophagus: A stone box used for burial, containing the coffin and body of the deceased, or sometimes only the body.

scribe: Someone hired to write down the language, to copy a manuscript, or record a spoken passage.

script: Writing.

sedentary: Settled; living in one place.

shaman: A religious leader or priest who communicates with the spirit world to influence events on earth.

smallpox: A severe contagious viral disease spread by particles emitted from the mouth when an infected person speaks, coughs, or sneezes.

stela: (plural: stelae) A stone pillar carved with images or writing, often used to provide historical details or for religious or political purposes.

stonemasonry: The work of a skilled builder who expertly lays cut or otherwise fitted units of stone in construction.

subordinate: Subject to someone of greater power; lower in rank.

succession: The system of passing power within the ruling class, usually upon the death of the current ruler.

surplus: The excess above what is needed; the amount remaining after all members of a group have received their share.

syllabograms: Symbols that represent the sounds of a language (usually a combination of a vowel sound and consonants).

T

terrace: One of a series of large horizontal ridges, like stairs, made on a mountain or hillside to create a level space for farming.

theorize: Create an explanation based on scientific evidence or historical analysis that has not yet been proven.

tlatoani: A Nahuatl word meaning "speaker" or "spokesperson" used by the Aztecs to refer to their rulers, or "they who speak for others." The Aztec emperor was often called *huey tlatoani,* or "great speaker."

trance: An altered mental state.

transformation: Changing into something else.

tribute: A payment to a nation or its ruler, usually made by people from a conquered territory as a sign that they surrender to the imposed rule; payment could be made in goods or labor or both.

trophy head: The head of an enemy, carried as a token of victory in combat.

U

urbanization: The process of becoming a city.

ushnu: A large platform in a central part of a city plaza, where the king or noblemen stood to address the public or view public festivities.

V

Valley of Mexico: A huge, oval basin at about 7,500 feet (2,286 meters) above sea level in north central Mexico, covering an area of about 3,000 square miles (7,770 square kilometers) and consisting of some of the most fertile land of Mexico.

vicuña: A South American mammal related to the llama and having a fine silky fleece, often used by the Andeans for making textiles. The early Andeans hunted vicuña for skins and meat.

vigesimal: Based on the number twenty (as a numeric system).

Villac Umu: Inca term for chief priest.

W

welfare state: A state or government that assumes responsibility for the welfare of its citizens.

Y

yanacona: A commoner who was selected and trained in childhood to serve the Inca nobility, priests, or the empire in general; the position was a form of slavery.

Yucatán: A peninsula separating the Caribbean Sea from the Gulf of Mexico, which includes the nation of Belize, the Petén territory of northern Guatemala, and the southeastern Mexican states of Campeche, Quintana Roo, and Yucatán. Yucatán is also the name of a state of Mexico, in the northern portion of the Yucatán peninsula.

Z

ziggurat: A platform or terrace with a tall temple tower or pyramid atop it in ancient Mesopotamia.

Research and Activity Ideas

The following ideas and projects are intended to offer suggestions for complementing your classroom work on understanding various aspects of the early civilizations in the Americas:

Plan a tour of historic Inca sites: Imagine that you are a travel agent and you are preparing a tour for a family that wishes to see the famous historic sites of the ancient Inca civilization in the Andes Mountain region of South America. What Inca cities should they travel to and why? Find a copy of a map of the area of the Inca civilization and plan their tour for them. Make a numbered list of at least six scenic stops they will want to make, marking the map with the corresponding number. Write down the highlights of what they will see there and why it is of interest. When you have completed the Inca tour guidebook and map, you may plan tours for people wishing to see the ancient Maya sites and the ancient Aztec sites as well. Find a map of the Mesoamerican region and start the plans.

Memoirs of a Maya teenager from 750 C.E.: You are a Maya teenager who lives in the year 750. Write an autobiography: what is your name? What city do you live in? Describe the details of everyday existence. What kinds of clothes do you wear and what other adornments do you use to make you look more attractive? Describe the food you eat, the house you live in, and other interesting facts about things like your religion and school. Please feel free to use your imagination to fill in the facts, but base your report on information you find in this book, other books about the Mayas you find at the library, and web sites about the life of the Maya people.

Discussion panel topic—Cities: Some archaeologists believe there were real cities in the Andes Mountains as far back as 2500 B.C.E. Form a group and try, as a group, to come up with a list of factors that make a city. Why is New York or Chicago a city, for example? Then discuss the evidence archaeologists have found in the Andes that might demonstrate that there were cities in the Americas so long ago. In what ways were the ancient cities like modern cities today? In what ways were they different? Can you imagine what life was like in Caral or in Chavín de Huantár?

Research topic—Pyramids: Write a report on the pyramids of the Americas. Research for your report can begin with this reference set, but it should include a trip to the library to find books on the ancient civilizations of the Americas and pyramids in general. You may also use the Internet for your research. What were the biggest pyramids of the Americas? How large were they? When were they built? How do they compare in size and in the time they were built with the pyramids of ancient Egypt? Who built them and how did the builders accomplish their work?

Travel diary of an Aztec merchant: The year is 1460 and you are a trader who has traveled into the Aztec city of Tenochtitlán for the first time to sell your produce. In an essay, describe how you would get into the city and what you would see when you got there.

Maya glyph poster: Make a Maya glyph poster. First you will need to look at some examples. There are some excellent web sites and books at your library that demonstrate Maya glyphs and their use. If possible, check out one of the following:

- "How to Write Your Name in Mayan Glyphs" at http://www.halfmoon.org/names.html

- Ancient Scripts.com http://www.ancientscripts.com/maya.html

- *Reading the Maya Glyphs,* by Michael D. Coe and Mark Van Stone. London and New York: Thames and Hudson, 2001.

Or find any other resource with pictures of Maya glyphs and explanations of their meanings. Find a glyph or a glyph phrase (your name or the date, for example) that appeals to you and make a poster using the Maya glyph design. Using colored pencils or crayons, draw the glyph and then color it in. Feel free to add your own style to the design. Be sure to label the poster, showing the glyph's meaning.

Early Civilizations of America Food Festival: Plan an Early Civilizations of America Food Festival. Set up booths for Maya, Aztec, and Inca foods. Make a batch of one kind of food and serve it in small portions so everyone can taste it. Read about the foods you are serving: be prepared to tell visitors to your booth all about the way the foods were prepared and eaten by the Mayas, Incas, or Aztecs. You may make any variety of dishes using corn, tortillas, beans, avocados, chili peppers, squash, pumpkin seeds, or chocolate. Here are some suggestions:

Maya booth:

- Popcorn

- Hot chocolate: Recipe

    2 ounces unsweetened bakers' chocolate, chopped into small pieces

    6 cinnamon sticks, broken into several pieces

    4 cups water

    3 tablespoons honey

Heat one cup of water in a saucepan until hot but not boiling and add the chopped chocolate. Stir until the chocolate melts. Add honey. With a wire whisk, beat the hot chocolate while gradually adding 3 cups of hot water from the tap.

When it's good and foamy, pour small portions into cups with cinnamon sticks in each one and serve.

Inca booth:

- Baked sweet potatoes or baked potatoes, cut into large bite-sized pieces with butter, salt, and pepper served on the side

- Quinoa: Recipe

You will need to purchase a box of quinoa (pronounced KEEN-wah), a grain available in the rice section of most grocery stores. For plain quinoa, simply follow the instructions on the back of the package. For variety, try toasting the quinoa before cooking it. Place 1 teaspoon of vegetable or corn oil on a nonstick frying pan and place over medium heat, stirring constantly until the quinoa is golden brown. Then cook according to package instructions. Try adding canned or frozen corn to the quinoa in the last few minutes of cooking for a real Inca dish.

Aztec booth:

- Corn tortillas (store bought; and cut into pieces) or tortilla chips to serve with refried beans and chilies

- Refried Beans: Recipe

Open two 15-ounce cans of pinto beans. Heat one tablespoon of vegetable oil in a heavy frying pan over medium heat. When it is hot, put several large spoonfuls of beans into the pan, sprinkle lightly with salt and pepper, and then mash them with a fork until they are hot and mashed. Then place them in a covered bowl and do another batch until the beans are used. Serve on tortilla pieces or tortilla chips with diced chilies, if desired.

- Canned chilies, diced into small pieces, served on the side.

Stage a play—The Historic Meeting of 1519: With a team of eight to ten people, write a short play about the first meeting between Aztec emperor Montezuma II and Spanish conqueror Hernán Cortés in Tenochtitlán in 1519. First do your research: make sure you know who was there and where the meeting took place. Find out whatever you can about how people were dressed and how they spoke with one another. Write the words that you imagine they spoke. Assign roles for each member of the group and then enact the scene for your class.

Debate—The acts of the conquerors: After the Spanish conquerors had defeated the Inca and Aztec empires and the Maya societies, they destroyed many important aspects of the native cultures, including the people's books, arts, and religious buildings and shrines, as they attempted to convert the people to Christianity and to educate them in European customs. Were the intentions of the Spanish honorable, and can their actions be justified? Stage a debate over these questions. Split the class in half; one half debates that the Spanish were not justified and the other half argues that they were (regardless of personal beliefs on these issues). Consider how much damage the Spanish did and what possible causes they might have had for their actions.

Early Civilizations in the Americas
Almanac

Introduction to Early American Civilizations

In world history, modern human beings (those human ancestors who fall under the category homo sapiens and are most like human beings today) go back about 150,000 years. For at least 142,000 of those years, Earth's people were nomadic (roaming from place to place without a fixed home); they traveled in small family groups or lived in tiny, temporary villages without government (a political organization, usually consisting of a body of people who exercise authority over a political unit as a whole and carry out many of its social functions, such as law enforcement, collection of taxes, and public affairs). Within the last eight thousand years, humans began to develop complex societies with political structures and dense populations. However, even after these complex societies first developed, thousands of years passed before civilizations arose.

What is a civilization? According to most dictionaries, civilization is a level of advancement and complexity in a society's technology, economics, politics, religious organization, arts, and sciences. Some scholars say that civilizations arise as a result of urbanization—the development of cities. Other scholars point out that some early societies did not

Words to Know

Agriculture: The science, art, and business of cultivating the soil, producing useful crops, and raising livestock; farming.

Archaeology: The scientific study of digging up and examining artifacts, remains, and monuments of past human life.

Artifact: Any item made or used by humans, such as a tool or weapon, that may be found by archaeologists or others who seek clues to the past.

Ceremonial centers: Citylike centers usually run by priests and rulers, in which people from surrounding areas gather to practice the ceremonies of their religion, often at large temples and plazas built specifically for this purpose.

City-state: An independent self-governing community consisting of a single city and the surrounding area.

Culture: The arts, language, beliefs, customs, institutions and other products of human work and thought shared by a group of people at a particular time.

Egalitarian: A society or government in which everyone has an equal say in political, social, and economic decisions and no individual or group is considered the leader.

Empire: A vast, complex political unit extending across political boundaries and dominated by one central power, which generally takes control of the economy, government, and culture in communities throughout its territory.

Excavation: The process of carefully digging out or uncovering artifacts or human remains left behind by past human societies so that they can be viewed and studied.

Government: A political organization, usually consisting of a body of people who exercise authority over a political unit as a whole and carry out many of its social functions, such as law enforcement, collection of taxes, and public affairs.

have true cities yet still had distinguishing features that are present in every civilization. At base, a civilization is a complex political, economic, and social structure in which people work at a variety of occupations and are divided into social classes by their wealth, power, or prestige. The ruling power of a civilization often dominates a large region from a central urban area, and a military force usually backs the central ruling power. Large monuments, such as temples or pyramids, and public works, such as irrigation or highway systems, indicate a civilization, because they are evidence that people have worked together in an organized fashion for a

Inca: The word Inca originally meant "ruler" and referred to the king or leader. It is also used to mean the original group of Inca family clans that arose to prominence in the city of Cuzco (pronounced KOO-sko). As the empire arose, the supreme ruler was called the "Sapa Inca," and members of the noble class were called "Incas."

Mesoamerica: A term used for the area in the northern part of Central America, including Guatemala, Honduras, El Salvador, and Belize, and the southern and central parts of present-day Mexico, where many ancient civilizations arose.

New World: The Western Hemisphere, including North and South America.

Pre-Columbian: Existing before Spanish explorer Christopher Columbus arrived in the Americas in 1492.

Prehistory: The period of time in any given region, beginning with the appearance of the first human beings there and ending with the occurrence of the first written records. All human history that occurred before the existence of written records is considered prehistoric.

Sedentary: Settled; living in one place.

Specialize: To focus on one thing in order to become very good at it.

Surplus: The excess above what is needed; the amount remaining after all members of a group have received their share.

Urbanization: The process of becoming a city.

Valley of Mexico: A huge, oval basin at about 7,500 feet (2,286 meters) above sea level in north central Mexico, covering an area of about 3,000 square miles (7,770 square kilometers) and consisting of some of the most fertile land of Mexico.

Ziggurat: A platform or terrace with a tall temple tower or pyramid atop it in ancient Mesopotamia.

common cause. Because the amount of labor involved in these projects is great and required many people and difficult work, it could not be accomplished without some kind of governmental authority and direction. Formal or organized religious institutions, writing systems, and scientific advances are other identifying features of a civilization.

The transition from nomadic to urban life

Before there were civilizations in the world, humans spent most of their time working for their own survival, usually gathering wild plants to eat and hunting for meat. Those who lived on the coast fished. Early humans lived in small groups, or bands. Bands were usually made up of a few families, and they were egalitarian (everyone had an equal say in political, social, and economic decision making and no one was considered the leader). The hunting-gathering lifestyle requires a great deal of land per person. Bands hunted game and gathered wild plants within one area until these resources were depleted; then they moved to a new area. The hunter-gatherers avoided other human groups because they did not want to have to compete for sources of food. The human population in any given area was therefore sparse, and people generally had little contact with anyone outside their own small family band. This was the basic human lifestyle worldwide until about 8000 B.C.E.

Agriculture

Sometime between 13,000 and 10,000 B.C.E. the world's first farmers began planting a few crops. Starting out slowly, probably as a series of experiments, farming did not become a main source of food until thousands of years later. Eventually, people who farmed became sedentary (settled down to live in one place), because they wanted to be in the area when the crops they had planted were ready to harvest. Other farmers were semi-sedentary, returning to the place where they planted their crops season after season. Between 8500 and 7000 B.C.E. farmers began growing grains, which provided different types of nutrients and in time would be ground and stored. Farming villages appeared, first in what is now Turkey and other parts of the Middle East, then in China, and later in Europe.

Agriculture or farming, including cultivating the soil and the planting and harvesting of crops, as well as raising animals, is considered an essential step in the rise of civilization because people who farm tend to settle into one location and to live and work with other people. A farmer who takes the trouble to plant crops will be sure to be there to harvest them when they are ready. Although farmers may work their land alone, in most cases the job is done better with neighboring farmers. To dig an irrigation canal, for example, is such a large job that it requires the effort of a group of people working together. Projects like irrigation canals or terracing (making large steps in the sides of a hill for farming) necessitate leadership and organization for planning and division of labor. Agriculture also allows denser populations in a single area. (Growing food crops requires relatively little space compared to the area needed to support hunter-gatherers.) When large numbers of people reside in one area, they must agree on how to live together peacefully in a community, and some form of government—a keystone of civilization—becomes necessary.

Division of labor

Once a community begins to grow crops and raise animals, food surpluses become common; that is, communities frequently produce enough food that there is extra food left over after all members of the community have taken their share. If a community has enough extra food, some of its members can be freed from the labor of finding or growing food and can specialize (focus on one thing to become very good at it) in other jobs, especially jobs that will help the community. When a community has people dedicated solely to political rule, religious leadership, arts, or trade, it usually results in advances within the community, because there are people who can spend their time planning how to utilize the labor and resources available to them. As the community advances, leaders generally begin to put together public projects, such as building religious monuments or creating new irrigation canals. These projects demand large amounts of labor, so the community must grow more surplus food to provide for the people who will shift from agricultural work to work on the

 ## The World's First Civilizations

The definition of civilization is not simple or universally agreed upon, but most experts do agree on which of the world's early societies developed into the first civilizations. These civilizations arose between 3500 and 2000 B.C.E. They were located in the following six places:

- Mesopotamia: c. 3500 B.C.E.

- Egypt: c. 3100 B.C.E.

- The Central Andes, South America: c. 2600 B.C.E.

- Indus Valley (present-day Pakistan): c. 2500 B.C.E.

- China: c. 2500–2000 B.C.E.

- Mesoamerica: c. 2000 B.C.E.

These first civilizations apparently developed independently of one another, with little or no contact between them. Why civilizations would arise in distant parts of the world at close to the same time is a puzzle. Human life had existed for more than a hundred thousand years before these civilizations developed.

Steps to Civilization: Worldwide Firsts

8000 B.C.E.: The first farming of grain crops takes place along the Nile River in Egypt and along the Tigris and Euphrates Rivers in Mesopotamia.

8000 B.C.E.: The first pottery is made in the Middle East, or possibly Japan.

6000 B.C.E.: The Chinchorro people of Chile create the world's first mummies.

5000 B.C.E.: In Egypt and Mesopotamia, the first known irrigation methods for watering crops are put to use.

4000 B.C.E.: The wheel is invented in Mesopotamia.

3500 B.C.E.: The first number system is developed by the Sumerians in Mesopotamia.

3300 B.C.E.: The first writing system is developed by the Sumerians in Mesopotamia.

3000 B.C.E.: The Egyptians create the first accurate calendar.

2550 B.C.E.: The Egyptians build their first known pyramids about the same time that the pyramids of Caral are built in the Andes.

public projects. Surpluses also allow for trade. Surplus products can be traded with people from different regions, ensuring that a variety of foods and other necessities are available even in times of crop failure or other natural disasters.

Social classes

As people in a community begin to take on different jobs, certain groups gain more power than others. This generally leads the community to become divided into social classes. Wealthy and powerful people, such as religious and government leaders and people in charge of trade, reside at the top of the class system. Farmers with ample land, merchants, and artisans (craftspeople) live comfortably in the middle tier of the class system. People who own little or no property or who possess less valuable skills form the working class. Members of this group usually live in the most basic homes and receive the least material rewards. Many experts believe that class systems are necessary in the development of civilizations, mainly because it takes a lot of power to encourage or sometimes force groups of workers to do the vast amounts of labor required for public projects.

Law, order, culture, and religion

As increasingly dense populations develop and cities begin to form, community members have to create some type of government to direct public affairs, such as festivals and ceremonies. They also need a system of law and law enforcement to protect the individual members of the community and the community as a whole. Community leaders usually direct the formation of a military force to protect the community from attack by outsiders.

Once law and order are established, community members can focus on projects or activities that improve community life. Rulers may hire architects to build large structures for public events or to design great monuments that commemorate religious figures or powerful leaders. Scientists begin to study and understand plant and animal life and the stars in the sky. Others develop irrigation or sewage systems. Artisans create pottery, which can be used to cook, serve, and store food. Surpluses of food and the production of cloth, ceramics, jewels, and other products enable a community to trade with other societies. The new products that arrive through trade, as well as new ideas from other cultures, contribute to more advances in technology. (Culture is the arts, language, beliefs, customs, institutions, and other products of human work and thought shared by a group of people at a particular time.) In most, but not all, developing civilizations, writing and record-keeping are necessary to keep track of taxes, resources, population numbers, and property rights.

An organized religious system—in which community members shared practices and worshiped many of the same gods under the direction of a priest, or shaman—was central to the establishment of early civilizations. Priests were often the first leaders of these civilizations. They were thought to have a special relationship with the gods that allowed them to control the forces of nature—earthquakes, plagues, floods—and protect the people.

Along with the positive aspects of civilization came the negative: Some civilizations created huge military forces, and wars became increasingly destructive and violent. Rulers often commanded with terrifying power, including the power to end the lives of their subjects. Common people had little choice in how they lived. Men were routinely drafted to carry out the huge public projects, like building pyramids or digging canals, which demanded exhausting and dangerous physical labor over long periods of time. The nomadic hunting and gathering life allowed for individual freedom and an egalitarian society; in the working classes of the developing civilizations of the Americas there was little personal freedom and virtually no hope of rising above their current social status.

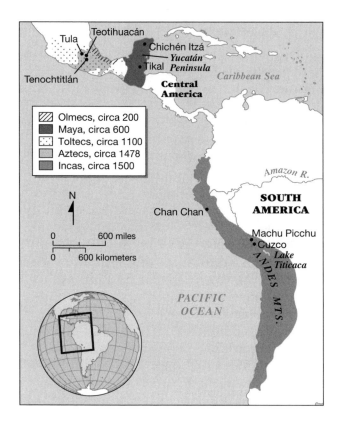

Map showing the sites of major ancient civilizations in Mesoamerica and South America. *Map by XNR Productions. The Gale Group.*

The ancient civilizations of the Americas

Two early civilizations developed in the Americas—specifically, in Mesoamerica (term describing a 400,000-square-mile [1,036,000-square-kilometer] area in the northern part of Central America, including Guatemala, Honduras, El Salvador, and Belize, and the southern and central parts of present-day Mexico) and in the central Andes Mountains of South America, including the part of the Andes in present-day Peru, and part of Bolivia, northern Argentina, and Ecuador. The geographic features of these regions made them extremely difficult to navigate and harder yet to farm. Although the two regions differ geographically, they both contain harsh physical environments, including parched desert-like plains at sea level and steep, frigid highlands at very high altitudes. However, despite these difficult conditions, people not only survived, but managed to forge two of the world's first civilizations. Many experts believe that the harsh physical environments of the Andes and Mesoamerica may have actually propelled the development of civilizations, because people had to work together to develop systems for survival.

Early civilization in the Andes mountain region

In 1532 Spanish explorer and conqueror Francisco Pizarro (c. 1475–1541) and his forces entered the Inca (pronounced ING-kuh) empire in present-day Peru, seeking the gold and treasures rumored to abound there. (The term *Inca* originally was used to refer to the supreme ruler and the original group of family clans that arose to prominence in the city of Cuzco [pronounced KOO-sko]. As the Inca empire

Sumer, Mesopotamia: The Cradle of Civilization

The first known civilization in the world was established by the people of Sumer in southern Mesopotamia. The rise of civilization there evolved over thousands of years. Mesopotamia is located in the Fertile Crescent, a broad plain watered by the Tigris and Euphrates Rivers, slightly inland from the spot where the two rivers dump their waters into the Persian Gulf. The early Sumerians developed a system of irrigation by putting up levees (embankments or walls at riverbanks) to control the two rivers, thus making it possible to get water to their crops as needed and preventing floods from destroying them. With their new method of irrigation and very fertile land, the Sumerians obtained surpluses of food from their farms.

The Sumerians' success in agriculture meant plenty of food was available for the growing communities of the region. Food surpluses allowed some people to stop farming and specialize at other jobs. Some became artisans, traders, administrators, or laborers. Others began to organize trade expeditions to supply the growing communities with needed materials. For example, the Mesopotamian plain had no stone, metals, or timber, so these materials had to be imported (brought from another region to be used in one's home region where it can be acquired by trade or purchase).

The farming villages of Sumer eventually developed into a system of twelve city-states. City-states were independent, self-governing communities that included a city and its surrounding farmlands. A ziggurat—a platform or terrace on which temples to the gods were erected—lay at the center of each city-state. (Because they lacked most other building materials, the Sumerians used clay from the rivers to build these structures. They cut and shaped the clay into bricks and then dried the bricks in the sun until they hardened. Then they stacked the bricks to form the ziggurat.) The homes and workshops of Sumerian craftspeople clustered around the base of each ziggurat. These artisans cast bronze tools and weapons or fashioned their wares on potter's wheels. Social classes developed; the homes of the priests, rulers, and wealthy merchants were located in central areas of the city and were far more luxurious than those of the laborers and farmers. Houses for farmers lay on the outskirts of the city-state.

By about 3500 B.C.E. other characteristics of civilization developed in Sumer, including a system of writing and record keeping and a style of art that represented people and their activities. Most authorities note these developments as evidence of the world's first civilization.

arose, the supreme ruler was called the "Sapa Inca," and members of the noble class were called "Incas.") As the Spaniards approached the temporary quarters of Atahuallpa

The snow-capped peaks of
the Andes Mountains.
Blackbirch Press Photo Bank.
Reproduced by permission.

(pronounced AH-tah-WAHL-pah; c. 1502–1533), the Inca emperor, they observed an army of forty thousand Inca soldiers.
Before Pizarro and his company conquered the capital city of
Cuzco and killed Atahuallpa, they had a chance to witness
the workings of a civilization that was in many ways as advanced as the civilization they knew in Europe.

The Inca empire was populated by some twelve million people in the early 1500s and spanned an area that ran
2,600 miles (4,183 kilometers) down the western coast of
South America, from present-day Ecuador to central Chile.
(An empire is a vast, complex political unit extending across
political boundaries and dominated by one central power,
which generally takes control of the economy, government,
and culture in communities throughout its territory.) Inca architecture was impressive: The monumental size of the structures and the precision of the stonework of the walls had
clearly demanded tremendous planning, labor, and skill.
Within the empire there were some 18,000 miles (28,962 kilo-

meters) of good, paved roads; thousands of storehouses scattered throughout the empire held vast amounts of surplus food; people living within the empire paid taxes, and skilled accountants kept track of the economy. Inca farmers used complex irrigation and terracing systems to meet the extraordinary demands of the high mountain slopes and the coastal deserts. The hardworking people of the empire generally specialized in their field—as artisans, bureaucrats, traders, accountants, warriors, textile makers, farmers, or fishermen.

This vast, populous, and complex civilization that the Spanish witnessed was not just the work of the Incas; after all, the Inca empire had been in place for only about one hundred years, since 1438. The Incas' advanced way of life was the result of thousands of years of effort and innovation by ancient civilizations in the Andes region. Among the earlier peoples were the Chavín (900–200 B.C.E.), Nazca (pronounced NAHZ-cah; 100 B.C.E.–700 C.E.), Moche (pronounced MO-chay; 100–800 C.E.), Tiwanaku (pronounced tee-wah-NAH-coo; 200–1200 C.E.), Wari (pronounced wah-REE; 600–1000 C.E.), and Chimú (pronounced chee-MOO; 1150–1470 C.E.).

Map of Cuzco, the capital of the Inca empire. *The Bridgeman Art Library. Reproduced by permission.*

Recent archaeological excavations have shown that cities and organized religion existed in the Andes even before the rise of the Chavín. Large ceremonial centers (city-like centers usually run by priests and rulers, in which people from surrounding areas gather to practice the ceremonies of their religion, often at large temples and plazas built specifically for this purpose), monumental architecture, and residential areas, all of which date back nearly five thousand years, have been found in the Norte Chico area of Peru. Pyramids, or temple mounds, were built in Peru's Supe Valley at about the same time the Egyptians were building their pyramids (around 2550 B.C.E.). These amazing buildings and the complexity of Andean social structures and religious organization have surprised the experts; such developments usually arise only after a community achieves other steps toward civilization, such as the making of pottery to store food supplies. There is no evidence that these early Andean people knew how to fire clay for pottery; instead, they appear to have made an unusual leap from relatively simple village life to complex organization.

Many scholars now believe that these Andean sites represent the first American cities and that this part of the Andes appropriately may be called the cradle of civilization in the Americas. Historians and anthropologists did not expect to find evidence of ancient civilization in the region, because the early Andean peoples did not have iron, a writing system, the wheel, or the plow—things previously thought to be essential to the development of civilization. However, the discovery of ancient Andean sites has prompted new questions about how civilizations arise. Many excavations in the area are continuing in the first decade of the twenty-first century. Only a small portion of the Andean area has been examined by archaeologists, and undoubtedly there will be new information—and many more surprises—in the years ahead.

The early civilizations of Mesoamerica

When the Spanish explorer Hernán Cortés (1485–1547) arrived at the great Aztec (more properly known as the Mexica; may-SHEE-kah) capital city of Tenochtitlán (pronounced tay-notch-teet-LAHN) in 1519, two hundred thousand to three hundred thousand people lived there. The city was built on a series of islands in the center of Lake Texcoco and was connected to the mainland by three major causeways (roads built like bridges over the water that connected the island to the shore). Cortés and many of his escorts wrote of the beauty and the wonders of the city, including its grand religious temples and monuments and other impressive architecture, its orderly streets and canals, and its floating gardens called *chinampas*. However, beauty did not protect Tenochtitlán from attack. Spain was determined to conquer Mexico, and Spanish forces soon destroyed the Aztec capital and built their own Spanish capital, Mexico City, on top of it.

In the years before the Spanish invaded the Americas, some thirty civilizations rose and fell in Mesoamerica, each with its own distinct languages, religious customs, and artistic styles, but still sharing in many general Mesoamerican traditions. The first of the civilizations to arise, as far as scholars know, was the Olmec (pronounced OLE-meck) culture, which flourished from about 1200 B.C.E. to 1200 C.E. (some new evidence suggests that it may have arisen much earlier). The Zapotec people of ancient Oaxaca (pronounced wah-HAH-kah), Mexico, existed at about the same time as the Olmec. A people known as the Teotihuacáns (pronounced TAY-uh-tee-wah-KAHNS), or lords of Teotihuacán, began building the first true city in Mesoamerica around the first century C.E. The great, peaceful cultural center of Teotihuacán (Place of the Gods) survived

Map of Tenochtitlán, capital of the Aztec empire. *The Bridgeman Art Library. Reproduced by permission.*

for about six centuries before it collapsed sometime after 750 C.E. One of its outstanding features is the 200-foot-high (61-meter-high) Pyramid of the Sun, the largest stone pyramid in all of pre-Columbian (existing before Spanish explorer Christopher Columbus arrived in the Americas in 1492) America and the third tallest pyramid of the ancient world.

The Maya (pronounced MY-uh) civilization of Mesoamerica grew out of a very early agricultural way of life, beginning around 2500 B.C.E. The Maya built great cities with stunning temples and pyramids throughout southern Mesoamerica. Maya priests and scholars, both men and women, were numerous, and they studied such subjects as astronomy, astrology, and mathematics. They developed the only complete writing system, in which the written text could fully reproduce the spoken language, in the ancient Americas. Most of the Maya civilization had collapsed before the Spaniards arrived in Central America and Mexico in the early sixteenth century. What was left of the great civilization

The Aztec city of Tenochtitlán was surrounded by Lake Texcoco and connected to the mainland by bridge-like roads. © Charles & Josette Lenars/Corbis.

was destroyed by the Spanish, who demolished Maya cities, burned the written records kept by the Maya, and forced the people to convert to Christianity. The Maya people still live in Central America in the twenty-first century, retaining their culture as farmers and artisans.

In about 950 C.E., the Toltecs (pronounced TOHL-tecks), a warlike people, took control of many of the Maya regions and other parts of Mesoamerica. They brought with them the culture of the earlier Teotihuacán peoples. Then, in the thirteenth century, the Aztecs arrived in the Valley of Mexico, a huge, oval basin at about 7,500 feet (2,286 meters) above sea level in north central Mexico, covering an area of about 3,000 square miles (7,770 square kilometers) and consisting of some of the most fertile land of Mexico. They were such a nuisance with their raiding and stealing that the residents of the valley banished them to an island in the center of Lake Texcoco, which they fortified and used as a base of operation. On the island they built their own magnificent

city, Tenochtitlán. The Aztecs continued to wage war on the other communities in the Valley of Mexico, and eventually established an empire that extended well beyond the valley. By the time the Spaniards arrived, the Aztec emperor Montezuma II (pronounced mohk-the-ZOO-mah; 1466–1520) ruled over a very large and powerful Aztec empire.

The Pyramid of the Magician in Uxmal, Mexico, is a stunning example of Maya advancement in architecture. © *Danny Lehman/Corbis.*

Reading about prehistory

Human history in North and South America began at least thirteen thousand years ago, but written records from ancient times are scarce and difficult to decipher. When the Spanish arrived in the Americas in 1492, they began to record history in a style of writing that contemporary people can easily understand. The period before the Spanish began their written documentation of life in the Americas—more than ten thousand years of history—is called American prehistory. It is important to note, however, that historians

An archaeologist uncovers skeletal remains and pottery dating to pre-Columbian times. *AP/Wide World Photos.*

learned to read Maya glyph-writing at the end of the twentieth century. (Glyphs are figures, often carved into stone or wood, used as symbols to represent words or ideas.) The distinction between American history and prehistory is not as clear cut as it has previously been described.

On the whole, materials other than written texts are usually the fundamental sources of information about pre-Columbian civilizations. Most historians base their view of the prehistoric past on evidence that comes from science, particularly from the field of archaeology. Archaeology is the scientific recovery and study of artifacts (objects made or used by humans) of earlier human life, such as burials, buildings, and pottery. By examining artifacts, archaeologists try to reconstruct the daily lives of the people of early cultures. Reading about prehistoric times often involves reading about discoveries made during a series of excavations (carefully digging out or uncovering artifacts or human remains left behind by past human societies so that they can be viewed and studied). In prehistory, there are few names or faces for the millions of individuals who lived in ancient times, and there are many mysteries that remain unsolved.

Historians have accumulated many more details about the Incas, the Aztecs, and the Mayas than they have for other Andean or Mesoamerican peoples. The Mayas, Incas, and Aztecs were still around in large numbers at the time the Spaniards arrived. Many accounts from the conquistadors, the soldiers who overthrew the native civilizations, describe the people and their habits. Although these are helpful, they are the words of the conqueror about the defeated. It was not in the best interest of the Spaniards to depict the native civilizations as sympathetic after they destroyed them; nor did they wish to paint the Americas as a place of advancement, since Spain was intent on establishing colonies and ruling over the residents.

Those who survived the invasion were able to tell the story of their people, or at least the portion of the story that they knew. Some of the survivors learned to write in Spanish and recorded the stories that had been passed down to them by the elders of their communities. Unfortunately, the Spanish were intent on destroying these cultures and converting the native people of America to Christianity and European culture. Many native people who learned to read and write had been taught that the things their ancestors believed were wrong. Recounting their stories for Spanish missionaries and others who might judge them harshly, they were often apt to change them to make them more agreeable to their new rulers, priests, and teachers. The written records are very valuable, if not always factually accurate, in understanding the ancient peoples and their traditions. Historians usually verify these accounts with the knowledge gained through archaeology to create a more balanced study of prehistory.

For More Information

Books

Adams, Richard E. W. *Ancient Civilizations of the New World.* Boulder, CO: Westview Press, 1997.

Coe, Michael D. *Mexico: From the Olmecs to the Aztecs.* 4th ed. London and New York: Thames and Hudson, 1994.

Katz, Friedrich. *The Ancient American Civilizations.* London: Phoenix Press, 2000.

Morris, Craig, and Adriana Von Hagen. *The Cities of the Ancient Andes.* London and New York: Thames and Hudson, 1998.

Morris, Craig, and Adriana Von Hagen. *The Inka Empire and Its Andean Origins.* New York: Abbeville Press, 1993.

Schobinger, Juan. *The First Americans.* Grand Rapids, MI: William B. Eerdmans, 1994.

Web Sites

"Ancient Indians." *Kid Info.* http://www.kidinfo.com/american_history/ancientamericasculture.htm (accessed on October 18, 2004).

Hooker, Richard. "Civilizations in America." *World Civilizations.* http://www.wsu.edu:8080/~dee/CIVAMRCA/CIV.HTM (accessed on October 18, 2004).

Before the Rise of Civilization: The First Americans

2

Thousands of years ago groups of people traveled to North and South America from far-away homes, and they stayed, becoming the first Americans. These migrations (movements of groups of people from one home to another) remain covered in mystery. How long ago did the first people come? Did they come by foot over a land bridge? Did they come by boat from the Pacific coast of Asia, or did they sail across the Atlantic? Were the early migrants from northern Asia, Southeast Asia, Australia, Japan, or Europe? Was there one large migration, or were there many migrations? The short answer to all of these questions is that no one knows. In some ways, scientists and historians seem to know less in the twenty-first century than they did at the end of the twentieth century. New evidence is emerging on a regular basis that disproves long-accepted views about the first immigrants to the Americas. Experts in the early twenty-first century are coming up with many intriguing new theories—educated guesses based on an abundance of new evidence and research. Their ideas present exciting possibilities about the history of the ancient Americas.

Words to Know

Aboriginal: Native to the land; having existed in a region from the earliest times.

Amerindian: An indigenous, or native, person from North or South America. The term "Amerindian" is used in place of the terms "American Indian" or "Native American" in these volumes, as the term "Native American" is often associated with the United States and the term "Indian" is offensive to some people.

Anthropology: The study of human beings in terms of their social structures, culture, populations, origins, race, and physical characteristics.

Archaeology: The scientific study of digging up and examining artifacts, remains, and monuments of past human life.

Arctic: The areas centered on the North Pole consisting of the Arctic Ocean and the lands in and around it.

Artifact: Any item made or used by humans, such as a tool or weapon, that may be found by archaeologists or others who seek clues to the past.

Controversial: Tending to evoke opposing views; not accepted by everyone.

Culture: The arts, language, beliefs, customs, institutions, and other products of human work and thought shared by a group of people at a particular time.

Evolution: A process of gradual change, from a simple or earlier state to a more complex or more developed state.

Excavation: The process of carefully digging out or uncovering artifacts or human remains left behind by past human societies so that they can be viewed and studied.

Indigenous: Native to an area.

Oral tradition: History and legend passed from generation to generation through spoken accounts.

Prehistory—the thousands of years in the human past when writing did not exist and therefore no written records of human history or events were left behind—poses a tremendous challenge to historians. Although in the twenty-first century scientists can send cameras to the planet Mars, they simply cannot look back with any certainty into the prehistoric past of the Americas. The two major sources of evidence about the unrecorded past are oral traditions (history and legend passed from generation to generation through spoken accounts) and science, in particular the sciences of archaeology (the study of digging up and examining artifacts, remains, and monuments of past human life) and anthropology (the

Paleoamerican: A member of a theoretical first population group in the Americas; scholars use this term to make a distinction between this group and the Paleo-Indians, a later group, who are generally considered to be the ancestors of modern Amerindians.

Paleo-Indian: A member of the group of people who migrated to the United States from Asia during the last part of the Great Ice Age, which ended about 10,000 years ago; Paleo-Indians are thought to be the ancestors of modern Amerindians.

Patagonia: A vast barren flat-land spreading through Argentina and into Chile between the Andes Mountains and the Atlantic Ocean.

Pre-Columbian: Existing before Spanish explorer Christopher Columbus arrived in the Americas in 1492.

Prehistory: The period of time in any given region, beginning with the appearance of the first human beings there and ending with the occurrence of the first written records. All human history that occurred before the existence of written records is considered prehistoric.

Radiocarbon dating: A method of testing organic (once living) material to see how old it is. Radiocarbon dating measures the amount of carbon 14 found in a sample. All plant and animal matter has a set amount of carbon 14. When an organism dies, the carbon 14 begins to decay at a specific rate. After measuring the extent of the decay, scientists can apply a series of mathematical formulas to determine the date of the organism's death—and consequently the age of the organic matter that remains.

Remains: Ancient ruins or fossils, or human corpses or bones.

study of human beings in terms of their social structures, culture, populations, origins, race, and physical characteristics).

This chapter is about the first migrations that "peopled" the Americas. According to the oral traditions of most Amerindian (indigenous, or native, person from North or South America) tribes, there were no migrations resulting in the "peopling of the Americas." Most native traditions relate that their people originated on the American continents. Some of the creation stories of ancient American civilizations will be covered in later chapters.

Archaeologists and anthropologists, on the other hand, are certain that people arrived in the Americas as the

Mammoths, elephant-like creatures, roamed across the Americas during the Great Ice Age. © *Jonathan Blair/Corbis.*

result of migrations from other continents; they do not think that human life in the Western Hemisphere evolved gradually, the way it did in other parts of the world. They feel certain of this because no remains (bones) of early forms of human beings have ever been found in the Americas; such remains have been found in Africa, Asia, and Europe. This chapter presents an overview of some of today's scientific theories and debates about the first people to migrate to the North and South American continents.

The Great Ice Age in the Americas

According to scientists, in the times before people existed in the Americas, the North and South American continents looked very different from any place modern humans have ever seen. Throughout Earth's history, there have been ice ages, long periods when the climate is very cold and large masses of ice (called glaciers) build up from snow accumulations. The last full ice age, the Pleistocene, began about two million years ago and ended about ten thousand years ago. The coldest period of the Pleistocene occurred about twenty thousand years ago; that period has come to be known as the Great Ice Age (with capital letters to set it apart from the term "ice age," referring to the longer eras). Two huge ice sheets covered a large part of North America, from Greenland to British Columbia. In those times extremely large animals roamed the Americas. For example, ice age beavers were as large as the brown bears known to modern people, and armadillos were as big as cars. Massive, tusked elephant-like creatures called mammoths and mastodons wandered across the two continents. Dangerous saber-toothed tigers and wild horses were also part of the ice age population.

The Bering Land Bridge and the "Clovis First" theory

When glaciers form, they freeze up vast quantities of water that would otherwise return to the oceans. This causes water levels to go down, and as the waters recede, land that was once under water becomes exposed. Scientists believe that glacial periods beginning about one hundred thousand years ago created a sea level that was 300 to 400 feet (91 to 122 meters) lower than present-day sea level. They theorize that the low water level exposed a vast land bridge spanning the distance across the Bering Strait, from Siberia in northern Russia to the northwest tip of North America (present-day Alaska). The land bridge, called Beringia, probably remained exposed until about twelve thousand years ago. Then it vanished beneath the rising waters as the Great Ice Age ended.

Since the Europeans first arrived in the Western Hemisphere, people have been interested in the origins of the natives of the land. In 1589 José de Acosta (1539–1600), a Jesuit missionary (a member of the Roman Catholic Society of Jesus, a religious order dedicated to spreading the Roman Catholic religion) stationed in South America, theorized that the first Americans had migrated on a route by land from Siberia. At that time the Bering Sea had not yet been discovered. In the late 1800s scientists expanded this theory, suggesting that human hunters might have followed big game

Hunters migrating from Asia across the Bering Land Bridge. *The Art Archive/ National Anthropological Museum Mexico/Dagli Orti.*

from Siberia out onto a land bridge spanning the Bering Sea between Siberia and Alaska and then continued across present-day Alaska and farther into the Americas.

Until the 1920s most people thought the land bridge migration had taken place between four thousand and six thousand years earlier. Then, in 1926, a cowboy in Folsom, New Mexico, discovered a stone spear point embedded in the rib cage of a type of bison that has been extinct for nearly ten thousand years. This proved that human hunters had been living in North America for at least ten thousand years. Ten years later, in Clovis, New Mexico, stone spear points were found in the remains of a mammoth. These remains were discovered in a layer of earth that was deeper than the site of the Folsom spear points, indicating that they came from an even earlier age. The older spear points, which came to be known as Clovis points, were radiocarbon-dated (tested for carbon 14 level to see how old they were) and found to be about 11,500 years old. After the first of these spear points were found, many more Clovis points and tool kits were discovered throughout North America. The sharpened rocks, attached to lances or spears for hunting, could be easily identified because they were fluted or grooved at the base and showed remarkable craftsmanship. They proved that humans had been living throughout the area that is now the United States and parts of Central America since at least 9000 B.C.E. For several decades most scientists thought that the Clovis points signaled the earliest period of human life in the Americas. This later became known as the "Clovis First" theory.

From the late 1950s to the recent past, most scholars accepted the theory that the first people in the Americas migrated from northeast Asian areas such as China, Siberia, and Mongolia. People from these regions were very specialized ice age hunters, who had developed a nomadic lifestyle, following big game wherever the animals roamed. According to the theory, within about one thousand years, the American continents—from Canada to the southernmost tip of South America—were populated with these big game hunters, who gradually developed into what is now called the Clovis culture. (A culture is the arts, language, beliefs, customs, institutions, and other products of human work and thought shared by a group of people at a particular time.)

Clovis spear points, which, for many years, were thought to be artifacts from the earliest period of human life in the Americas. © *Warren Morgan/Corbis.*

Pre-Clovis archaeological sites

During the decades following the 1950s, scholars generally accepted the Clovis First theory of the peopling of the Americas, even though there were archaeological finds of earlier settlements that conflicted with the theory. In 1977 archaeologist Tom Dillehay (1947–) began digging at a site at Monte Verde in south-central Chile. The site had been completely covered by a peat bog (a wet covering of decomposing vegetation), which preserved it in almost the same way that lava from volcanoes preserved ancient sites in Europe. Under the bog Dillehay discovered the remains of a small ancient village, where approximately twenty or thirty people had lived in twelve tent-like homes covered in mastodon hides. Extensive testing showed the artifacts at the Monte Verde site to be 12,500 years old. The skeptical archaeological community, though, had believed for many years that Clovis humans had been first. Many highly respected archaeologists had built their theories based specifically on the Clovis First theory and were unwilling to even consider conflicting evidence. Though the evidence was there to be seen and tested, it took some archaeologists decades to accept the Monte Verde findings. By 1997 the evidence had held up through an assault of criticism and analysis. Most of the scientific community now accepts that the artifacts from the site are at least a thousand years older than those from the Clovis sites.

Other sites in North and South America have yielded artifacts dating back before the Clovis period, though some have been discredited and most have not reached the level of acceptance of Monte Verde. In South America, the Taima-Taima site on the coast of Venezuela dates back 13,000 years; the Los Toldos and Piedra Museo sites in Argentina date back about 12,500 years; Lapa de Boquete in Brazil dates back about 12,000 years; and the Tibitó site in the Colombian Andes dates back 11,700 years. There are quite a few other possible pre-Clovis South American sites as well. North America has a few of its own possible pre-Clovis sites. Notably, the Meadowcroft Rockshelter in Pennsylvania, excavated by archaeologist James M. Adovasio (1944–) beginning in 1973, contained artifacts between 14,000 and 17,000 years old. Some extremely convincing evidence at the Topper site in South Carolina is currently under intense investigation. What appear to be human-made tools were dug from a hillside next to the Savannah River; some scientists suggest the tools date back at least 16,000 to 25,000 years. While many noted archaeologists find these artifacts compelling, others claim there is no way to ascertain that the tools found are actually human-made.

Other American artifacts have been radiocarbon-dated to extremely early times. The artifacts dating back more than 15,000 years are considered more controversial than those dating much later. Renowned archaeologist Richard "Scotty" MacNeish (1918–2001) began excavations in 1990 at a site called Pendejo Cave in southern New Mexico. Scientists found baskets, a piece of jewelry, simple stone and bone tools, and the remains of extinct animals. There was also direct evidence of human habitation—what appears to be human hair and fingerprints. MacNeish's analysis indicates that the site was inhabited by humans as long as 50,000 years ago (some say 30,000 years ago). At a site called Pedra Furada in Brazil, French-Brazilian archaeologist Niede Guidon (1933–) announced that she had found cave paintings that were 17,000 years old and stone tools that dated back as many as 32,000 years. In one section of the Monte Verde site in Chile, Dillehay found evidence of life dating back well before the now-accepted 12,500 years ago; in fact, some artifacts at the site are thought to be 33,000 years old.

In the early twenty-first century, archaeologists continue to unearth ancient American artifacts that do not fit into the Clovis First theory. Having confirmed that the accepted dates for the peopling of the Americas were probably wrong, many scholars have gone on to develop new theories about human life on the American continents before the Clovis era. A host of scientists have presented alternatives to the Bering Land Bridge theory of migration. Others are finding evidence that the earliest populations may have come from other origins than northeast Asia.

Alternatives to the Bering Land Bridge migration theory

Seaworthy boats have been around in some parts of the world for at least forty thousand years. Many experts believe that immigrants from northeast Asia may have traveled by boat along the coast of Asia during the Great Ice Age and then sailed south along the American Pacific Coast to their place of settlement. According to the Bering Land Bridge theory, early Americans took about one thousand years to walk the 10,000-mile (16,090-kilometer) distance from the far north near the Bering Strait to the far southern reaches of South America. Although one thousand years is a very long time, the motivation for each generation to keep moving at this rate bothered many experts. Some have theorized that at least some migrants undertook some part of their journey in boats, traveling down the coast by island-hopping or by navigating among icebergs or along shorelines. It is nearly impossible to prove this, though, because the shores that existed during the ice age have long since been submerged under water, and evidence that may have supported the theory is hidden under the sea.

One set of prominent archaeologists has compared the stone tools of the Clovis culture to the tools of the Solutrean culture, a European culture that developed in France and the Iberian Peninsula (the region of Europe presently occupied by Spain and Portugal) for about a three thousand-year period starting about twenty thousand years ago. These archaeologists note a distinct similarity between the stone tools of the Solutrean culture and the Clovis culture. Finding no other likely origins of the Clovis culture's distinctive tools and points, these scholars believe that ancient Europeans traveled across the Atlantic Ocean, navigating along glaciers and islands, to populate the area that is now the southeastern United States. According to this "Solutrean" theory, these early immigrants from Europe were in fact the ancestors of the Clovis people. No one knows exactly when they might have arrived, but presumably it would be around twelve thousand years ago, when the Clovis culture appeared in the southeast of present-day United States. Many archaeologists dispute the Solutrean theory for its lack of evidence.

Paleoamericans and other origin theories

Scientists and historians have long assumed that the first people who came to the Americas were northern Asians from Mongolia, Siberia, and China. They knew that these people were the ancestors of modern Amerindians, because northern Asians and Amerindians share certain physical characteristics (Mongoloid, or Asian, features) that indicate they come from the same racial stock. However, new techniques for evaluating human remains have convinced some experts in the field that people from what appear to be racial groups other than Mongoloid were present in the Americas before the northern Asians. Using a precise computerized method of measuring skulls—called craniometric analyses—archaeologists and other scientists have discovered that some ancient American people had Caucasoid or Negroid features, not Mongoloid features—that is, they came from white racial stock or black racial stock, not Asian stock. An advanced form of radiocarbon dating, which can date tiny fragments of bones and other organic (once living) matter with a high degree of accuracy, has helped them determine that some of the Caucasoid and Negroid remains are older than the remains of the ancient Asian migrants, the Amerindians' ancestors. These new techniques have greatly altered the field of American prehistory in just a few years' time, and many fresh theories have emerged.

Some experts suggest that the first Americans may have come from Southeast Asia. Scientists developed this idea after studying ancient human remains found in South America. In 1996 the 11,500-year-old remains of a young woman (named "Luzia" by her discoverer) found in Brazil were determined to have Negroid features rather than Mongoloid features. In other words, her face had features that were characteristic of a member of the black (Negro) race; she did not have the Asian (Mongoloid) features that were typical of other early American remains. Later, about fifty more ancient skeletons were found nearby in Brazil with similar Negroid features. Some scientists classified these skeletons, including Luzia, as Paleoamericans, proposing that they were actually early Americans who arrived before the Mongoloid people of Northeast Asia. Proponents of this theory claim that one or more groups probably left Southeast Asia and migrated to Australia about forty thousand years ago by boat, perhaps establishing the aboriginal society that still lives there in the early twenty-first century. Others may have traveled by boat northward along the coast of Asia and then crossed into the Americas at the Bering Strait. According to this theory, Luzia's ancestors probably arrived in the Americas about fifteen thousand years ago.

Since the findings about Luzia were published, many more ancient skeletons dating back more than eight thousand years have been found in the Americas that apparently do not have Mongoloid features. Some scientists have found remains that have similarities to a native Japanese group called the Ainu; others have found remains that resemble Southeast Asians; others have remains with similarities to those of Europeans. The scientists pursuing these alternative origins theo-

Native American Graves Protection and Repatriation Act

There has been relatively little research on the remains of ancient peoples in the United States in the past decades. This is because, by law, the remains of pre-Columbian peoples (existing before Spanish explorer Christopher Columbus arrived in the Americas in 1492) have to be turned over to Amerindian groups for reburial. Congress passed the Native American Graves Protection and Repatriation Act (NAGPRA) in 1990. The law was created in response to disrespectful handling of Amerindian remains in the past; it was designed to protect the right of Amerindian groups to bury the remains of their dead. Amerindian groups welcomed this law, because it forced U.S. museums and government agencies to return the remains of their ancestors and many cultural objects that belonged to them. In the early twenty-first century, NAGPRA was at the center of the Kennewick Man trial, a conflict between scientists who wish to examine recently discovered ancient remains that may add to the knowledge of pre-Clovis inhabitants of the Americas and Amerindian groups who wish to treat the remains in a traditional manner.

The Kennewick debate began in July 1996 when two men watching a boating race on the Columbia River near the eastern Washington town of Kennewick found part of a human skull in the river. When most of the complete skeleton was found, the local coroner (a public official who makes inquiries into the circumstances of mysterious deaths) and an anthropologist found the remains to

ries propose that groups of people—the Paleoamericans—migrated to the Americas at an unknown date and lived there before the northeast Asians—the Paleo-Indians—arrived. Many experts have shown that skeletons dating back more than eight thousand years are predominantly from the group showing Paleoamerican features, and skeletons from periods after that time have the predominantly Mongoloid features of modern-day Amerindians. Some proponents of this "Paleoamerican" theory have speculated that the earlier group of Paleoamericans perished in warfare with the newcomers, the Paleo-Indians. It is also possible that the two groups merged through intermarriages and gradually their descendants took on the current physical traits of Amerindians.

It is important to note that, despite the evidence, many archaeologists and historians do not believe that there were migrations from places other than Northeast Asia. They argue

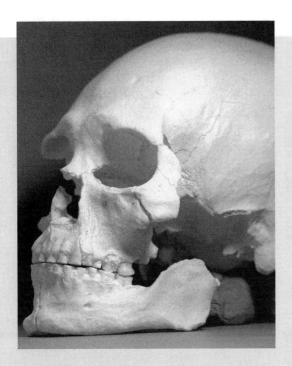

Skull of Kennewick Man. *AP/Wide World Photos.*

be more than nine thousand years old, making the Kennewick Man one of the oldest and most complete skeletons ever to be found in the United States. The anthropologist described the remains as Caucasoid, meaning that the Kennewick Man had features that were characteristic of a member of the white, or Caucasian, race (someone whose ancestors come from Europe, North Africa, or southwest Asia). A highly publicized court battle took place, with a group of scientists on one side and a group of Amerindians on the other, each contending their right to the Kennewick bones. On February 4, 2004, a three-judge panel upheld a 2002 ruling, stating that there was no substantial evidence that Kennewick Man had been an ancestor of modern Amerindians. The ruling will allow further scientific study of Kennewick Man unless it is stopped by an appeal.

that the differences in physical traits between the ancient and modern skeletons are due to adaptations to the environment and other evolutionary processes. That is, according to the critics of the Paleoamerican theory, the ancient ancestors of today's Amerindians simply had different features when they arrived in the Americas. They underwent gradual hereditary changes as one generation succeeded another. Given the changes in world wide climate and local conditions, evolutionary changes could have accounted for the changes that make the older skeletal remains appear to be from a different race.

Other evidence: Genetics and dental comparisons

Some scientists have attempted to learn more about American prehistory by comparing the genetic makeup of

An anthropologist examines the skull of "Luzia." *AP/Wide World Photos.*

Amerindians and the genetic makeup of Asians who come from some of the places that may have been the native lands of early Americans. Put very simply, genes are the basic units of heredity; they determine the traits that are passed from one generation to another. According to the genetic analysis, modern Amerindians are all genetically related to one another, and they are very closely related to the people of northeastern Asia. They are not genetically related to Europeans or southwest Asians. These tests have shown few variations in the genetic makeup of all Amerindians. Similarly, dental studies have shown that modern Amerindian teeth are most like the teeth of people in northern China but not like the teeth of people in European Russia or certain areas of Siberia in modern or ancient times. According to one dental theorist, people of northern Chinese origins may have migrated to the Mongolia area in east central Asia about eighteen thousand years ago, traversing it over thousands of years and finally crossing the Bering Land Bridge into Alaska about twelve thousand years ago.

Linguistic evidence

In 1989 linguist Johanna Nichols (c. 1944–) began a study of Amerindian languages. She found 150 language families on North and South America and quickly determined that this many languages could not possibly have developed in the 11,000-year time frame proposed by the Clovis First theory. Nichols believes that the Americas had to have been inhabited by humans for at least 30,000 to 40,000 years to account for the language development that occurred. She has proposed the following sequence of migration, based on language variations: Humans crossed the Bering Land Bridge about 30,000 to 40,000 years ago and traveled down to South America; between 22,000 and 14,000 years ago, the glaciers in the north spread, and humans were forced to stay in the warmer climate of South America; about 14,000 years ago, humans in South America began to spread north, inhabiting North America; around 12,000 years ago, another migration came across the Bering Land Bridge and spread down the coast; 5,000 years ago, another migration occurred through the waters near Beringia, and the people settled in Alaska, Greenland, and Canada.

Life for America's early settlers

In the past, most history books have described the earliest settlers in the Americas as a rugged group of hunters of ice age mammals, particularly mammoths. In recent years, most historians have expanded their views of the first Americans. While some of the first immigrants certainly killed the occasional mammoth, they also fished, gathered sea products, wove cloth and nets, gathered plants, made baskets, and built boats. The first Americans were not all alike. Traveling in small groups that adapted to the wide variety of environments, they developed diverse skills. At the Meadowcroft site in Pennsylvania, where humans are believed to have been living at least thirteen thousand years ago, Adovasio excavated tools for hunting small game, baskets for carrying plants, and bone tools probably used for working with textiles and hides. Unusual habitats in other regions, such as the frigid Arctic (the areas centered on the North Pole consisting of the Arctic Ocean and the lands in and around it) and the dry deserts of southwest North America, made survival especially challenging. Tools for chopping ice and killing whales in the Arctic differed greatly from the tools of small game hunters and wild plant gatherers of more southern regions.

For all early settlers in the Americas, survival was dependent on occupying vast expanses of land with few other people in the area. Anthropologist Michael D. Coe estimates that hunter-gatherers require about 25 square miles (64.8 square kilometers) of land per person to survive. The basic social unit was a very small group of families. For any given territory, it would not take long for a group of settlers to deplete (use up) the wild plants and animals. Then it was necessary to move on. Thus, in the years before farming came to any given region, humans were not very social. Contact with other humans was avoided, since it meant competition for food. As these first Americans spread out in pursuit of their needs, they populated the most remote corners of the two American continents. In the Andes and in parts of Mesoamerica (the area in the northern part of Central America, including Guatemala, Honduras, El Salvador, and Belize, and the southern and central parts of present-day Mexico, where many ancient civilizations arose), some of these groups were heading down the long path toward civilization.

For More Information

Books

Adovasio, J. M., with Jake Page. *The First Americans: In Pursuit of Archaeology's Greatest Mystery.* New York: Random House, 2002.

Coe, Michael D. *Mexico: From the Olmecs to the Aztecs.* 4th ed. London and New York: Thames and Hudson, 1994.

Coe, Michael, Dean Snow, and Elizabeth Benson. *Atlas of Ancient America.* New York: Facts on File, 1986.

Dewar, Elaine. *Bones: Discovering the First Americans.* New York: Carroll and Graf, 2001.

Periodicals

Wade, Nicholas, and John Noble Wilford. "New World Ancestors Lose 12,000 Years." *New York Times* (July 25, 2003): p. A19.

Wright, Karen. "First Americans (Origins of Man)." *Discover* (February 1999): p. 52.

Web Sites

Begley, Sharon, and Andrew Murr. "The First Americans." *Newsweek,* April 26, 1999. Available at http://www.abotech.com/Articles/firstamericans.htm (accessed on September 13, 2004).

Dillehay, Tom D. "Tracking the First Americans." *Nature,* September 4, 2003. Available at http://www.nature.com/cgi-taf/DynaPage.taf?file=/nature/journal/v425/n6953/full/425023a_fs.html (accessed on September 13, 2004).

Lovgren, Stefan. "Who Were the First Americans?" *National Geographic,* September 3, 2003. Available at http://news.nationalgeographic.com/news/2003/09/0903_030903_bajaskull.html (accessed on September 13, 2004).

Early Andeans:
From Nomads to City Folk

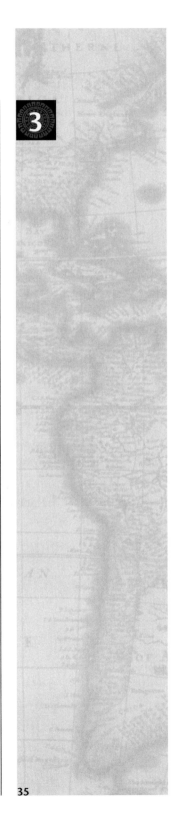

3

People have been living in the Andean region for at least twelve thousand years, and probably much longer. From the time of the earliest inhabitation of the region until about 7000 B.C.E. most Andean people were nomadic or semi-nomadic, roaming through the vastly different environments of the dry coastal plains, foothills, highland meadows, and mountain peaks. They hunted large and small game, fished, and gathered edible plants. Late in this era some Andean people began to grow a few crops; others began to raise camelids (family of mammals that, in the Americas, includes the llama, the alpaca, the vicuña, and the guanaco). Between 7000 and 3000 B.C.E. the Andean people began to settle into rough homes, initially caves or rock shelters, and ultimately formed small farming villages.

Things changed greatly around 3000 B.C.E., when the Andean people in a number of different areas began building very large ceremonial complexes (citylike centers in which people from surrounding areas gathered to practice the cere-monies of their religion, often at large temples and plazas built specifically for this purpose) many that required de-

Words to Know

Alpaca: A member of the camelid family; a domesticated mammal related to the llama that originated in Peru and is probably descended from the guanaco. The Andeans used the long silky wool of the alpaca in their textiles.

Altiplano: A high plateau; also referred to as a puna. In the central Andes Mountains of South America, where early Andean civilizations arose, the altiplano is about 12,000 to 16,500 feet (3,658 to 5,029 meters) high.

Architecture: The art or practice of designing and constructing buildings or other large structures.

Ayllu: A group of extended families who live in the same area, share their land and work, and arrange for marriages and religious rituals as a group; the basic social unit of the Andean peoples.

Camelid: A family of mammals that, in the Americas, includes the llama, the alpaca, the vicuña, and the guanaco.

Ceremonial centers: Citylike centers usually run by priests and rulers, in which people from surrounding areas gather to practice the ceremonies of their religion, often at large temples and plazas built specifically for this purpose.

Chicha: A kind of beer that Andean peoples made from maize or other grains.

Drought: A long period of little or no rainfall.

Ecosystem: A community of plants and animals and the physical environment (including geographic location, altitude, climate, and soil) where they live.

El Niño: An occasional phenomenon in which the waters of the Pacific Ocean along the coast of Ecuador and Peru warm up, usually around late December, sometimes bringing about drastic weather changes like flooding or drought.

Excavation: The process of carefully digging out or uncovering artifacts or human remains left behind by past

tailed planning and engineering and required hundred of thousands of human hours of labor to build. At that time, the Andean peoples were apparently fairly unsophisticated. Their farming was simple and there was no pottery for cooking and storing food. Nonetheless, during the years between about 3000 B.C.E. and 1800 B.C.E., the Andeans made great advances in art, religion, politics, and trade. From the foundations laid by the ceremonial centers, the first Andean cities were established. According to many scholars, it was during this period that civilization was born in the Americas.

human societies so that they can be viewed and studied.

Frieze: A band of decoration running around the top part of a wall, often a temple wall.

Guanaco: A member of the camelid family; a South American mammal with a soft, thick fawn-colored coat, related to and resembling the llama.

Huaca: A sacred place, usually used for a temple, pyramid, or shrine.

Llama: A member of the camelid family; a South American mammal that originated in Peru and probably descended from the guanaco. Llamas were used for their soft, fleecy wool, for their meat, and for carrying loads.

Monumental architecture: Buildings, usually very large, such as pyramids or temple mounds, that are used for religious or political ceremonies.

Radiocarbon dating: A method of testing organic (once living) material to see how old it is. Radiocarbon dating measures the amount of carbon 14 found in a sample. All plant and animal matter has a set amount of carbon 14. When an organism dies, the carbon 14 begins to decay at a specific rate. After measuring the extent of the decay, scientists can apply a series of mathematical formulas to determine the date of the organism's death—and consequently the age of the organic matter that remains.

Sacrificial offering: Something precious given to the gods. In early civilizations, sacrificial offerings often involved killing an animal or sometimes even a human being; the life that was taken was offered as a gift to the gods.

Vicuña: A South American mammal related to the llama and having a fine silky fleece, often used by the Andeans for making textiles. The early Andeans hunted vicuña for skins and meat.

The Andes: A region of extremes

The Andes Mountains are one of the world's longest and highest mountain ranges, running the entire 4,500-mile (7,241 kilometers) length of South America's western coast, from Colombia in the north to Argentina and Chile in the south. The ancient Andean civilizations arose in the central portion of the Andes and along the coastal plains to the west; this area included almost all of present-day Peru and parts of Bolivia, northern Argentina, and Ecuador. In this region there are a variety of extreme climates and geographies, rang-

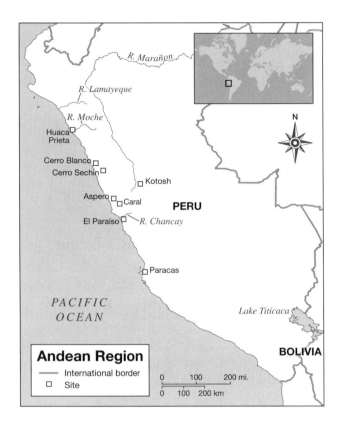

R. Marañon

R. Lamayeque

R. Moche

Huaca
Prieta

Cerro Blanco
Cerro Sechin

Kotosh

Aspero
Caral

PERU

El Paraíso
R. Chancay

Paracas

*PACIFIC
OCEAN*

Lake Titicaca

BOLIVIA

N

Andean Region

— International border
□ Site

0   100   200 mi.

0   100 200 km

Map showing the sites of ancient civilizations in the Andes region of Peru. *Map by XNR Productions. The Gale Group.*

ing from arid coastal deserts to high mountain peaks and volcanoes to fertile highland plains.

A narrow and extremely dry strip of coastal plains runs along the coast of Peru. There is virtually no rainfall on these plains. Cutting through this coastal desert are about fifty rivers running down from the nearby mountains, which create the system of valleys. Many of the rivers did not run all the way to the coast, and some were dry part of the year. The coastal people of ancient times settled in these river valleys. Good water sources in the dry coastal area were fundamental to the early Andean societies. Water played a major part in their religions, politics, arts, and economy.

The foothills (hills at the base of a mountain range) of the Andes rise abruptly out of the dry plains. Beyond them is the steep ascent to the mountain peaks, which rise to elevations as high as 20,000 feet (6,096 meters) in some places. In the central part of the Andes, a high plateau lies between two parallel ranges (the Cordillera Occidental and the Cordillera Oriental). This plateau—called an altiplano or puna—stands at a dizzying altitude of 12,000 to 16,500 feet (3,658 to 5,029 meters). Areas above 15,000 feet (4,572 meters) are extremely cold and covered in snow year round. Between the mountain peaks, there are fertile valleys ranging from 7,500 to 12,000 feet (2,286 to 3,658 meters) in elevation. The mountains, like water, were sacred to many of the early Andean societies. Temples and pyramids often faced nearby peaks and were sometimes built in their image. East of the Andean mountain range lies dense tropical rainforest, marking the end of the Andean civilization region. Although these regions were never incorporated (or added into) Andean societies, they provided many essential products and profoundly influenced Andean arts and religions.

Extreme changes in altitude and climate were not the only environmental challenges to the Andean people. The Andean region has long been the center of volcanoes and earthquakes, and it also experiences periodic weather changes brought on by El Niño (an occasional phenomenon in which the waters of the Pacific Ocean along the coast of Ecuador and Peru warm up, usually around late December, sometimes bringing about flooding or drought [long periods of little or no rainfall]). All of the early Andean civilizations and societies were profoundly affected by earthquakes and El Niño, droughts and floods; in fact the decline of several civilizations is thought to have been the direct result of both events occurring one after the other. Additionally, off the coastal area of Peru there is a cold ocean current known as the Humboldt Current. The cold water causes deep waters to rise up, creating excellent conditions for all kinds of seafood. Unfortunately, when El Niño conditions warm up the coast, much of the seafood disappears.

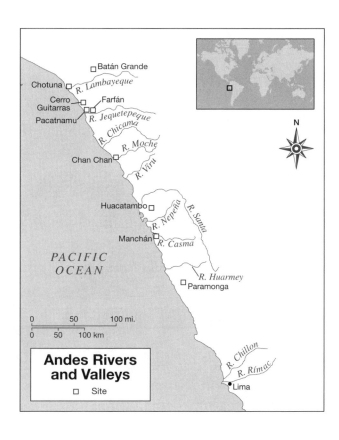

Map showing the sites of ancient Andean civilizations in Peru, including Andes rivers and valleys. *Map by XNR Productions. The Gale Group.*

The earliest Andeans

No one knows exactly when or how the first humans arrived in South America (for more information, please see Chapter 2). The earliest humans known to have lived in the Andean region were hunter-gatherers who developed special skills for the dramatically varied environments of the area. Using artifacts from the Monte Verde site in Southern Chile, which dates back at least 12,500 years, archaeologists have developed an idea of how some of the earliest Andean people lived. The camp at Monte Verde was strategically positioned. It lay within a day's walking distance of several different ecosystems (communities of plants and animals and the distinct physical environments where they live): a wetland area, where people could gather edible plants; the ocean, which

The altiplano, or open puna, lies below the snow-covered peaks of the Andes.
© Kevin Schafer/Corbis.

provided early humans with food from the sea—fish, other sea animals and birds, and seaweed; and the foothills of the Andes, where hunters tracked down vicuña, guanaco, and occasionally a mastodon (a very large mammal, now extinct, that resembled an elephant). Monte Verde inhabitants gathered plants, including wild potatoes, berries, seeds, nuts, and leafy vegetables, which were an important part of their diet.

Most early Andean people were semi-nomadic, following their game high into the mountains in the summer and then spending winters at camps in the lowlands. During the hunting season, hunting groups moved up into the altiplano, the cold and dry grassy plateau at about 13,000 feet (3,962 meters). There they hunted for camelids and other game, living in rock shelters or caves until it was time to move on.

In the lowlands and coastal areas west of the Central Andes, where rain seldom falls, people hunted and gathered in mangrove swamps (mangroves are plants that grow in

The First Mummies

Archaeologists look carefully at how ancient peoples treated their dead, because this information helps them determine how complex a particular society was. In general, as a society becomes more complex, its burial procedures and rituals (formal acts performed the same way each time, usually used as a means of worship by a particular group) also become increasingly complex. In some ancient societies these burial procedures included mummification (preservation) of the body. Beginning about 7,800 years ago, the Chinchorro people of Chile developed a process of mummifying the bodies of their dead. Their early mummies are thought to be the world's first mummies. With tools made of stone and shell, the Chinchorro removed the internal organs and flesh of the body and then filled the body cavity with earth, feathers, or grass. Often they placed a rod within the body to support it. The Chinchorro frequently covered the body (or just the face) in clay and painted it, placing a wig on the head. Bodies were often propped up and kept above ground long after death. Scholars believe that the practice of mummifying bodies eventually spread into other parts of the Andes.

Mummification and other early burial customs are evidence of the fundamental Andean tradition of ancestor worship. Most Andean civilizations believed that their dead ancestors actively worked for the well-being of their living descendants. Early Andean people often kept the bodies of their ancestors around for many years after death, and they sometimes prayed to the body of a dead ancestor or asked its advice. Andean social groupings, in which groups of families worked together and formed small villages, were usually organized around a long-deceased ancestor from whom everyone in the group could trace their family lines. The remains of a deceased ancestor could be used as proof of an individual's heritage, ensuring that he or she had a right to land or other benefits in a village.

wetlands along ocean shores; these wetland areas provide a habitat for fish and small animals). Hunter-gatherers also found small animals and a variety of edible (able to be eaten) plants in desert meadows called lomas meadows. These green areas in an otherwise arid environment owed their existence to the moisture brought in by fog banks from the sea and provided a vital portion of some coastal dwellers' diet.

Settling into Andean homes

By about 7000 B.C.E. on, some Andean groups had begun to settle into year-round homes, often in rock shel-

New World Camelids

Llamas and alpacas belong to a group of animals called camelids. Their early ancestors lived in North America forty million years ago. Ancient camelids were only about 1 foot tall. Thousands of years ago some of them migrated into the highland plateaus of the Andes, where they adapted to the severe freezing and windswept conditions. Over time, these animals evolved into the vicuña and the guanaco. (Scientists believe that other ancestors of the llama crossed the Bering Land Bridge, leaving North America for Asia, where they evolved into the modern camel.)

Early humans in the Andes hunted guanaco and vicuña as well as deer for their skins and for meat. Cave paintings in the Andes that date back more than ten thousand years show humans hunting the camelids. By about 6000 B.C.E. humans had begun to domesticate (raise and breed) the vicuña and guanaco. After these camelids were domesticated, about six thousand years ago, llamas and alpacas evolved from the domesticated species but did not replace them, so there were four kinds of camelids in the region.

Eventually, llamas and alpacas would become central to Andean civilization. The llama is 4 to 7 feet tall (about 3.5 feet at the shoulder) and weighs between 150 and 350 pounds. An herbivore (plant-eater), it grazes on grasses, herbs, and any other plants or moss it can find in the high plains. Like camels, llamas can go without water for days at a time, getting most of the water they need from the plants they eat. They are strong and agile and were extremely well adapted as pack animals for the early Andeans, carrying their trade goods along treacherous mountain paths. Although llamas cannot be ridden like horses, they are bred to be strong enough to carry large loads that are too heavy for

ters or caves. Even for those who continued to move from place to place, hunting had become highly specialized, and people tended to stay longer in one place. At this time the Great Ice Age was ending, so there were significant changes in the climate and environment. The large mammals—the mastodons, giant sloths, native horses, giant armadillos, and many others—became extinct. People branched out into different environments: Some adapted to life in the tropical rainforests hunting and gathering over wide territories; others settled on the coast, where the sea provided an abundance of fish and other sea creatures to eat; others moved into the highland areas of the Andes, hunting deer and camelids.

A llama grazes in the Andes. © *Alex Steedman/Corbis.*

wool is finer than llama wool. The Andeans bred alpacas solely for this wool, which was (and still is) woven into beautiful textiles (cloth).

When the Spanish arrived in South America during the sixteenth century, they replaced llamas and alpacas with cows and sheep. The Spanish and Andeans then hunted the wild guanacos and vicuñas nearly to extinction, and they are still endangered in the early twenty-first century. After the Spanish conquest of Peru, few people in Peru or Bolivia bothered to breed llamas and alpacas, and for many years they were largely forgotten. In recent times, however, llamas are once again being bred for their meat, and alpaca for their wool, which has regained its place as a luxury item. Because llamas were such a central part of life before the Spanish conquest, the modern-day people of the Andes value camelids as a symbol of their heritage.

humans. Without the llama, much of the early trade in the Andes would have been impossible. The meat of the llama was an important part of the Andean diet, and llama wool was woven into cloth. Alpaca

Simple farming and animal domestication started in the Andean region. By 6000 B.C.E. camelid-raising had begun in some areas. In the fertile areas where rivers brought the mountain rainwater onto the coastal desert, people began to experiment with growing a few types of plants. In northern Peru and northern Chile, beans were grown, probably by hunters in the off-season. On the coast by about 4000 B.C.E. people were growing peppers, lucuma fruit, and bottle gourds. Over time, new plants were introduced to the Andes region, including squash, avocados, peanuts, and cotton. Grains such as amaranth and buckwheat were grown in some areas and tubers such as potatoes in others.

The Cotton pre-Ceramic era: 3000 to 1800 B.C.E.

By 3000 B.C.E. the people on the coast and in the highlands had settled into communities and were regularly exchanging their goods. The highland people, far from the sea, enjoyed ocean fish in their diet; the people on the Peruvian coast regularly used fishing nets made of highland cotton, which became an important new crop, and ate potatoes and other foods grown in the highlands. They benefited from the extreme differences in climate and environment of neighboring regions by this exchange of goods. The people in all climates were able to ensure food throughout the seasons, because, for example, if the crops weren't producing in the river valleys, the Andeans could still trade cotton nets or bottle gourds to acquire fish from the coast or llamas from the highlands.

At this stage, the Andean peoples lacked many of the advancements that other ancient civilizations had developed. For example, although the Andeans were using simple forms of irrigation, few Andean areas were growing grains. In addition, no one in the Andes region was creating pottery at this time. Without pots, people cooked food by placing hot stones into baskets of food or broth. The Andeans had not discovered the wheel either, so travel and transporting heavy goods were time-and labor-consuming. Nonetheless, this era, now known as the Cotton pre-Ceramic era—from about 3000 B.C.E. to about 1800 B.C.E.—is considered by some scholars to be the period of the birth of civilization in the Americas. During this time, the Andeans made great advances in art, religion, politics, and trade. The most remarkable development in these years, though, was the building of elaborate monumental buildings—large shrines or mounds that became the trademark of early Andean civilizations.

Monumental architecture

Before 3000 B.C.E., most of the architecture in the Andean region was fairly simple, mainly consisting of houses and small buildings used for religious practices. Around 3000 B.C.E., however, the Andeans began building large-scale mounds in the highlands and coastal areas; these were public structures built for ceremonial use. The monumental mounds were very large (in fact, some of the largest monuments ever built in the Andes come from these early times). Some looked like hills; some had terracing (a series of horizontal ridges or stairs) ascending them; some looked like the pyramids of Egypt. They were often built to face a mountain; some are believed to have been made in the image of the mountains. Temple mounds were often built on top of an older building or temple. A community might first have a small temple. Then laborers would cover over the first building and build a temple on top of it. Rooms at the top of temple mounds were places for persons of higher status and used by the most important rulers or priests. Most of the pre-Ceramic temple mounds that have been found on the coast are rectangular, while those that were built in the highlands are more rounded or oval.

The construction of these huge temple mounds would have required hundreds of thousands of human hours of labor. For armies of men to have left the crops or hunting to spend months building a pyramid or monument required a surplus of food in the region to feed the laborers. The different skills involved in construction—from dragging heavy blocks of stone to organizing the laborers to designing and preparing the architectural plans—shows that a system of dividing skills and labor was in place. A ruler or government powerful enough to force or persuade the laborers to do this work and to reward the architects and planners for their efforts was also required. Pre-Ceramic settlements and centers with religious monuments have been found throughout the Andean region. Three examples are sites at Huaca Prieta in the Chicama Valley, Aspero in the Supe Valley, and El Paraíso in the Chillón Valley.

Huaca Prieta. The village of Huaca Prieta, on the northern coast of Peru, had a single monumental mound about 40 feet (12 meters) high. (This is highly unusual for an early Andean community; most had several mounds.) By 3000 B.C.E. notable advances in the art of weaving had taken place in Huaca Prieta. Villagers once wove simple reed mats, but when cotton was introduced to the village, they began weaving fine Peruvian cottons. The textiles found at Huaca Prieta bear intricate geometric designs as well as the shapes of animals and humans, all woven into the fabric in a variety of shades. These designs, which included crabs, double-headed snakes, a condor with a snake in its stomach, and others, may have represented figures from a religious system. The designs are often considered to be the first art created in the Americas, and some are still used in Peruvian textiles today. The people of Huaca Prieta buried their dead wrapped in reed mats and often placed grave offerings of dried gourds cut into bowls or other vessels with designs carved on them or other items with the body. This care in sending a deceased person to the other world with offerings to the gods and other materials to aid him or her on their way indicates a belief in the afterlife.

Aspero. Overlooking the Pacific Ocean on the northern side of Peru's Supe Valley was the large village of Aspero, covering more than 30 acres (.12 square miles /.08 square kilometers) and densely populated by about 2800 B.C.E. Aspero had plazas and terraces surrounding seventeen ceremonial mounds; the two largest mounds—Huaca de los Sacrificios (Shrine of the Sacrifices) and Huaca de los Idolos (Shrine of the Idols)—were about 98 feet (30 meters) tall by 164 feet (50 meters) wide. The top areas of these mounds held a number of rooms and courts. Both shrines were used for religious rites. In Huaca de los Sacrificios, archaeologists have found the remains of offerings to the gods, including textile and feather work, beads, carved wood, and burnt seeds. There is also evidence that human beings may have been sacrificed to the gods (killed to honor or appease the gods). In Huaca de los Idolos, archaeologists found small figurines made from unbaked clay. Most of the figurines represent females, several of which are pregnant. Archaeologists believe these were used in fertility rites (religious practices in which people ask the gods to grant them fruitfulness in crops and in human reproduction). The walls of the mounds at Aspero were made of rock that was carried to the building sites in woven bags called *shicra*. Workers filled these bags with heavy rocks and set them in place within the wall, leaving the bag with the rocks. The walls were then coated with adobe mortar and plaster and sometimes painted. Many Andean villages used *shicra* in building their monumental architecture, though the bags were never used in the construction of homes or non-ceremonial buildings.

El Paraíso. Located in the Chillón Valley in central Peru near the present-day capital city of Lima, El Paraíso (the Paradise) dates back to 1800 B.C.E. It was long thought to be the largest pre-Ceramic center in the Andes. Covering an area of about 125 acres (.20 square miles/.51 square kilometers), El Paraíso probably had a population of fifteen hundred to three thousand people in its peak years. Unlike most of the early coastal centers, it was built more than a mile inland. Fish from the sea were the primary food of the people of El Paraíso. Villagers gathered wild plants and dug up the roots of sedges and cattails at the riverside for food as well. They also had farms where they grew squash, beans, peppers, and some fruit. The main crop was cotton, which the residents of El Paraíso used for making fishing nets and tackle, clothing, and other prized possessions.

El Paraíso lacked grains, pottery, and metalwork, and yet from this simple society arose tremendous architectural accomplishments that demanded organized labor, leadership, urban planning, and engineering. El Paraíso was made

Ruins of El Paraíso in central Peru. *Daniel H. Sandweiss/University of Maine.*

up of thirteen or fourteen temple mounds; seven of them formed a U shape, defining the town center. The buildings at El Paraíso were made from an estimated 100 tons (90.7 metric tons) of rock that had been carried some distance in baskets and *shicra* bags, like those used at Aspero. The two largest constructions are mounds measuring about 165 feet (50.3 meters) wide, 26 feet (7.9 meters) high, and a quarter of a mile long. Between these two monuments is a very large plaza, and at one end is a smaller structure. It appears that El Paraíso was both a ceremonial center and a place where people lived. Within the mounds, stairways and hallways led to a variety of rooms and courts, some used for ceremony and others, most likely, for living quarters. The seven temple mounds of El Paraíso are one of the earliest examples of the U-shaped monument design, a design that would come to be heavily used in the early Andean civilizations, particularly in the highlands.

Many of the known pre-Ceramic centers like Aspero and El Paraíso were large, and archaeologists have found clear evidence that complex social institutions were present there. However, these centers are generally not considered cities. Many of the people in these places were not permanent residents, but rather travelers who went there to pay tribute (a gift, payment, or other acknowledgement of gratitude or respect) to the gods of worship. In addition, archaeologists have found little evidence that any business transactions went on in these centers, even in places where the population was more permanent. The primary purpose of the centers was to host religious ceremonies and public events rather than day-to-day business. Because the ceremonial centers showed no signs of city life, many archaeologists do not consider them to be the sources of early Andean civilization.

Norte Chico discoveries

In the early twenty-first century, major archaeological discoveries were made in the Norte Chico region of Peru—an area along the coast, about 100 miles (161 kilometers) north of Lima (the present-day capital of Peru). The discoveries there, described below, are still being explored today, and they are changing the way many archaeologists think about early civilization in the Americas. Many archaeologists believe the first cities and the cradle of American civilization are being uncovered there today.

Caral: America's first city?

Many ancient sites are known to exist throughout the Andes, but only a small portion of them have been excavated. One such site, Caral, was discovered in the Supe Valley of Peru in 1905, in a remote desert location. At that time, the large temple mounds of Caral were thought to be the work of people of fairly recent times, and the site was ignored for years. During those years, the mounds were covered by sands that the wind swept into hill-like formations. Ninety years later, in 1994, Peruvian archaeologist Ruth Shady Solís made her way to Caral. What appeared to her at first to be huge hills made of sand turned out to be gigantic temple mounds, or pyramids, covering a vast area—160 acres (.25 square miles/.65 square kilometers). Intrigued, Shady Solís and a team began to sift through the region surrounding the pyramids. They discovered a mysterious lack of ceramic artifacts, indicating that Caral had almost certainly existed and thrived before ceramics came into use in the Americas (which began around 1800 B.C.E.).

Shady Solís decided to begin an excavation of the Caral pyramids, a huge undertaking for which she recruited the Peruvian army. Caral's largest pyramid—"the size of four football fields and … 60 feet (18.3 meters) tall," according to John F. Ross in a 2002 *Smithsonian* report—was excavated first. In the walls of this pyramid, the archaeological team found, among many other things, the reeds from *shicra* bags that had been used to carry stones to the building site (the stones were left in the bags and piled up to form the walls). Because reeds are organic (once living) matter, scientists were able to use a special testing procedure called radiocarbon dat-

An archaeology student examines the *shicra* bags found in the ruins at Caral, which is believed to be the oldest city in the Americas. *AP/Wide World Photos.*

ing to determine the age of the *shicra* materials. The test results showed that the materials came from a range of years between 2600 and 2000 B.C.E. This information meant that the site was older than anyone had believed possible. It proved, to the surprise of archaeologists everywhere, that the pyramids of Caral were built at about the same time as the pyramids of ancient Egypt.

A complex society

The surprises continued. Caral's pyramids were huge and very complex, and the artifacts in them revealed a complicated society that previous archaeological work had not indicated. Shady Solís's team uncovered six pyramids around a central plaza. Piramide Mayor, the largest, was terraced and had huge staircases leading up to a platform. At the top were rooms that were probably used for ceremonies. Altogether there were three huge, sunken circular plazas, one of which was about 150 feet (46 meters) in diameter. In one plaza there were numerous houses. Next to the plaza and pyramids stood a temple and a sunken amphitheater (a large circular building with rising seating surrounding an open space), which was large enough to accommodate hundreds of people attending public events. In the amphitheater the team found thirty-two flutes carved from the bones of large birds. Later many more musical instruments were found in the amphitheater, made from the bones of deer and llamas. Just outside the central area encompassing the buildings and plazas described above there were residential areas. Perhaps this was where the workers lived. The size of the monuments indicates that there were probably thousands of laborers working constantly at this public monument over a period of many years.

Tourists view a room with a circular oven-type pit at the Caral site. The room may have been part of a residential building. *AP/Wide World Photos.*

The architecture of Caral provides evidence that there were distinct social classes within the community. The smaller pyramids had rooms at their tops to house the community's most powerful families—the priests and political leaders. A variety of neighborhoods surround the center. Neighborhoods with adobe houses and buildings not unlike modern apartment buildings, with units for different families' use, were probably home to the middle class—the artisans, or craftspeople (particularly weavers), administrators, and traders. In other neighborhoods, houses made of cane or thatch and mud probably gave shelter to the working-class residents of Caral, people who worked on farms or labored building the monuments. Although no one knows how many people lived in Caral in its heyday, most experts agree that its permanent residents numbered in the thousands.

Caral's economy

Caral's system of long-distance and short-range trade or exchange remains somewhat mysterious. Although Caral was

20 miles (32 kilometers) inland from the Pacific Ocean, its trash heaps were full of fish bones and residue from sea products, indicating that a major part of the diet there was fish—sardines and anchovies in particular. Despite the desert climate of the coastal area, the people of Caral managed to raise crops. Experts believe that farmers in Caral irrigated the dry soil by hoeing paths from nearby riverbeds to their land. The people grew beans, nuts, vegetables, and fruits, but apparently no grains or corn. The major crop in Caral was cotton. Archaeologists believe that the cotton was used to make fishing nets, which were then traded to coastal communities in exchange for fish. Shady Solís believes, in fact, that Caral was a major trade center with a long-distance trade network. Artifacts found in Caral provide support for this theory, because many of the raw materials and goods found there are known to have come from distant areas surrounding the Andes. It is also possible that Caral was a religious center visited by people from surrounding regions, pilgrims who brought tribute or offerings with them.

A city without violence

Interestingly, Caral does not appear to have engaged in any type of warfare or other violence. Scholars include warfare on the list of factors usually associated with civilization because at some point, most complex societies must defend themselves against competing communities; or conversely, some powerful societies feel the need to raid or conquer new territory and the people living there. However, there is no evidence in Caral of any defensive walls or of military action. Nor is there, so far, any evidence of human sacrifice. One grave, found within the large temple at Caral, held a baby who had died of natural causes. By all indications, the baby had been gently handled; he was wrapped in fine cloth and buried with stone beads to accompany him to the next life. The burial grounds of Caral and other nearby sites will almost certainly provide more information on this in the future. Meanwhile, the idea of a complex society without violence continues to be an intriguing possibility in the history of human civilization.

Surrounding urban centers

After the dramatic discoveries in Caral, other archaeologists launched large-scale efforts to excavate other ruins in the Norte Chico area. They have turned up about thirty urban (city) centers in three of the region's four river valleys—the Supe, Patavilca, and Fortaleza. Seventeen of these urban centers are in the Supe Valley, near Caral. Most of them have been radiocarbon-dated to the period between 2700 and 2000 B.C.E., almost exactly the same period when the Caral pyramids were built. This suggests that Caral was a city within a larger civilization, which may have had one central government and a shared religion. Shady Solís, the archaeologist who made the most recent discoveries in Caral, believes that Caral was the administrative and religious center of a civilization that included all the settlements and cities in the Supe Valley and possibly beyond. She also believes, and many other experts concur, that Caral was the first American city.

The abandonment of Caral

Caral and the urban centers around it thrived for several centuries. Sometime between 2000 and 1600 B.C.E., the residents of Caral painted their buildings black and then abandoned the city. The residents had time to cover over some of the treasured monumental buildings before they left. It is not clear why the people of Caral left their city. Drought and famine are likely causes. In the centuries that followed, many Andean peoples revered the abandoned city of Caral. They left treasures as offerings outside its borders but never tried to occupy it. Thousands of years later the Incas (pronounced ING-kuhs) would build temples just outside the city of Caral.

The Staff God

One of the important findings of the Norte Chico excavations is a four-thousand-year-old depiction of the Staff God, carved into part of a bowl made from a gourd. The artifact was found in a burial ground in the Patavilca River Valley. The engraved figure is a short, fanged creature with splayed (spread apart) feet; it is holding what appears to be a staff in one hand and a snake in the other. The Staff God, long known to archaeologists and historians, was previously thought to have originated in about 1000 B.C.E. among the Chavín people of the Andes (see Chapter 4 for more information on the Chavín). The most famous representation of the Staff God is on the stone gateway at the city of Tiwanaku (pronounced tee-wah-NAH-coo) and dates to about 200 C.E. The Staff God engraved on the bowl found at Norte Chico was radiocarbon-dated to 2500 B.C.E., a date that falls within the pre-Ceramic period. It is the oldest known religious artifact in the Andean region.

Most archaeologists and historians attach a profound significance to the discovery of the Staff God in Norte Chico, especially in connection with the discovery of the city of Caral nearby. It proves that some form of the central religion of the Andes that existed 4,300 years later was already in place in 2500 B.C.E. Archaeologist Jonathan Haas, a member of the research team in Norte Chico, commented in the *Christian Science Monitor* that in 2500 B.C.E. there were "small hunter-gatherer bands and fishing villages [in the Andean region].... Then you find this giant monster in Norte Chico—cities with large circular plazas, monumental architecture, and now a divinity figure. That's extraordinary." Because scholars consider a central religion one of the key elements in the development of a civilization, the ancient Staff God artifact provides more evidence that civilization in the Americas came into being in the pre-Ceramic Andes.

After Caral

Around the time that the city of Caral was abandoned, sometime after 1800 B.C.E., many people living in the coastal area of the Andes region moved inland to farm. Irrigation techniques spread throughout the region, allowing farmers to grow more than one crop each year and produce surplus food. With more food available, populations in each community became denser. The surplus food could be used to feed laborers who created public works. Huge stone and earthen ceremonial centers were built at an ever-increasing rate.

At this time people in the Andes region began firing clay to create pottery. Pottery had been used in the Caribbean and Ecuador for centuries, but most archaeologists believe it was discovered independently in the Andes. Pottery made it possible to store the surpluses of food that farmers were producing with their new irrigation methods. It also allowed Andean peoples to cook their food and to brew a fermented drink made from maize (corn). The drink, called *chicha,* was a kind of beer; it remained an Andean staple (produced regularly and used by many people) for thousands of years.

Pottery was an important new development in the Andes region, and its appearance marks the beginning of the Ceramic period (1800 B.C.E.) in the Americas. At this time the people in the Andes developed new social patterns due, at least in part, to the continued stability provided by new technology in farming, stored food surpluses, and trade.

Development of the *ayllu*

Some historians and archaeologists believe that the *ayllu* (pronounced EYE-yoo), the basic social unit of the ancient Andean region that would later be central to the Incas, existed in some form by around 1800 B.C.E. An *ayllu* was a small community made up of several family groups that claimed a common ancestor and generally lived together in a rural village. The members of the *ayllu* owned land in common and ensured that all member families had land. The people within an *ayllu* usually socialized and worshiped together.

Alliances and warfare

Archaeologists speculate that by 1800 B.C.E., the Andean communities were beginning to organize themselves by river valleys. The people of the various villages and centers within one river valley exchanged goods among themselves, usually not venturing out to other river valleys. More ceremonial centers were built in each river valley, and the people of the surrounding communities were able to gather on a regular basis at their nearest center for area-wide religious ceremonies. Because they shared goods and religious practices, the people within the valley felt a strong connection. Though most were probably not united by a common government or ruler, alliances among the villages and urban centers grew.

As the Andean people's focus extended out beyond their own villages, they developed friendships, as well as hostilities with other people. Water was always an issue and wars were probably sparked by competition for water sources. The

A warrior adorns a carving found in Cerro Sechín.
© *Kevin Schafer/Corbis.*

new, warlike mood showed up in Andean art by the thirteenth century B.C.E. At the site of a small urban center called Cerro Sechín in the Casma Valley, about 250 miles (402 kilometers) north of present-day Lima, Peru, archaeologists found four hundred carved slabs forming a mosaic (a decoration made by using pieces of various materials to create a picture or pattern) on the face of a stone temple dating back to about 1290 B.C.E. The mosaic depicts a group of armed warriors. The largest friezes (bands of decoration running around the top part of a wall, often a temple wall) show the victorious soldiers marching along triumphantly, while some of the smaller friezes portray the bodies of the defeated soldiers, naked and often mutilated (cut up or dismembered) or cut in half. Most of the slabs display the decapitated heads of the defeated warriors. This is one of many Ceramic monuments indicating the rise of military violence in the Andean region.

For More Information

Books

Adams, Richard E. W. *Ancient Civilizations of the New World.* Boulder, CO: Westview Press, 1997.

Coe, Michael D. *Mexico: From the Olmecs to the Aztecs.* 4th ed. London and New York: Thames and Hudson, 1994.

Katz, Friedrich. *The Ancient American Civilizations.* London: Phoenix Press, 2000.

Morris, Craig, and Adriana Von Hagen. *The Cities of the Ancient Andes.* London and New York: Thames and Hudson, 1998.

Morris, Craig, and Adriana Von Hagen. *The Inka Empire and Its Andean Origins.* New York: Abbeville Press, 1993.

Moseley, Michael E. *The Incas and Their Ancestors: The Archaeology of Peru.* London and New York: Thames and Hudson, 1992.

Schobinger, Juan. *The First Americans*. Grand Rapids, MI: William B. Eerdmans, 1994.

Web Sites

"The Lost Pyramids of Caral." *BBC: Science and Nature: TV and Radio Follow-Up.* http://www.bbc.co.uk/science/horizon/2001/caraltrans.shtml (accessed on September 22, 2004).

Ross, John F. "First City in the New World? Peru's Caral Suggests Civilization Emerged in the Americas One Thousand Years Earlier Than Experts Believed." *Smithsonian,* August 2002. Available at http://www.smithsonianmag.si.edu/smithsonian/issues02/aug02/caral (accessed on September 22, 2004).

Spotts, Peter N. "Religion in the Americas Began 2250 B.C." *Christian Science Monitor,* April 17, 2003. Available at http://www.csmonitor.com/2003/0417/p02s02-woam.html (accessed on September 22, 2004).

Chavín Culture

4

Chavín de Huántar (pronounced chah-VEEN deh WAHN-tar) probably does not fit the definition of a true city in the eyes of most scholars, but at this ancient bustling ceremonial center (citylike center usually run by priests and rulers, in which people from surrounding areas gather to practice the ceremonies of their religion, often at large temples and plazas built specifically for this purpose), many of the seeds of Andean civilization were sown. Functioning primarily as a religious center, Chavín de Huántar became an increasingly complex society, with a robust economy, social classes, job specialization, and an elite group of rulers. Between 500 and 200 B.C.E. the Chavín people made remarkable innovations in religion, the arts, engineering, architecture, and trade, and their advancements spread to other cultures throughout the Central Andes. The Chavín cult (a group that follows a living religious leader [or leaders], who promotes new religious doctrines and practices) was responsible for uniting a large part of the region for the first time. The cultural influence of the Chavín helped the entire Central Andes region take a large step toward true civilization.

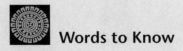

Words to Know

Administrator: A person who manages or supervises the day-to-day operations of business, government, and religious organizations.

Ceremonial centers: Citylike centers usually run by priests and rulers, in which people from surrounding areas gather to practice the ceremonies of their religion, often at large temples and plazas built specifically for this purpose.

Cult: A group that follows a living religious leader (or leaders) who promote new doctrines and practices.

Culture: The arts, language, beliefs, customs, institutions, and other products of human work and thought shared by a group of people at a particular time.

Deity: A god or goddess, or a supreme being.

Dates of predominance

900–200 B.C.E.

Name variations and pronunciation

Spelled Chavín; Chavin. Pronounced chah-VEEN. The term refers to a style of art and a religious cult that was widespread in the Andes between 500 and 200 B.C.E.; it also refers to the people who introduced these cultural developments. The main Chavín center, as far as archaeologists can tell, was Chavín de Huántar, pronounced chah-VEEN deh WAHN-tar.

Location

Chavín de Huántar is located in the northern highlands of present-day Peru at the head of the Marañón River valley, about 250 miles (402 kilometers) north of Lima, the capital of Peru.

At its height, the Chavín culture spread throughout much of present-day Peru, from present-day Ica, southeast of Lima on the southern coast, to the northern border of Peru and into the northern highlands.

Feline: A member of the cat family; or resembling a member of the cat family.

Frieze: A band of decoration running around the top part of a wall, often a temple wall.

Hallucinogenic drug: A mind- and sense-altering drug that may create visions of things not physically present.

Iconography: A method of relaying meaning through pictures and symbols.

Pantheon: All of the gods that a particular group of people worship.

Pilgrim: A person who travels to a holy place to show reverence.

Stela: A stone pillar carved with images or writing, often used to provide historical details or for religious or political purposes.

Tribute: A gift, payment, or other acknowledgement of gratitude or respect.

Chavín de Huántar

Chavín de Huántar lay at an altitude of nearly 10,000 feet (3,048 meters) at the meeting place of two rivers, one flowing down from a tall, snow-capped mountain peak called Huantsán. The center of the site was positioned on a roadway through the mountains that lay about halfway between a tropical forest region to the east and the desertlike coastal plains to the west. The route had been used by traders for years. The center of Chavín de Huántar was occupied and built in three phases over a period of nearly seven hundred years. The size and population of the center grew during each phase.

The Old Temple

During the first phase of construction in Chavín de Huántar, the Chavín people created the magnificent Old Temple as a center of religion and authority. Like many earlier, Pre-Ceramic monuments (built between 3000 B.C.E. and 1800 B.C.E.), the Old Temple had a U-shaped design, with the open part of the U facing the mountains. Three platforms of differing heights (from 36 to 53 feet [11 to 16 meters] tall) formed the U, and a sunken circular courtyard stood within. From the outside, the Old Temple appeared to be made of solid rock. No doors or windows were visible. To a pilgrim (someone who travels to a holy place to show reverence) arriving in the city

ECUADOR

BRAZIL

N

Chavín de Huántar

PACIFIC
OCEAN

PERU

Lima

0   100   200 mi.

0   100   200 km

Chavín

International border

□   Site

Map showing the site of the ancient Chavín civilization in Peru. *Map by XNR Productions. The Gale Group.*

from afar, the front wall of the central platform must have inspired great awe, if not fright: About 35 feet (10.6 meters) from the temple floor, a series of very large carved stone heads protrude from the wall. The heads are part animal and part human, with menacing bared fangs. In *Chavín and the Origins of Andean Civilization* (1992), Richard L. Burger, one of the principal scholars of the Chavín, theorizes that these heads may represent the different stages of transformation, or visions, of a Chavín priest, also called a shaman. Shamans sometimes took a hallucinogenic drug (a mind- and sense-altering drug that may create visions of things not physically present) in order to achieve a sense of transformation (change in form or appearance). While in this drugged condition, the shaman might see himself as an animal or a deity (god) figure (see also Religion in this chapter).

Inside the Old Temple is a remarkable network of passageways, secret chambers, tunnels, and air vents, none of which can be seen from the outside. Strategically placed ducts bring in odd geometric patterns of light and shadow as well as fresh air. Underneath the temple there is an elaborate system of water canals. The water came from the two nearby rivers, and experts believe that when it was released through special floodgates into these canals, it produced a mighty roar, perhaps like that of a jaguar; to the people of that time, it might have seemed that the temple itself was roaring. Pilgrims gathering in the courtyard of the temple may have been equally awestruck by what they saw and heard: Secret passages allowed the Chavín shaman to suddenly appear at the top of the platform, as if by magic, to proclaim their messages from the gods. In some of the inner rooms that were open to the public, air vents allowed voices to carry over long distances, so that someone in a central area could be heard in a remote room as if they were standing in it. In the courtyard of the Old Temple was a stone frieze (a band of carved decoration running around the top part of the temple wall) depicting half-human, half-animal figures. Like the protruding heads on the outer temple wall, these figures probably represent the transformation of a priest.

At the center of the Old Temple, reverently placed in a dark, cross-shaped chamber, is what appears to be the temple's main religious object: the Lanzón, a 15-foot-tall (4.5-meter-tall) pillar, or stela, carved out of granite. Engraved in the stone is the form of a god, perhaps the main deity of the Chavín. It is a humanlike form with a feline (catlike) face; the hands and feet have claws. The human earlobes on this deity are heavy with pendants or ear spools (large, round ear ornaments). Snarling with thick lips, the deity displays the fierce-looking fangs common to many Chavín images. Its

A stone face adorns a wall at the Old Temple of Chavín de Huántar.
© Ric Ergenbright/Corbis.

eyebrows and hair are snakes. The top part of the Lanzón extends through the ceiling and into the room above it. When visitors prayed to the Lanzón, a priest hidden from view in the room above may have answered them, making it seem as if the engraved image of the god had spoken.

The Lanzón is still in its place in the ruins of the Old Temple; two other stone carvings from the Old Temple were long ago removed and taken to another location. One is the Tello Obelisk (an obelisk is a tall, narrow pillar topped by a pyramid shape); the other is the Raimondi Stone. The Tello Obelisk depicts another animal deity, the caiman (a South American animal similar to an alligator); this was a common deity figure in the Chavín cult. The Raimondi Stone is carved with an image of the Staff God. This Andean deity is usually shown from the front and often has a catlike head with a fanged mouth and clawed feet that are spread apart. Its hair (or headdress) is often made up of snakes or snake heads. The Staff God always holds one staff and sometimes two. This

The Lanzón, a 15-foot-tall carved stone pillar, stands in the center of the Old Temple at Chavín de Huántar.
© Richard List/Corbis.

deity did not originate among the Chavín; its image has been found on at least one artifact that dates back to much earlier times. In the Norte Chico area of Peru, scientists found an easily recognizable image of the Staff God etched into a gourd that is about four thousand years old. This is believed to be the oldest identifiable religious image ever found in the Americas (see Chapter 3 for more information). The Staff God remained a central part of many Andean religions until the Spanish invaded the region in the sixteenth century.

The New Temple

By about 400 B.C.E., Chavín de Huántar had grown considerably. It probably had about three thousand residents and covered an area of more than 100 acres (0.16 square miles/.41 square kilometers). The populations in the surrounding areas had increased as well. At this time the Chavín people decided to create the New Temple by enlarging and remodeling the south building platform of the Old Temple. Construction of the new building, which was also modeled on the U-shaped design, was in the works for many generations. The Old and New Temple were both used for religious ceremonies and events. In time they came to be known as the Castillo (pronounced cah-STEE-yoe), or Castle.

The Chavín de Huántar site has captivated observers throughout history. The buildings of the Chavín required precise planning, skillful artistry, and substantial knowledge of engineering, acoustics (sound), and hydraulics (science that deals with water and other liquids at rest or in motion). The complexity of the structures and of the religious symbols portrayed in Chavín architecture indicate that this was a highly advanced culture. The extraordinary features of the Castillo seem to go far beyond the needs of a standard ceremonial center. The question still looms in the early twenty-

first century: Who planned such a fabulous center, and what was their purpose? Burger has offered the idea that Chavín de Huántar may have been the headquarters of an oracle or a family of oracles. Oracles are people, usually priests or priestesses, through whom the gods are believed to speak; an ordinary member of the public would have consulted an oracle for advice or help in making an important decision. Whether or not this theory is accurate, it is evident that religion and religious practices exercised an unusual amount of influence at Chavín de Huántar.

Ruins of Chavín de Huántar.
© Ric Ergenbright/Corbis.

History

The Chavín people are thought to have originated in small farming communities that may have been developing as far back as 3500 B.C.E. By 800 B.C.E., many of the ceremonial centers along the Peruvian coast and in the Andean highlands had been abandoned or had suffered huge losses of population. Around that time, in a mountain pass in the northern Central Andes, the Chavín began building their ceremonial center. About five hundred Chavín people were living in the area at the time. When the center, Chavín de Huántar, was completed, people from a wide surrounding area worshiped there, while making their living by farming in the valley or herding llamas or hunting in the highland meadows.

Chavín de Huántar drew many visitors. A compelling religious cult arose there, and soon people from distant valleys were making long treks up treacherous mountain roads to visit the awe-inspiring temple, which roared with an eerie force and magically produced priests from its doorless and windowless walls (see The Old Temple earlier in this chapter). The religion practiced at Chavín de Huántar began to take hold across the Andean region. (Archaeologists have found artifacts in quite a few unrelated regions across the Andes that bear distinctly recognizable Chavín religious images: the Staff God, the jaguar, the monkey, and various birds of prey.) The people who came to this center from afar brought tribute (gift, payment, or other acknowledgement of gratitude or respect) to the gods. No one knows exactly how the tribute was collected or how it was used in the city's economy, but some scholars believe that the tribute goods enriched the center's economy and stimulated interest in exchanging goods with distant communities. In time, Chavín de Huántar developed extensive trade and its people prospered.

By about 400 B.C.E., the religious cult of the Chavín had spread to remote parts of the Andean region. Chavín technology in tiles, ceramics, dyeing techniques, metalwork, stonework, and other fields found its way into distant settlements. Chavín religious imagery appears on artifacts—ceramics, textiles, and carvings—from as far south as Nazca (pronounced NAHZ-cah) and throughout the northern coastal and highland communities.

It is very unusual for religion to spread in this way without military conquest, but there is little evidence of war among the many groups that adopted the Chavín culture. Most scholars believe that the disappearance of pre-Ceramic (3000 B.C.E. to 1800 B.C.E.; see Chapter 3 for more information) ceremonial centers created a spiritual need and that the Chavín religion was alluring to the Andean people because it filled that need. Many scholars also believe that the spread of the Chavín culture marked the first time that the ancient Andean communities were united. This union of diverse Andean communities of the Chavín culture was a pivotal event in the history of Andean civilization.

According to Adriana Von Hagen and Craig Morris in *The Cities of the Ancient Andes* (1998), Chavín de Huántar was never more than a ceremonial center and does not seem to have had any central governing body or military enforcement. Von Hagen and Morris note that, even so, Chavín de Huántar was the center of culture and ideas for a vast area. The exchange of religious ideas and imagery with other areas developed into a system of goods exchange, and this connection of religion and economy was a crucial contribution to later Andean civilizations. Von Hagen and Morris conclude:

> *The exchange system was tied to religion and ceremony, and production was geared to providing the goods the religion and the elites required. Artistic innovation created the designs and symbols for communicating religious ideas and marking the identities of the religious elite, and technological innovations introduced new ways of producing the goods that the religion required. This fusion of the ceremonial and the economic would become a fixture of Andean cities.*

Government

Little is known about the governing of Chavín de Huántar, but such a large and powerful ceremonial center must have had a strong administrative system in place. (Administrators are people who manage or supervise the day-to-day operations of business, government, and religious organizations.) The priests in Chavín de Huántar almost certainly had a great deal of power. The priests, the administrators, and wealthy traders probably made up an elite group of rulers in the community. There also must also been a big pool of laborers to build the large temples of Chavín de Huántar. It is likely that nearby farming villages sent crews of workers to public building projects as a kind of tribute payment to the religious center.

Economy

At the time Chavín de Huántar was built, most of the people in the area were farmers, herders, and hunters who had successfully adapted to the mountainous terrain. By about 500 B.C.E. the economy of the region seems to have been driven by

Oracles

Chavín scholar Richard L. Burger theorizes in *Chavín and the Origins of Andean Civilization* that the Chavín religious cult may have spread in the same manner that a sixteenth-century religious cult spread in the Andes. Because the sixteenth-century event happened right before the Spanish invaded the Andes region, it has become part of recorded history, and it may shed some light on the operations at Chavín de Huántar.

Pachacamac was a ceremonial center in the Lurín Valley of Peru during the sixteenth century. It was home to a powerful and admired oracle who collected tribute from the people to offer to the Pachacamac deity. The deity, who was believed to control earthquakes, was greatly feared, and people from far and wide brought goods such as llamas, textiles, gold, and dried fish to keep the god happy. The trip was long, though, and soon remote villages asked the religious establishment at Pachacamac for permission to build branches of the religious center closer to their homes. They offered to provide local oracles to substitute for the oracle at Pachacamac. In this way, a form of religious state government with regional centers developed as the religion spread. Scholars believe that a similar arrangement was reached between the priests at Chavín de Huántar and the people of Paracas, who built a branch ceremonial center at Karwu.

the temple. As the Chavín religion spread, people traveled to Chavín de Huántar from all over the Andes, bringing gifts and tribute for the priests and oracles and greatly enriching the city. Traders who lived in or near the ceremonial center also traveled, taking Chavín goods and ideas to remote parts of present-day Peru.

As Chavín de Huántar began to prosper, its people continued to develop their skills in the arts and technology. Eventually, at the height of the center's prosperity, many people specialized in their own fields and carried on businesses in their homes, creating goods that could be exchanged to people in far-off places. Aside from being expert stone carvers, the Chavín people were potters, bead makers, weavers, and metalworkers. Within the temple, new kinds of occupations arose. Some temple workers created religious imagery that artists were to reproduce on Chavín artwork, which was then dispatched throughout the region. The temple also employed administrators, whose job was to keep the place running smoothly.

Because of its mountain location, Chavín de Huántar initially had limited trade. It took a tremendous effort to carry goods up to the ceremonial center. Around 500 B.C.E., however, people began to herd llamas (South American mammals that originated in Peru) and use them as pack animals. A llama driver could handle as many as thirty animals at a time, and each llama could carry a heavy load up the mountain trails. Thus, trade in the city increased greatly. As more and more teams of llamas headed up the trail, it became necessary to build better roads.

Remains discovered by archaeologists show that after 500 B.C.E. the residents of Chavín de Huántar were eating more llama purchased from herders and more fish brought up from the coast. This indicates that their trade was good, and some people in the center were getting quite rich. But life was not necessarily good for everyone. From the refuse left behind, it is clear that the people who lived closer to the temple ate a healthier diet than the people who lived on the outskirts of town. While the people who lived nearer the center ate their food off ceramic serving dishes and owned many goods from foreign places, the houses on the edges of the town had none of these goods and conveniences. People who lived on the outskirts of town were clearly not as wealthy. Social classes, in which certain groups of people were more privileged than others, had emerged.

Religion

The nature of the Chavín religion will probably always remain a mystery, but it is of great interest because some of the distinct features that emerged helped form the basis of all the major Andean religions. The Chavín religious imagery, the idea of sacred geography and *huacas,* or shrines, and the act of transformation, particularly into an animal spirit, are early developments in the complex Andean religion.

Scholars have tried to gain some understanding of the Chavín belief system by interpreting the depictions of Chavín gods on art objects. The three deities found on artifacts in the Old Temple—the "snarling" god of the Lanzón, the caiman of the Tello Obelisk, and the Staff God of the Raimondi Stone—are certainly major deities in the Chavín pantheon (the recognized gods of the Chavín). Scholars believe that by the time of the New Temple, another god had taken the "snarling" god's place but its image was lost. Other deities, particularly feline (catlike) figures, are depicted in stone carvings, in textiles, and on ceramics. Images of animals and portraits of half-human, half-animal figures abound. Many of the apparently religious images involve a creature with a combination of human, cat, bird, and

The Raimondi Stone depicts the catlike head, fanged mouth, and clawed feet of the Staff God, a central Andean deity. © *Gianni Dagli Orti/Corbis.*

snake features. Most have fangs and appear to be snarling and ferocious.

When the builders of Chavín de Huántar erected their city, they expressed a sense of "sacred geography," placing their buildings in positions aligned with the surrounding features of nature that the Chavín considered sacred. The people revered the mountain peak, Huantsán, that loomed over their city as sacred. They felt connected to the mountain through the Moqsna River, which flowed down from the mountain and right through their city. The site of their city was also the meeting point of the Moqsna and another river; this meeting of the rivers, too, was considered a lucky or even sacred feature of nature. The shrine or *huaca* built upon a sacred place was considered the most direct link to the gods who had the power to help the Chavín people or destroy their lives. People considered it a wise investment to travel to the sacred sites and deliver their tribute. They were also ready to provide labor in the building or repair of the *huaca*. In return, they expected the supernatural beings to make them safe and provided for them.

The shamans of Chavín de Huántar used a type of hallucinogenic cactus—San Pedro cactus—to achieve visions, or hallucinations, which they interpreted as messages from the spirit world. In Peru, San Pedro cactus has been used in this way continuously for the past three thousand years. Some of the carved pictures of beings that are half-human and half-animal may represent the visions the shamans had when they were under the influence of the hallucinogen and saw themselves transforming into animals or deities.

Arts and sciences

When experts refer to "Chavín style," they are referring to the style the Chavín used in their stone sculp-

tures. Through trade, other communities became familiar with Chavín style and adopted it in their own artwork; thus, some art pieces done by peoples other than the Chavín may also be said to have Chavín style. The stone carvings made by the Chavín—both the huge monuments and the small sculpted pieces—are considered the most notable artwork of the culture. However, the Chavín were also master artists in metalwork, especially gold, and in textiles and ceramics.

The administrators of the Chavín de Huántar ceremonial center in its heyday were apparently actively working to distribute their religious ideas through a complicated system of artistic imagery. Using a system of iconography (a method of relaying meaning through pictures and symbols) the Chavín artists expressed a variety of religious concepts that would be understood in far off places by placing traditional religious images in certain orders and repeating them in a variety of ways. The creators of these figures intended them to

Felines, such as the gold one pictured here, were regarded as divine in the Chavín culture and were often portrayed in metalwork. *The Art Archive/Museo del Oro Lima/Dagli Orti.*

be understood and interpreted in combination with each other. Only people who knew what the figures were intended to represent would have been able to interpret this art. In this way, the art was somewhat like written text, in that some of the depictions may have had a literal (factual or real) meaning. According to anthropologist John Howland Rowe in his undated lecture at the University of California, Berkeley, called *Form and Meaning in Chavín Art,* the most common icon, or religious image, used by the Chavín was the snarling, fanged mouth of a cat. The Chavín gave human, snake, and even bird figures this feline mouth. Rowe explained that the cat, or jaguar, mouth probably signifies that the creature in the picture is either divine or mythological (relating to an imaginary story, being, or thing). This is an example of how religious ideas were conveyed.

Decline

The Chavín influence only lasted for about three hundred years. No one knows for certain what caused its demise, but sometime after 300 B.C.E. the building of monumental centers in the surrounding region suddenly ceased. People scattered, abandoning the areas of the large ceremonial centers, including Chavín de Huántar. Without the unifying religious and trade network of the Chavín in the years following its abandonment, the Andean region was once again divided into small communities that remained independent of each other.

For More Information

Books

Burger, Richard L. *Chavín and the Origins of Andean Civilization.* London and New York: Thames and Hudson, 1992.

Davies, Nigel. *The Ancient Kingdoms of Peru.* London: Penguin, 1997.

Morris, Craig, and Adriana Von Hagen. *The Inka Empire and Its Andean Origins.* New York: Abbeville Press, 1993.

Moseley, Michael E. *The Incas and Their Ancestors: The Archaeology of Peru.* London and New York: Thames and Hudson, 1992.

Von Hagen, Adriana, and Craig Morris. *The Cities of the Ancient Andes.* London and New York: Thames and Hudson, 1998.

Web Site

"Form and Meaning in Chavín Art." *Eighth Emeritus Lecture Honoring John Howland Rowe, Anthropology Emeritus Lecture Series at U.C. Berkeley.* http://sunsite.berkeley.edu/Anthro/rowe/pub/chavin/ (accessed on September 28, 2004).

Nazca Society

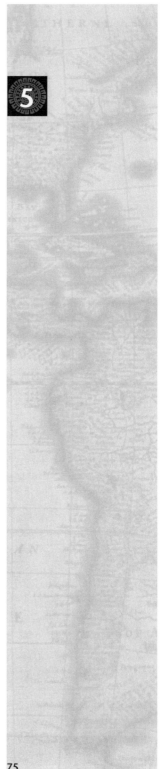

5

The Nazca (pronounced NAHZ-cah) were a small, independent society that flourished between 100 B.C.E. and 700 C.E. The Nazca people worked as farmers, skilled potters, and basket makers, and as a group they made significant advances in underground irrigation systems. They also made large-scale line drawings in the desert, which have endured into the twenty-first century. Many similar independent communities existed in the Central Andes during the same period as the Nazca, but the Nazca are more famous, mainly because of these amazing drawings. If a modern traveler flies over the arid (dry, with little or no rainfall) southern coastal plains of present-day Peru he or she will see a vast display of straight lines that are miles long, huge geometric shapes, and gigantic animal and plant figures. The drawings are so large that it is difficult to see them from the ground. Why did the Nazca sketch out these enormous pictures in the sand—pictures that they could not easily view themselves? This question has puzzled all kinds of investigators. Some of them offer scholarly theories to explain the drawings; others have

75

Words to Know

Aqueducts: Human-made channels that deliver water from a remote source, usually relying on the pull of gravity to transport the water.

Astronomical observatory: A place designed to help people observe the stars and planets and all celestial phenomena.

Bioglyph: A symbolic animal or plant figure etched into the earth.

Ceremonial centers: Citylike centers usually run by priests and rulers, in which people from surrounding areas gather to practice the ceremonies of their religion, often at large temples and plazas built specifically for this purpose.

Geoglyph: A symbolic figure or character etched into the earth.

Pampa: The partly grassy, partly arid plains in the Andean region.

Pilgrim: A person who travels to a holy place to show reverence.

Pre-Columbian: Existing before Spanish explorer Christopher Columbus arrived in the Americas in 1492.

Trophy head: The head of an enemy, carried as a token of victory in combat.

come up with alternative explanations involving extraterrestrial beings and the supernatural.

Dates of predominance
100 B.C.E.–700 C.E.

Name variations and pronunciation

Spelled Nazca; Nasca. Pronounced NAHZ-cah. The term refers to the people who lived in the Nazca Valley at that time.

Location

The Nazca exercised power over the people in the desertlike southern coastal plains, or *pampa,* from the Chincha River Valley in the north to the Acari Valley in the south, about 250 miles (402 kilometers) south of present-day Lima, Peru.

Important sites

Cahuachi

Cahuachi was built in the Nazca Valley around 100 C.E. Though it may have arisen as a small village, it eventually became the major religious center for the Nazca. It was a place where pilgrims traveled to pay their respects or tribute to their priests and gods. Cahuachi stands at the site where the Rio Grande de Nazca changes from an aboveground river to an underground river. Most scholars believe that the Nazca saw this place as a sacred spot; they think the Nazca built their ceremonial center (citylike center usually run by priests and rulers, in which people from surrounding areas gather to practice the ceremonies of their religion, often at large temples and plazas built specifically for this purpose) there so that they could worship the creators of the water supply.

The ceremonial center at Cahuachi covered about 370 acres (.58 square miles/1.5 square kilometers). About forty adobe (sun-dried earthen brick) temple mounds still exist at Cahuachi. Most are simply adobe caps that were placed on the tops of hills. The Great Temple, Cahuachi's biggest structure, was created from an existing hill and towers about 100 feet (30.48 meters) over the town. Most archaeologists believe that Cahuachi was only used for ceremonies and burials and that it was never a place where common people lived or worked. Sometime in the fourth or fifth century C.E., great natural disasters struck Cahuachi—drought (long period of little or no rainfall), followed by flooding and mud slides, and possibly an earthquake as well. It appears that the Nazca people purposely burned and then abandoned Cahuachi in the sixth century and moved their religious center to the north, where they had already begun to mark gigantic line drawings on the surface of the *pampa*.

Map showing the sites of the ancient Nazca civilization in Peru. *Map by XNR Productions. The Gale Group.*

Ventilla

In the Ingenio River valley, a Nazca center called Ventilla arose while Cahuachi was still inhabited. Unlike Cahuachi, Ventilla was probably the residential city of the Nazca, a place where people lived and did business. Ventilla was much larger than Cahuachi and had many buildings. There is little left of the ruins of Ventilla. Its history, independent of the Nazca lines, is very sketchy.

The dry, desert conditions of the Nazca Valley. © Yann Arthus-Bertrand/Corbis.

History

The story of the Nazca people revolves around the geography and water sources in the area where they lived, one of the driest places on the planet. The southern rivers of Peru are smaller than those in the north and tend not to stretch all the way from their mountain sources to the sea; hills block their path to the Pacific Ocean. The Nazca Valley is the inland meeting point of several such rivers. In the lower valley, the Rio Grande de Nazca and some of the other rivers actually run underground in certain places, avoiding the hot sun of the desert plains, which would otherwise evaporate their waters. The Nazca people adapted to their harsh, dry environment by developing an irrigation system that followed the example of the rivers: They located and tapped into the water table (the upper limit of the portion of the ground wholly saturated with water) and then directed the water—underground—to the places it was most needed. The Nazca built underground aqueducts, channels that delivered the water to far-off reservoirs (chambers used for storing water) and irrigation canals. Some of these channels are as deep as 30 feet (9 meters) underground and measure up to a half-mile long. A few of these aqueducts, called *puquios,* are still in use in the early twenty-first century.

Even with the Nazca innovations in irrigation, the southern coastal climate was too dry to provide enough food for dense populations. Scholars estimate that the population of the Nazca Valley probably never rose above twenty-two thousand people.

Government

Little is known about the government of the Nazca. The images on Nazca ceramics do not indicate that there was a hierarchy, or classification of the people according to ability or to economic, social, or professional standing within the society. The people who participated in the Nazca culture shared customs, a style of art, and a religion, but they probably lived in fairly small social units that were governed independently.

Religion

Like other pre-Columbian (existing before Spanish explorer Christopher Columbus arrived in the Americas in 1492) groups, the Nazca seem to have based their religion on the forces of the natural world. On their pottery and on the ground of the desert, they drew images that represent the godly forces of rain and climate. According to archaeologist Donald Proulx, as quoted in a 2000 *Discover* article, these images were "representations of supernatural forces—not deities [gods] in the Western sense but powerful forces of sky and earth and water whom they needed to propitiate [satisfy] for water and a good harvest."

The Nazca lines

The best-known artifact (any item made or used by humans, such as a tool or weapon, that may be found by archaeologists or others who seek clues to the past) of the

The Nazca people created an amazing system of lines that remains on the coast of present-day Peru. © Yann Arthus-Bertrand/Corbis.

Nazca is the amazing system of lines that the Nazca people drew on the coastal plains, or *pampa,* north of Cahuachi. The drawings extend over an area of about 400 square miles (1,036 square kilometers). The *pampa* has a fine dark crust that covers much whiter sand below. By brushing away the crust, the Nazca created well-defined lines of pale sand. Because the *pampa* receives so little rain and is protected from winds by the mountains, the Nazca lines are still there and mostly intact in the early twenty-first century, two thousand years after they were created.

The Nazca lines are called "geoglyphs." They represent a kind of writing or expression drawn directly on the earth's surface. There are about a thousand Nazca geoglyphs in all, including straight lines, odd shapes, and "bioglyphs," or animal and plant images. Some of the perfectly straight lines are 9 miles (14.5 kilometers) long. Viewed together, some of the straight lines form gigantic geometric shapes. There are also unknown symbols and zigzagging lines.

Among the bioglyphs are huge birds, spiders, and plants. Most scholars of ancient Andean cultures believe that the animal images were done first, and that the straight lines and geometric shapes were probably created in, or even before, the earliest known Nazca settlements in the area, possibly between 200 and 300 C.E.

The people who made these lines probably worked in groups over a period of many years. They may have been fulfilling a public work commitment to the rulers or priests at Cahuachi or elsewhere. To make the lines, the workers cleared rocks from their path and piled them up for later use. Then, with branches or their feet, they swept off portions of the dark crust, exposing the white sand below it. Finally, they piled the stones along the borders between the light and dark sand. The creators of the lines must have drawn them out ahead of time in small sketches. Using mathematics, they enlarged their sketches into the huge figures on the ground, laying them out with stakes and ropes.

Purpose of the Nazca lines

The Nazca drawings were not discovered by modern people until the 1920s. Since that time there have been many theories about their creation. Scholars disagree about the specific purpose of the lines, but almost all of them believe that the lines had a religious function and were used as sacred pathways and grand-scale monuments to gods associated with natural resources and good harvests. The lines were probably used as walkways by pilgrims (people who travel to a holy place to show reverence).

Among the first scholars to study the Nazca lines in depth was historian and anthropologist Paul Kosok (1896–1959). Beginning his work in the 1930s, long before there was public interest, Kosok theorized that the lines represented the Nazca perception of the movements of the stars and planets. Suggesting that the lines were a kind of astronomical observatory (a place designed to help people observe the stars and planets and other celestial phenomena), Kosok called them "the largest astronomy book in the world" (as quoted in a 2000 *Discover* magazine article). One of his followers, German mathematician and archaeologist Maria Reiche (1903–1998) spent fifty years studying the Nazca lines.

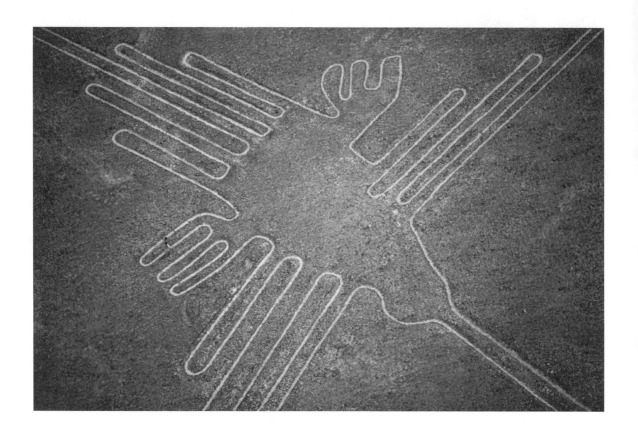

A bioglyph, an animal or plant image, in the form of a hummingbird is seen from this aerial view. © *Yann Arthus-Bertrand/Corbis.*

She rented a small house in the desert nearby and until the age of ninety spent her days alternately measuring and tidying up the mysterious lines. Working from a mathematical viewpoint, Reiche sought to prove that the lines functioned as a calendar that helped Nazca farmers time the planting of their crops. She believed that the Nazca lines aligned with the positions of the sun and planets. In the late 1960s, the theories of Kosok and Reiche were put to the test in a sweeping computer analysis. The results of this analysis seemed to prove that the Nazca lines did not correspond in any way to the position of the sun, the planets, or other celestial bodies.

In the 1980s, archaeologist Johan Reinhard (1943–) began to study the ways of the modern Andean people in Peru, Bolivia, and Chile. Reinhard witnessed their ceremonies and he noted that during these ceremonies the people gave offerings to mountain gods in hopes of obtaining badly needed water. Reinhard believes that the Nazca lines are sacred walkways that symbolically connect the various aboveground and

An Alternative Idea about the Nazca Lines

Since the late 1960s, Swiss writer Erich Von Däniken (1935–) has sold 56 million copies of his books, which relate his ideas on the beginnings of civilization on Earth. His theory is that well-meaning and very advanced beings from outer space traveled to Earth in spaceships thousands of years ago. When they arrived on Earth, according to Von Däniken, they found the ape-like ancestors of humans living here. By interbreeding with them, they created modern human beings. While they were here, the aliens built many monuments, such as Stonehenge in England (a circular setting of large standing stones dating back to about 2500 B.C.E.), the pyramids in Egypt, and the great Maya (pronounced MY-uh) temples in Mesoamerica. These aliens had become the gods of human religions before they left Earth for good thousands of years ago.

Von Däniken believes that the set of Nazca lines served as airport runways for the space gods as they arrived and departed in their spaceships. He reasons that people on the ground could not have drawn such perfectly straight lines and concludes that the lines must have been drawn from the air. (Many scientists who have studied the ancient Andean civilizations find this line of thinking insulting to ancient peoples, who accomplished many sophisticated things.) When Von Däniken published the first of his books promoting his spaceport theory in 1968, the empty desert landscape around the lines suddenly became a major tourist destination, and the new stream of people quickly became a danger to the fragile environment and the ancient lines themselves.

Scientists and historians have found thousands of holes in Von Däniken's reasoning, and most scholars are very critical of his work. Still, in 2003, the writer opened Von Däniken's Mystery Park, a huge theme park in the Swiss Alps that features high-tech displays of the wonders and mysteries of the world. The park was an immediate box-office success, drawing large crowds when it opened. A display featuring the Nazca lines is one of the main attractions at the theme park.

underground water sources to the mountain gods. He suggests that the Nazca made their line drawings extra large so that the gods could see them from their positions in the sky.

David Johnson offered yet another theory in the late 1990s. Johnson had been working in the area of the Nazca lines, trying to help the residents of small villages on the *pampa* find water. He noticed that whenever he found a fresh source of water underground, he also found a Nazca trape-

This Nazca spouted vase depicts birds, which were often featured in Nazca ceramics. *© Gianni Dagli Orti/Corbis.*

zoid figure (a four-sided figure with only two sides parallel) drawn in the sand. Johnson believes the lines are an elaborate system of mapping the locations of water tables.

Astronomer and anthropologist Anthony Aveni (1938–) believes that the Nazca bioglyphs were created five hundred years before the geoglyphs and that the later line drawers wrote right over the earlier markings. Aveni suggests that the earlier lines and the later lines may have had different purposes. Using a reproduction of the lines, Aveni began his analysis by removing the earliest of the Nazca lines, the bioglyphs, so that he could view only the geoglyphs, the lines that were made hundreds of years later. By looking at just the later geoglyphs, Aveni found that the straight lines branch out in spoke patterns and that an aboveground water source is at the hub of each group of spokes. Experts have long thought that the Nazca intended their lines to be seen from above, but Aveni believes that the lines were created as walkways, probably used as part of a ritual for seeking help from the godlike forces of rain and fertility. Aveni's theory does not account for the purpose of the Nazca bioglyphs.

Arts

The Nazca society is thought to have its origins in the culture of the Paracas people, who lived from about 475 to 175 B.C.E. on the Paracas Peninsula, which extends off the coast just north of the Nazca region. The Paracas society is known for its beautifully woven and embroidered textiles and extravagant clothing. The Nazca people were not as adept at textiles, but they excelled in pottery. Many of the images that adorn Paracas textiles also appear on Nazca ceramics. During the Nazca years, ceramists developed topnotch technical skills and began to use brilliant colors on their pottery, sometimes as many as eight colors per piece. Nazca pottery often features images of birds, fish, beans, or peppers. One of the common images is a man with a serpent tongue and a trophy head (the head of an enemy, carried as a token of victory in combat) at the end of the tongue.

Decline

The Nazca society had dissolved by about 700 C.E. The demise of the Nazca may have been caused by earlier natural disasters—severe drought followed by flooding brought about by El Niño. (El Niño is an occasional phenomenon in which the waters of the Pacific Ocean along the coast of Ecuador and Peru warm up, usually around late December, sometimes bringing about drastic weather changes like flooding or drought.) It is also possible that the Nazca were overwhelmed by neighboring peoples. The Wari (pronounced wah-REE) people (see Chapter 8 for more information) were in the process of spreading their empire, and they may have been in some way responsible for the demise of the Nazca. However, there is little evidence to support this.

For More Information

Books

Davies, Nigel. *The Ancient Kingdoms of Peru.* London: Penguin, 1997.

Fagan, Brian. *Kingdoms of Gold, Kingdoms of Jade: The Americas before Columbus.* London and New York: Thames and Hudson, 1991.

Von Hagen, Adriana, and Craig Morris. *The Cities of the Ancient Andes.* London and New York: Thames and Hudson, 1998.

Periodicals

McClintock, Jack. "The Nasca Lines Solution." *Discover* (December 2000): p. 74.

Web Sites

"Mystic Places: Nazca Lines." *Discovery Channel Online.* http://www.exn.ca/mysticplaces/nazcalines.asp (accessed on October 18, 2004).

"Nazca." *E-Museum @ Minnesota State University, Mankato.* http://www.mnsu.edu/emuseum/prehistory/latinamerica/south/cultures/nazca.html (accessed on October 18, 2004).

Moche Culture

6

The Moche (pronounced MO-chay) people unified a section of the northern coastal area of the Central Andes region, spreading a unique culture. It is believed that the Moche imposed strict political and administrative rule upon outlying regions, governing through local headquarters or capitals. The Moche prospered for several hundred years by skillfully manipulating scarce water sources, but they lived under the constant threat of natural disasters—earthquakes and the legendary El Niño that periodically ravaged their lands with floods and droughts (a long period of little or no rainfall). The Moche are best known for their beautiful artwork—and for their grisly practices in human sacrifice. Their artwork often depicts events and people that correspond to their actual history. From artifacts (items made or used by humans, such as tools or weapons), archaeologists have put together a profile of the way the Moche state operated, and most conclude that the Moche state had many of the important features that characterize civilization: social classes, specialized large-scale production of a number of goods, dense populations, trade, political organization, and regional administrative centers throughout the state.

Words to Know

Administrator: A person who manages or supervises the day-to-day operations of business, government, and religious organizations.

Adobe: Sun-dried earthen brick used for building.

Ceremonial centers: Citylike centers usually run by priests and rulers, in which people from surrounding areas gather to practice the ceremonies of their religion, often at large temples and plazas built specifically for this purpose.

Chiefdom: A social unit larger and more structured than a tribe but smaller and less structured than a state, which is mainly governed by one powerful ruler. Though there are not distinct classes in a chiefdom, people are ranked by how closely they are related to the chief; the closer one is to the chief, the more prestige, wealth, and power one is likely to have.

Culture: The arts, language, beliefs, customs, institutions, and other products of human work and thought shared by a group of people at a particular time.

Deity: A god or goddess, or a supreme being.

Drought: A long period of little or no rainfall.

El Niño: An occasional phenomenon in which the waters of the Pacific Ocean along the coast of Ecuador and Peru warm up, usually around late December, sometimes bringing about drastic weather changes like flooding or drought.

Elite: A group of people within a society who are in a socially superior position and have more power and privileges than others.

Huaca: A sacred place, usually used for a temple, pyramid, or shrine.

Pre-Columbian: Existing before Spanish explorer Christopher Columbus arrived in the Americas in 1492.

Dates of predominance
100–800 C.E.

Name variations and pronunciation
Spelled Moche; Mochica. Pronounced MO-chay; mo-CHEE-ca.

Location
The Moche people lived in the Moche and Chicama River valleys in the dry northern coastal plains between the

Andes Mountains and the Pacific Ocean in present-day Peru. At its height, the Moche civilization stretched approximately 330 miles (530 kilometers) down the coast, from the Piura River valley in the north to the Huarmey River valley in the south, generally extending inland no more than about 50 miles (80 kilometers).

Important sites

Peruvian archaeological sites have been subjected to looting for centuries, from the moment the Spanish arrived seeking gold in 1531 to modern times. Because of this, many of the Moche artifacts disappeared long ago. Burial sites of Moche nobility (who were buried with an abundance of riches) have been ransacked, and whole sites have been destroyed. Because of their unique beauty, Moche artifacts bring a lot of money to the looters and the people who deal in the stolen goods, so unfortunately, the looting will probably continue.

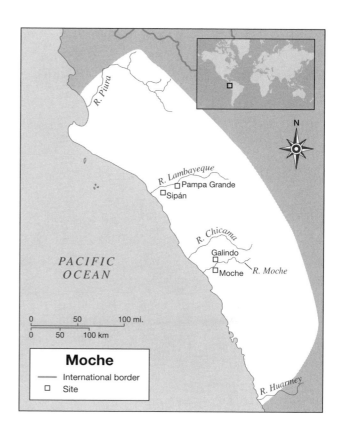

Map showing the sites of the ancient Moche civilization in Peru. *Map by XNR Productions. The Gale Group.*

Cerro Blanco: Huaca del Sol and Huaca de la Luna

Two huge terraced adobe monuments still stand at Cerro Blanco: Huaca del Sol (Shrine of the Sun) and Huaca de la Luna (Shrine of the Moon). They are in the lower midsection of the Moche River Valley, on the bank of the river, under the lofty mountain peak called Cerro Blanco, or White Mountain. Before falling into ruin, the cross-shaped Huaca del Sol was more than 1,100 feet (335 meters) long, 525 feet (160 meters) wide, and 130 feet (40 meters) tall (the height of a 10-story building). An estimated 143 million adobe bricks, arranged in column-like segments, were used to build the *huaca* or sacred place. Huaca de la Luna, only 1,600 feet (488 meters) away at the steep rise of Cerro Blanco, was a slightly smaller monument: 950 feet (290 meters) long, 690 feet (210

Huaca del Sol (Pyramid of the Sun) functioned as a center of business and government of the Moche state. © *Charles & Josette Lenars/Corbis.*

meters) wide, and 105 feet (32 meters) tall. It consisted of three large platforms connected by four large plazas. The monument was surrounded by thick adobe walls that extended all the way back to the mountain. The construction of Huaca del Sol seems to have been an ongoing process from about 100 to 450 C.E. Huaca de la Luna's construction went on even longer, taking about six hundred years; the initial buildings served as foundations for later monuments. The two *huacas* are believed to be the largest structures ever built in South America; in the Western Hemisphere they are second in size only to the pyramid at Cholula de Rivadia in Mexico.

Building the two *huacas* at Cerro Blanco required a large number of people. The work began with the making of adobe bricks. These were made by pressing mud into a four-sided form and setting it in the sun to dry. Workers making the adobe would then press the identifying mark of their community into each brick. About one hundred marks exist in the adobes of Huaca del Sol, suggesting that about one

hundred communities sent teams of men to build the monument.

The space between Huaca del Sol and Huaca de la Luna was a busy urban area with houses and businesses covering about 1 square mile (2.590 square kilometers). About ten thousand people lived there. The houses that have been excavated reveal that there were sharp differences between the social classes in the city. Some lived very well in stone and adobe houses close to Huaca de la Luna and the mountain. Their homes were equipped with fine ceramics and other manufactured goods. Others, who lived closer to Huaca del Sol, lived in cane houses patched with mud and had few luxuries in their homes. The businesses in the city were mainly workshops where pottery, metalwork, textile production, bead making, and many other crafts took place. Many of the raw materials that the Moche artisans used in making their crafts came from places too far away for the Moche to obtain by themselves. This indicates that some system of

Huaca de la Luna (Pyramid of the Moon) was considered the Moche center of religion. *© Charles & Josette Lenars/Corbis.*

long-distance trade, in which they exchanged some of their crafts for the raw materials to make them, was essential to their economy.

The two *huacas* had different functions. Most experts believe that Huaca del Sol functioned as an administrative headquarters, a place where officials carried out the daily business and governmental work of the Moche state. At the top of Huaca del Sol, there was a complex of rooms constructed with wooden poles; these rooms probably served as administrative offices for the city. Some rooms had raised seats that may have been thrones. Archaeologists excavating these upper rooms found trash left behind by the people who used the space. To experts this indicated that the rooms were not used as temples or priestly residences, because such places would have been maintained with great care. In contrast, experts think that Huaca de la Luna functioned as a center of religion and ritual (a formal act performed the same way each time, usually used as a means of worship by a particular group), because it was found perfectly clean during excavation. At Huaca de la Luna, human sacrifices were carried out in an elaborate, horrible ritual (see Religion: Human sacrifice rituals in this chapter).

Historians now believe that the Moche people originally were divided into at least two regions, which were separately ruled but united by a shared religious system. The southern region was ruled from Cerro Blanco, a religious center located in the Moche and Chicama Valley area. The northern region, in the Lambayeque Valley, may have had several independent government centers. Sometime around 550 to 600 C.E. the original Moche centers near the coast were abandoned. Galindo, a center about 12 miles (19 kilometers) inland from Cerro Blanco, and Pampa Grande, which lay inland from Sipán in the north, became the seats of power in the last years of the Moche civilization.

History

After the fall of the Chavín in about 200 B.C.E., the people of the Central Andes lost much of the unity that the Chavín culture had provided. Separated by threatening mountain peaks, they lived in isolation in many different river valleys, where they organized small, independent governments. At this time, the coastal population grew. The rivers were an important source of the population growth in the desertlike coastal plains, and new methods of irrigation brought the water where it was needed. The irrigation systems consisted of canals that were carved from the rivers at carefully chosen points to deliver the maximum amount of water to prepared fields on the desert plains.

By using every drop of water available and exploiting the resources of the sea by fishing, hunting the small sea animals and birds, and gathering shellfish and seaweed, the people who preceded the Moche were able to produce abundant food and accommodate large populations within each valley. However, there was no central ruling power that could coordinate the use of the limited water supply, and it was difficult to ensure that the water in each valley was being used wisely and fairly and not stolen or diverted by intruders from other valleys. In fact, during this era, conflict among the Moche leaders (usually referred to as Moche lords by scholars) of the different valleys grew, probably over the use of water sources. By about 1 C.E., armies developed in the valley communities, and some towns put up defensive walls in preparation for attack. Military actions became widespread in the northern coastal region.

Within the valleys, chiefdoms arose. (A chiefdom is a social unit larger and more structured than a tribe but smaller and less structured than a state, which is mainly governed by one powerful ruler.) Most chiefdoms supported a small but powerful group of nobles, or elite, who enjoyed many privileges that common workers did not. From the lavish burial chambers of the elite it is clear that some nobles were extremely wealthy, even in the early years of the Moche state. The simple burials of the commoners indicate more meager circumstances for the majority. The political leaders within the valleys were often priests. The people of the valleys expected their leaders to provide more than political guidance; they expected them to negotiate with the gods— that is, to ask the gods for adequate rain and protection from earthquakes and floods. In return, the common people were willing to work for the state. Local communities put together gangs of workers who would spend a portion of the year

Finding the Lord of Sipán

Near the coastal city of Chiclayo in present-day Peru, a Moche center called Sipán took its place among the northern Moche headquarters around 100 C.E. At Sipán there was a ceremonial center (city-like centers usually run by priests and rulers, in which people from surrounding areas gather to practice the ceremonies of their religion, often at large temples and plazas built specifically for this purpose) called Huaca Rajada that had three pyramids. Until 1987 archaeologists knew Huaca Rajada only as a center of the later Chimú (pronounced chee-MOO) people, and they were not very interested in the site, because the ruins there had been destroyed many years before. There are few jobs in the area near Huaca Rajada; severe poverty is the norm. Faced with this dire economic situation, local looters, called *huaqueros,* try to make a living by digging through the ancient ruins, looking for a stray gold medallion or a piece of ancient ceramics that they can sell to dealers.

In February 1987 *huaqueros* dug a shaft (a vertical opening or tunnel through the floors of a building) deep into a Huaca Rajada platform, hoping to find more buried treasures. As they began digging through the ruins, a ceiling in the tunnel roof collapsed, and a burial chamber containing an enormous collection of priceless treasures fell upon the looters. As they hurriedly tried to pack up the treasure, a fight broke out among them, and one of the

huaqueros was killed. After some bitter disputes among the rest of the looters, one *huaquero,* feeling betrayed, went to the police. Within a couple of weeks the police called archaeologist Walter Alva (1951–), the director of Peru's Bruning Museum in Lambayeque.

Alva was at first skeptical that the site had anything new to offer, but when he saw some of the artifacts the looters had left behind, he quickly identified them as Moche art and realized that Huaca Rajada was the site of a powerful Moche center. When Alva went to the site to investigate, he found the ancient ruins teeming with *huaqueros,* and they were not happy to see him there. Eventually, with the help of the police, Alva cleared the immediate area. Hoping to prevent any more looting of the site, he decided to stay there and begin his own dig with a small team of workers. Soon, one of the world's top Moche scholars, Christopher Donnan (1940–), joined him. Alva and his small team faced intense hostility from the local people, who understandably resented foreigners coming into their area and removing the treasures of their ancestors. In an effort to reduce this hostility, Alva made a museum of the artifacts on the spot and encouraged the local people to come in to pay their respects to the artifacts of their ancestors. Finally, through his persistence in engaging local people in his project, Alva received the community's support.

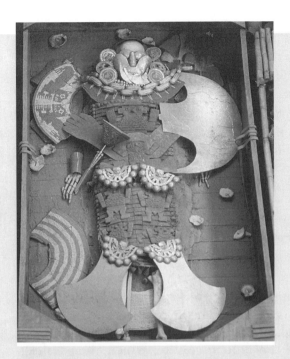

The tomb of a warrior-priest of Sipán. © *Kevin Schafer/Corbis.*

During the excavation at Huaca Rajada, Alva's team determined that the pyramid the looters entered in 1987 had been constructed by the Moche in different stages over hundreds of years. The two lead archaeologists on the dig, Alva and Donnan, believe that the first stage of construction began about 100 C.E. and ended in about 300 C.E. In the oldest portion of the pyramid, at various levels, the archaeological team found three royal tombs. These burial chambers proved to be among the richest tombs ever found in the Americas. Gold and silver artifacts, textiles, and other items in the tombs revealed that the early Moche people had artistic skills far surpassing anyone's expectations.

The lavish burial offerings indicated that the dead were people of great power and prestige; such offerings would not have been bestowed upon mere local lords. Donnan found one of the tombs particularly interesting, because he recognized many of the objects in it from scenes depicted on Moche pottery and in Moche murals. Moche art frequently depicts a warrior-priest who presides over a human sacrifice ceremony. The warrior-priest wears a distinctive costume, with a crescent-shaped warrior back-flap, a crescent-shaped headdress, and unusual ear spools— large, decorated tube-shaped plugs that were fitted into holes made in the ear lobes. Donnan noticed that the person buried in the tomb had the same attire and equipment as the warrior-priest depicted in many pieces of Moche art. Donnan and other experts believe that this person, who has come to be called the Lord of Sipán, was in reality a warrior-priest whose function was to preside over the human sacrifice ceremony. Finding the tomb of this person proved that the hideous sacrifice scenes archaeologists had seen depicted by Moche artists (see Religion: Human sacrifice rituals in this chapter) corresponded to actual events rather than depicting mythical events in religious tales that were passed from generation to generation. The royal tombs found at Huaca Rajada also indicated that the center had powerful local rulers and was probably not under the direct rule of leaders in the Moche Valley.

doing public jobs. These jobs included maintaining the irrigation canals, making adobes, or building *huacas,* the ceremonial centers that ranged from small public buildings to some of the biggest pyramids ever built in the Americas.

By about 100 B.C.E., in the far northern coastal plains, the Gallinazo, predecessors of the Moche, had settled in the Moche Valley. They built some cities in the mid-valley areas, particularly in the Virú Valley. During their reign, the population in the northern valleys increased significantly. The Gallinazo became master adobe makers and built huge adobe ceremonial mounds. They were probably responsible for beginning the construction of Huaca de la Luna (Shrine of the Moon) at Cerro Blanco, the site that became the capital of the Moche state.

Around the time that construction of Huaca de la Luna began, leaders in the Moche River valley and in the Chicama River valley united and formed a single state. This was the beginning of the Moche culture, which then quickly spread throughout the northern region. For many years, historians believed that the whole Moche state was ruled from Cerro Blanco. However, evidence of independent rule in the north has made them revise their theory. They now believe that the valleys in the southern part of the Moche state were directly ruled from Huaca del Sol in Cerro Blanco. The Moche may have conquered the people in these valleys, or they may have persuaded local leaders (through gifts, threats, or intermarriages) to join the Moche state. To impose their rule in the southern region, Moche leaders set up administrative centers in each southern valley. In the north, though, it seems that there were several centers of government and that the Moche established a form of indirect rule through local leaders.

Government and religion

Archaeologists are unclear about the religious practices of the Moche. Moche ceramic designs present many different gods. One of the most often depicted gods is an active god who may have lived among the Moche people. (Some gods were thought to live far off in the spirit world, removed from the daily concerns of humans.) Moche artists depict this god with a feline (catlike) mouth and a headdress formed of sunbeams radiating out from the head. The Moche relied on this god to send them sun, rain, and healthy crops.

Religion and politics were completely intertwined in the Moche culture. While exercising political power and gaining new territories, Moche leaders also built temples and staged rituals that were believed to protect the people. These leaders were more than priests in their ritual function; they became godlike in their promise to intervene, or get involved to help change events, in the supernatural world. They acted as intermediaries, or middlemen, between the common people and the gods. Scholars call the Moche rulers warrior-priests because they had both military and religious functions. Wearing elaborate ceremonial costumes, which were painstakingly crafted out of gold and other precious stones and metals, the warrior-priests held tremendous authority. To many Moche people, their rulers probably seemed to be gods themselves.

Human sacrifice rituals

Human sacrifice was one of the most central practices of many Andean religions, and this was apparently particularly true for the Moche. The Moche sacrifice ceremony began with one-on-one combat between Moche nobles. Such combat was probably staged in formal contests, with many fights going on at once. The combatants were heavily armed and elaborately adorned. Most experts agree that the purpose of these staged battles was to create prisoners of war who could be sacrificed to the gods. The combatants fought until one of them fell in defeat. The victor did not immediately kill the defeated man. Instead, he would strip the fallen warrior of his clothes and tie a rope around his neck. Then the defeated warrior was tied to other captives and the whole group was presented to a group of leaders. Afterward, the prisoners were taken in a procession or parade to the place where the sacrifice would be carried out. There, their throats were cut and the blood was collected in a bowl and then placed in an ornate goblet, which was passed to the warrior-priest and other priests and priestesses to drink.

People have long questioned the purpose of human sacrifice. In most of the later (and more documented) pre-Columbian (existing before Spanish explorer Christopher Columbus arrived in the Americas in 1492) cultures human sac-

Human sacrifice, as depicted by the combat scene in this Moche vessel, was a traditional practice for the Moche culture.
© Nathan Benn/Corbis.

rifice was performed as a way to satisfy the gods, and even to feed them, in order to make sure that the earth could continue to produce and its people flourish and multiply. For many ancient people, the act of sacrifice was deemed absolutely necessary for survival and the continuation of life on earth. Moche scholar Elizabeth Benson's explanation is quoted in *Discover* magazine: "I think that in the past, people thought they could change the world by ritual. We think we can change it with technology, so we've lost a lot of the sense of the importance of ritual. [P]eople thought that this was how you controlled the world, how you had enough food for your people. And a human being was the most important offering you could make."

The tradition of sacrificing humans went on in the Moche state for hundreds of years. To date, archaeologists have found the remains of about one hundred Moche sacrifice victims. About seventy of those victims were recently uncovered in a plaza behind Huaca de la Luna. It was apparent to the scientists examining the remains that the victims had been tortured at length before they were clubbed to death or decapitated. Scholars do not know why the Moche sacrifice ritual would have included such brutal measures.

Economy

Many artisans, traders, and administrators (people who manage or supervise the day-to-day operations of business, government, and religious organizations) lived in the cities surrounding the great Moche pyramids, but most Moche people were farmers and fishermen. The key to the Moche economy was water. Irrigation canals diverted streams from the rivers out into an expansive patchwork of agricultural fields. There the Moche grew corn, beans, potatoes, squash, chili peppers, and other food crops. There were many fields set aside for cotton as well; textiles were a major Moche product. Over time the network of canals became complex. The canal system required regular maintenance, so farmers who needed water for their crops would join labor gangs and do the maintenance work in exchange for irrigation water. Having rights to water sources (obtained through military force or perhaps simply by being the first to tap into the source and divert it) could make people and their communities very powerful. Conflicts erupted when the lord of one valley tried to use a water supply controlled by the lord of another valley. Tensions over water increased as the valleys became more and more crowded.

Though the land was very dry, the Moche's coastal location provided some very useful resources. Farming in the desert required fertilizer, or plant food. Moche men took boats made of reeds out to the islands off the northern coast to obtain seabird droppings called *guano,* which they spread over their fields as a highly effective fertilizer. With water and fertilizer, they were able to produce abundant crops. Along the coast, anchovies (small fishes resembling herrings) were abundant, and the Moche usually caught them in large nets. Anchovies could be dried and traded to the people in the highlands, adding needed protein to their diets.

Arts and sciences

The Moche had great skill in the arts, and the ceramics and metalwork they left behind bring very high prices

Stirrup spouted vessels were the most widespread ceramic pots in the Moche culture. © *Nathan Benn/Corbis.*

among dealers and collectors. The Moche excelled in many forms of art, but in ceramics, metalwork, and textiles, they are considered to be some of the best pre-Columbian artists of the Americas.

The Moche always used molds to shape the body of their ceramic pots; they were the first South Americans to do so. Most Moche ceramics are easily identified by their red and white finish. Along with their ceramic pots, Moche ceramists made sculptures, often producing highly realistic heads, or portraits, of their patrons (customers), usually members of the aristocracy. Sculptures were often placed in the burial chambers of wealthy deceased persons. Many of these lifelike portraits were inlaid with pearl or gold. Moche artists captured facial details in their portraits, conveying emotions rarely attempted in this art form.

The most widespread Moche ceramic pots were stirrup spout vessels (bottle-like pieces with two spouts) and flaring bowls. Artists often painted detailed scenes on these pieces, using fine brush strokes. There were battle scenes, human sacrifices, creation scenes, mythical tales, and scenes depicting sexual encounters. The research of archaeologist Christopher Donnan has revealed that the Moche ceramists painted only a limited number of themes. He believes that these themes arose from oral tales and rituals or pageants. Evidence found in the Moche center of Sipán (see the box on pages 94–95) indicates that some scenes depict actual people carrying out their roles in the Moche world.

The Moche had easy access to a number of precious metals and developed remarkably sophisticated technology as well as advanced artistic skills in metalwork. They knew how to work in most kinds of metals, but gold was their favorite. In *Kingdoms of Gold, Kingdoms of Jade* (1991) Brian Fagan explains: "The Andeans associated gold with the life-giving sun, the deity that brought warmth and fertility to the soil and to humans." The Moche used their metal craftsmanship for elaborate jewelry, masks, headdresses, figurines and other sculpted objects, and for some weapons and farming tools.

To create their metal sculptures, Moche artists often began with a wax model. Then they covered the wax figure in clay. When they fired the clay, the wax melted and flowed out of the surrounding clay, leaving a cavity in the fired clay figure. The artists then filled the cavity with molten copper or another metal. When the copper cooled, the sculptors would crack open the clay figure and take out a copper art piece. Artists often covered the copper piece in gold or silver. They used a technique called electrochemical replacement plating to adhere these precious metals to the art piece. This involved dissolving the gold or silver in some kind of acid solution and then dipping the copper piece in the liquid. The gold or silver would adhere to the copper surface and form a

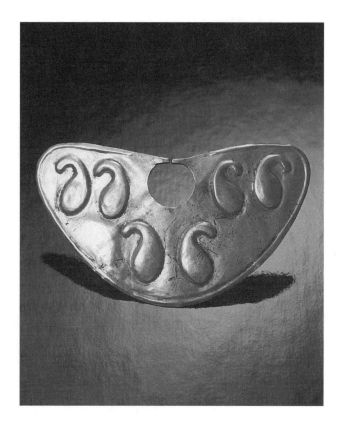

The Moche used their metal craftsmanship to make elaborate jewelry, such as this hammered gold nose ornament. © *Nathan Benn/Corbis.*

coating. With this process, the Moche crafted exquisite gold-plated sculptures.

The Moche are also noted for their exceptional weaving. They were skillful in their use of cotton, alpaca fur, and sometimes feathers. They wove intricate designs into their cloth, including symbolic representations of gods and mythical themes. They also created many different dyes to color the cloth.

Decline

From 563 to 594 C.E. a drought wasted the lands between the Pacific Ocean and the Andes Mountains. With less water, the Moche farms produced significantly less food, causing extreme distress as the people struggled to survive. The drought also led to long-term political insecurity, as the Moche probably began to question the power of their leaders to protect them. Scientists believe that an earthquake may have occurred at some point after the drought, perhaps in about 650 C.E. The earthquake would have caused landslides, possibly blocking the canals. Sand from the sea was probably washed ashore, forming huge sand dunes that covered coastal villages. Experts believe that sometime after these disasters, heavy rains hit the area. The rain created a terrible flood, with the rivers raging down the mountainsides, washing out canals and destroying the Moche fields and crops.

The Moche people coped with the flood damage, rebuilding their cities and irrigation canals and replanting their crops. Sometime between 550 and 650 C.E., though, the Moche rulers at Cerro Blanco abandoned their city and moved farther up the river valley. The rulers in the Lambayeque Valley in the north soon did the same. The precise chronology of events is not known but apparently at some point during the disasters the city of Galindo, about 12 miles (19 kilometers) inland in the Moche Valley, was the center of Moche rule and quickly became the largest Moche city. Later Pampa Grande, about 30 miles (48 kilometers) inland in the Lambayeque Valley, became the seat of power. For about one hundred years Moche lords at Pampa Grande ruled over the diminished and insecure state. Pampa Grande had an estimated population of twelve thousand people, and a huge shrine called Huaca Fortaleza rose up from the city floor as if to signify that power still remained.

However, according to historians, it is possible that another un-determined weather disaster may have struck the Moche some-time between 700 and 800 C.E.

Historians speculate that these incidents were more than the people could bear. For years the Moche people had brought offerings to their warrior-priests, trusting them to in-tervene in the supernatural world and protect them from natural disasters; now it seemed that the warrior-priests had failed them. Most historians think the Moche people rose up against the warrior-priests because archaeological evidence shows that large parts of Pampa Grande were burned and that the city was then abandoned. Other experts believe that the Wari (pronounced wah-REE) people from the east (see Chapter 8 for more information) invaded the city and were responsible for this final destruction. In any case, the end of the Moche state had arrived.

For More Information

Books

Davies, Nigel. *The Ancient Kingdoms of Peru*. London: Penguin, 1997.

Fagan, Brian. *Kingdoms of Gold, Kingdoms of Jade: The Americas before Columbus*. London and New York: Thames and Hudson, 1991.

Morris, Craig, and Adriana Von Hagen. *The Inka Empire and Its Andean Origins*. New York: Abbeville Press, 1993.

Moseley, Michael E. *The Incas and Their Ancestors: The Archaeology of Peru*. London and New York: Thames and Hudson, 1992.

Von Hagen, Adriana, and Craig Morris. *The Cities of the Ancient Andes*. London and New York: Thames and Hudson, 1998.

Periodicals

Donnan, Christopher B. "Iconography of the Moche: Unraveling the Mystery of the Warrior-Priest." *National Geographic* (October 1988): pp. 551–55.

Web Sites

"Las Huacas del Sol y de la Luna." http://www.huacas.com/index.html (accessed on September 28, 2004).

Pringle, Heather. "Temples of Doom." *Discover,* March 1999. Available at http://www.findarticles.com/cf_dls/m1511/3_20/54359911/p6/arti-cle.jhtml?term= (accessed on September 28, 2004).

Tiwanaku Culture

7

M any experts consider Tiwanaku (pronounced tee-wah-NAH-coo) and Wari (pronounced wah-REE; see Chapter 8) to be the first expansive empires of the Andean region. (An empire is a vast, complex unit extending across political boundaries and dominated by one central power, which generally takes control of the economy, government, and culture in communities throughout its territory.) Both held influence over large areas of the Central Andes—Tiwanaku in the southern region and Wari in the north—from about 650 to 1000 C.E. The concept of a Tiwanaku or Wari empire is controversial among scholars of ancient Andean cultures, particularly because no evidence of war or conquest has been found in the regions where Tiwanaku and Wari artistic style and religious imagery prevailed. Many believe that these so-called empires were independent communities that shared religion and culture but without direct rule from afar. Though Tiwanaku and Wari shared some cultural traits, it appears that they were independent of each other in many important ways. Scholars do not fully understand the relationship between these two leading governments of the Andes, but it is clear that both Ti-

Words to Know

Adobe: Sun-dried earthen brick used for building.

Ayllu: A group of extended families who live in the same area, share their land and work, and arrange for marriages and religious rituals as a group; the basic social unit of the Andean peoples.

Ceremonial Centers: Citylike centers usually run by priests and rulers, in which people from surrounding areas gather to practice the ceremonies of their religion, often at large temples and plazas built specifically for this purpose.

Colony: A group of people living as a community in a land away from their home that is ruled by their distant home government.

Ecosystem: A community of plants and animals and the physical environment (including geographic location, altitude, climate, and soil) where they live.

Empire: A vast, complex political unit extending across political boundaries and dominated by one central power, which generally takes control of the economy, government, and culture in communities throughout its territory.

Frieze: A band of decoration running around the top part of a wall, often a temple wall.

Guanaco: A member of the camelid family; a South American mammal with a soft, thick fawn-colored coat, related to and resembling the llama.

Llama: A member of the camelid family; a South American mammal that originated in Peru and probably descended from the guanaco. Llamas were used for their soft, fleecy wool, for their meat, and for carrying loads.

Pre-Columbian: Existing before Spanish explorer Christopher Columbus arrived in the Americas in 1492.

Sacrifice rituals: Ceremonies during which something precious is offered to the gods; in early civilizations, sacrifice rituals often involved killing an animal or sometimes even a human being—the life that was taken was offered as a gift to the gods.

Stela: A stone pillar carved with images or writing, often used to provide historical details or for religious or political purposes.

Stonemason: A skilled builder who expertly lays cut or otherwise fitted units of stone in construction.

Trophy heads: The head of an enemy, carried as a token of victory in combat.

wanaku and Wari greatly influenced the Incas (pronounced ING-kuhs), who built the largest native empire in the Americas about a thousand years later.

Tiwanaku was a huge and splendid city, the site of some of the most remarkable stonework in the Americas. An estimated fifty thousand people lived within the city, which prospered for about eight hundred years, thanks in part to an ingenious method of farming. Tiwanaku was perched so high in the mountains that modern tourists often have great difficulty catching their breath when they visit the site. The city was abandoned long before the Spanish invaded South America, and it has been looted for its artifacts (items made or used by humans, such as tools or weapons, that may be found by archaeologists or others who seek clues to the past) for centuries. Thus, with few clues available, it poses a mystery that captivates twenty-first-century archaeologists. They have many questions about the ancient city and the people who lived there. For example, how did this powerful and thriving capital arise in such a remote and inaccessible place? Furthermore, how did this society come to rule or influence faraway places?

Dates of predominance
c. 200–1200 C.E.

Name variations, pronunciation, and origins
Spelled Tiwanaku, Tiahuanaco, Tiahuanacu. Pronounced tee-wah-NAH-coo. The word refers to the city, its people, and their culture. The Tiwanaku people are believed to be the ancestors of the present-day Aymara people, who live in the area of the ancient site. According to local legend, the city of Tiwanaku was once called *Taypi Kala*, which means "The Stone in the Center."

Location
The city of Tiwanaku stood on the southern side of Lake Titicaca in present-day Bolivia, west of the capital city of La Paz. At an altitude of 13,861 feet (4,225 meters) above sea level, Lake Titicaca is perched between two major mountain ranges of the

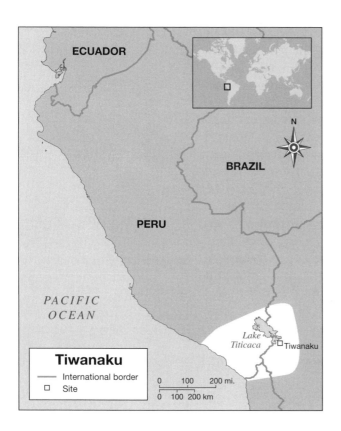

Andes Mountains: the Cordillera Oriental and the Cordillera Occidental. It is the highest navigable body of water in the world. Bordered on its northern shores by present-day Peru, the lake has a surface area of 3,210 square miles (8,314 square kilometers). It extends about 120 miles (193 kilometers) in length and 44 miles (71 kilometers) in width. The ruins of Tiwanaku stand about 9 miles (14.5 kilometers) from the lake, but experts believe that Tiwanaku was originally a port city on the lake's edge. Over time, the waters of the lake have receded significantly, creating the distance between the city's ruins and the lakeshore.

By the seventh century, the Tiwanaku empire, centered in the city of Tiwanaku, included other cities and centers around Lake Titicaca, as well as colonies (territories controlled by a central distant power) in outlying areas. Contained within this empire were a variety of ecosystems—that is, different physical environments and specially adapted plants and animals. The empire extended to the jungle lowlands in the east and to the coastal regions in the west; it reached south to the northwestern region of Argentina and north to settlements in the Pacific coastal desert of Peru, as well as part of Chile. The largest known Tiwanaku colony outside the Titicaca area was in the Moquegua Valley of southern Peru. There are almost certainly ruins of other cities and regions that were dominated by Tiwanaku; however, archaeologists have not extensively explored the south-central highlands of the Andes, so further information about these places remains buried with the artifacts.

Map showing the site of the ancient Tiwanaku civilization near the border of Peru and Bolivia. *Map by XNR Productions. The Gale Group.*

Tiwanaku

Tiwanaku was a precisely planned city that covered an area of about 1.5 square miles (3.9 square kilometers). In its heyday, it was a place of magnificent beauty. The

A view of Lake Titicaca from the hills. *© Hubert Stadier/Corbis.*

stonework, or masonry, of its many walls was so perfect that they still stand in the twenty-first century, even after earthquakes in the area have demolished modern buildings. Workers built the walls with massive blocks of stone that weighed up to 100 tons (90.7 metric tons); they often had to carry the stones over great distances. The stones were cut with sharp cutting stones to fit tightly together; the fit was so precise that they have held for centuries without mortar. Tiwanaku stone sculptures were also large and imposing. Many of the exterior walls of the city were adorned with carved stone friezes (bands of decoration running around the top part of a wall); some of these were covered in gold plate, and others were colorfully painted. When the sun shone on Tiwanaku, the city sparkled from its many gold surfaces.

Tiwanaku was both a sacred center of the Andes and a bustling city. Within the city, space was carefully divided between the ceremonial center (citylike center usually run by

The precisely cut stones in this wall of the Semi-subterranean Temple have stood the test of time.
© *Gianni Dagli Orti/Corbis.*

priests and rulers, in which people from surrounding areas gather to practice the ceremonies of their religion, often at large temples and plazas built specifically for this purpose) and the residential and business section. A moat separated the sacred area from the business area, making the sacred part seem like an island. Tiwanaku's Akapana is a huge, cross-shaped pyramid, measuring 50 feet (15 meters) high and 650 feet (198 meters) long. For many years, modern visitors to Tiwanaku thought the monument was a natural hill with human alterations at the top, but excavations proved that the entire hill was human-made. The base of Akapana consisted of stone blocks that had been skillfully cut and then joined to other stone blocks. A series of seven sandstone-covered terraces led up to a summit courtyard. Canals extended from the courtyard down to the moat that separated the ceremonial core from the rest of the city; these canals were built to carry rainwater and probably made a great roaring sound when water was present, like the water channel

system at Chavín de Huántar (pronounced chah-VEEN deh WAHN-tar; see Chapter 4 for more information). According to Alan Kolata, one of Tiwanaku's most dedicated archaeologists, as quoted in Adriana Von Hagen and Craig Morris's book *Ancient Cities of the Andes*: "the sound of the water cascading from one terrace to the next mimicked that of torrential rain falling on nearby mountains."

Akapana was the most sacred of the shrines at Tiwanaku. Victims of human sacrifice rituals (ceremonies during which human beings are killed and offered as gifts to the gods) have been found buried at the bottom of the structure. The monument was almost certainly the site of grand festivals, drawing people from a large surrounding area for celebrations and ritual ceremonies. During these events, the rulers of Tiwanaku would appear on the lofty terraces of Akapana, dressed elaborately in gold and carrying their trophy heads (the head of an enemy, carried as a token of victory in combat) on belts.

Ruins of Tiwanaku, near La Paz, Bolivia. © *Wolfgang Kaehler/Corbis.*

The Gateway God, a figure wearing a sunburst headdress and holding two staffs, appears on a portal in Tiwanaku. © Kevin Schafer/Corbis.

Not far from Akapana was the Semi-subterranean Temple, a sunken courtyard made of sandstone blocks, with sculptured stone heads protruding from the walls at regular intervals. In the center of this sunken courtyard, excavators found the Bennett Stela (a stela is a stone pillar carved with images or writing), a 24-foot-tall (7.3-meter-tall) statue of a man in an imposing headdress, probably the likeness of a Tiwanaku leader, or possibly the image of a god. West of this temple is a low-lying platform called the Kalasasaya, which many believe was the seat of the Tiwanaku government. Leading to the Kalasasaya is the Gateway of the Sun, a 10-ton (9.07-metric ton) portal, or doorway carved from a single massive block of granite. At the top of the portal is a carved figure, called the "Gateway, or Sun God," wearing a sunburst headdress. The figure holds two staffs and has tears running down its face; it is surrounded by winged attendants and what appears to be religious imagery. The Sun God has been associated with several pre-Columbian (existing before Span-

The Tiwanaku Ruins

After a revolution in Bolivia in the early 1950s, the nation's majority of indigenous people gained greater rights and were free to express their pride in the country's native heritage. The ruins of the ancient city of Tiwanaku became a symbol of that pride. Bolivia initiated many projects to excavate and restore some of the city's monuments, and public interest in the city increased. Since that time, Bolivian children learn about Tiwanaku early in their schooling. Most people in Bolivia visit the ruins of Tiwanaku at least once in their lives, and the entire nation holds the ancient city in deep regard as the sacred center of the region's first civilization.

By the late 1990s, increases in population and in the construction of homes and businesses near Tiwanaku threatened to destroy the ancient site. A village called Ti- wanaku, which is located near the ruins, was growing rapidly, fed by the new tourist business there. To make it easier for tourists to reach the area, planners created a highway that runs right through the ruins. Their disregard for the fragile site destroyed important monuments. Making matters even worse, the Bolivian government badly mismanaged the tourist business, so the money generated by tourism never reached the people who lived in the area; they continued to live in severe poverty. In 2000, after protesting the Bolivian government's handling of the ruins, leaders of the local communities near Tiwanaku quietly staged a takeover of the site, demanding that they be given the authority to manage it themselves, which they received. Whether or not they can stop the destruction at this late date remains to be seen.

ish explorer Christopher Columbus arrived in the Americas in 1492) Andean deities, all of which may be connected. It is often associated with the Staff God, a deity featured in the religious imagery at Chavín de Huántar. (The Staff God did not originate with the Chavín; the earliest known image of the Staff God dates back to 2500 B.C.E.) The Gateway God is also associated with Thunupa, a god of weather and the bringer of thunder, lightning, and rain. Many scholars believe that the Gateway God represents Viracocha, the god of creation (see Religion in this chapter).

There were large and elaborate residential palaces within the ceremonial core of Tiwanaku, no doubt the homes of the priests and rulers of the city. Many residential neighborhoods lay on the other side of the moat, outside the sacred center. Buried in the clay beneath the city was an advanced sandstone sewer (an underground canal system for carrying away human waste matter); Kolata believes that this sewer functioned well for five hundred years. Many homes were made from adobe (sun-dried earthen bricks) and had outdoor patios. Although most of the homes were more modest than the palaces in the sacred center, Kolata believes that Tiwanaku was an exclusive city that allowed only powerful people—the wealthy, the rulers, and the government or religious administrators—to live within its limits.

History

The Lake Titicaca basin (a depression in the earth, often with a body of water in it) in the Andean highlands has been inhabited by Andean peoples since before 1000 B.C.E. Before the Tiwanaku culture emerged, the societies living there had already built ceremonial structures and residences for a dense population. The Tiwanaku began building their center around 200 C.E. Within about one hundred years, the Tiwanaku prepared the stones for the ceremonial core of the city. The massive stones that made up the foundation and walls of the city were probably obtained in a quarry across Lake Titicaca (in present-day Peru), dragged by a large crew of men to the shore, and then placed on reed boats to cross the huge lake. At a port near Tiwanaku another large crew of men dragged the stones to their destination in the city. This work was done without the aid of the wheel, so it required a great number of people to accomplish the task. To direct such a large project, Tiwanaku must have had strong leadership with extensive organizational abilities. By about 500 C.E., Tiwanaku was a thriving urban center with many outposts in the southern sector of the Central Andes region.

Government

Powerful priest-rulers controlled the city of Tiwanaku. When they appeared before the public, they presented themselves dramatically, wearing ornate costumes and staging spectacular ceremonies and rousing festivals for their people. The people believed, as a matter of religious faith, that the elite ruling class had a right to rule over them. They believed that the priest-rulers could communicate with the gods and influence the forces of nature, and they expected the rulers to use these special powers to ensure good harvests. In return, the common people were willing to work hard and give some portion of their earnings—whether in crops, ceramics, or labor—to the elite. Thus, there were two basic social classes: the rich and powerful elite and the commoners. While the elite lived in lavish palaces and dined on llama (a native Andean mammal) meat, ocean fish, and corn (imported from faraway posts), the commoners ate quinoa (pronounced KEEN-wah; an Andean grain), potatoes, and fish from the lake.

Some experts believe that Tiwanaku had a strong and highly organized government. However, others believe that the "empire" was in fact a conglomeration of small, independently ruled groups that were united by shared beliefs and mutually beneficial trade relations. According to this theory, the *ayllu* (pronounced EYE-yoo)—the local kin group, usually made up of several family groups—remained the center of power and organization in Tiwanaku. Scholars who subscribe to this theory point out that the Tiwanaku culture could have easily spread without any central government influence. Tiwanaku was a major center of trade and religion, so its culture probably spread as traders and pilgrims (people who visit a holy place to show reverence) traveled between the city and distant valleys. In addition, large groups of Tiwanaku people relocated to places that had different climates and ecosystems; they went there to establish colonies that could supply necessary crops to Tiwanaku. Like the traders and pilgrims, these colonists carried the Tiwanaku culture with them as they traveled.

Many scholars believe that the Tiwanaku empire was simply a system of alliances between the smaller groups that came to share the artistic styles and religion of Tiwanaku. There is no solid evidence of Tiwanaku ruling directly over the many areas that shared its culture, but research and excavation continue.

Economy

In most pre-Columbian Andean regions, the basic social and economic unit was the *ayllu*. The main purpose of the *ayllu* was to organize work and to distribute land among its members. Each member of an *ayllu* had a work responsibility to the group. If a relative needed a house built or a field plowed, the members of his or her *ayllu* would gather to do the work, with the understanding that their labors would be paid back to them in kind at a later date. For the Aymara people living in the Titicaca area, this labor obligation was called *ayni*; for the Quechua-speaking (pronounced KECH-wah) people (such as the later Incas), it was called *mit'a*. *Ayllus* often split into two groups; one farmed in the highlands and the other in the lowlands. That way they could raise a wide variety of crops and make the *ayllu* more or less self-sufficient (able to produce everything needed for the group's survival).

The workers who built Tiwanaku's temples were probably fulfilling *ayllu*-based labor obligations. Massive slabs of granite and sandstone had to be transported over long distances to the city, and it would have taken a great number of people to accomplish this work. Each village probably sent a crew to carry out its part in such projects. The *ayllu's* division of farmers between highland and lowland areas was also carried out on a large scale, with whole colonies of Tiwanaku people established in other zones. Traders, often with herds of llamas, moved among the different settlements, bringing lowland crops, such as chili peppers, cotton, and cocoa, to the highlands and carrying highland products, such as quinoa, potatoes, and artworks, to the lowlands. As this trade system grew, the arts and products of Tiwanaku came into use in an ever expanding area.

Looking out upon the highland areas around Tiwanaku, it is difficult to imagine how the land could have produced enough food to support the estimated 250,000 people who lived in Tiwanaku and in the three valleys around it. The Lake Titicaca basin in which the city was located was perched at a high altitude. The dry, windswept plains, or altiplano, around the basin were vulnerable to frost and drought (long period of little or no rainfall). The secret to farming productivity around Tiwanaku was an ingenious irrigation system, unearthed by Bolivian archaeologist Oswaldo Rivera and fellow archaeologist Kolata in the late 1970s. When they began excavating Tiwanaku, they found the remains of 43 square miles (111.3 square kilometers) of raised fields that had been separated by irrigation canals. Raised farming was a perfect solution to the climate of the highlands, which get hot sun during the day but are often very cool at night, sometimes experienc-

A Little Help from the Ancients

When the city of Tiwanaku was deserted sometime between 1000 and 1200 C.E. its creative method of farming—using raised platforms surrounded by canals to regulate the climate—was abandoned and forgotten. Nearly a thousand years later, at the end of the 1970s, Bolivian archaeologist Oswaldo Rivera and U.S. archaeologist Alan Kolata found evidence of the raised farming system used at Tiwanaku; as their excavation progressed, they began to realize that the area had once been a fertile patchwork of productive fields. The Aymara people who were living in the floodplain (flatland bordering the lake and made up of soil deposited during floods) of Lake Titicaca in Bolivia in the 1970s were generally very poor, and malnutrition among them was common. Their lands in the highland area known as Pampa Koani were not productive or reliable. The two archaeologists tried to convince local farmers to try the ancient method, but for several years, the farmers resisted, regarding the archaeologists' ideas with intense suspicion.

In 1987 Rivera and Kolata convinced one Aymara farmer to dig canals and build raised planting surfaces. With the new method, his potato crop thrived. His neighbors lost their crops when the area was hit with frost; the daring farmer's crop was unaffected. By the next year the man's crops were astounding everyone—they were growing at a rate of about seven times the normal yield. Since then, the people of Pampa Koani have successfully returned to the raised farming system of their ancestors, and their farms have continued to produce at far better rates than they had imagined possible.

ing frosts that can destroy the crops. The farmers in Tiwanaku dug canals around earthen platforms that were between 15 and 50 feet (4.6 and 15 meters) wide and about 650 feet (198 meters) long. These were fed with water from the wetlands around Lake Titicaca. The canals made up about one-third of the surface area of a field. During the day, the water absorbed the sun's heat. At night, as the air cooled, the warmer water began to evaporate, creating an enveloping mist over the crops. The mist kept the temperature more stable and thus protected the crops from frost. Thanks to this irrigation system, harvests increased considerably, and surrounding Tiwanaku were vast areas of highly productive farmlands.

Llama-raising was another crucial industry in Tiwanaku and the surrounding areas. Llamas were raised for

Textiles, generally made from alpaca or llama fur, were important to the Tiwanaku economy.
© Burstein Collection/Corbis.

meat and their fur, but they were also invaluable pack animals that traders used to transport goods over vast areas. Textiles were an important part of the Tiwanaku economy. The fur of the alpaca (a South American mammal with a soft, thick fawn-colored coat, related to and resembling the llama) was used to weave a soft, warm wool, which was greatly valued in the cold mountain climate.

Religion

Hundreds of years after Tiwanaku was abandoned by its people, the Incas came across its splendid ruins. For the Incas, the very existence of Tiwanaku was a problem. According to their creation mythology (traditional, often imaginary stories dealing with ancestors, heroes, or supernatural beings, usually making an attempt to explain a belief, practice, or natural phenomenon), the Inca people were the first civilized people of the world; only lawlessness and savagery had existed before them. Because they believed themselves to be the first true civilization, the Incas felt they had divine justification for ruling their vast empire. Finding the ruins of an advanced civilization that had flourished many years before them contradicted their mythology and called their authority to rule into question. Therefore, the Incas decided to adapt their mythology to include Tiwanaku. According to the revised myth, the creator god Viracocha first created human beings made of clay or stone in Tiwanaku; this explained the existence of the great stone statues found in the city. After experimenting with clay humans in Tiwanaku, Viracocha made the Inca people, but it was in Tiwanaku that human beings first emerged, according to the Incas.

Stone figures stand in Tiwanaku's Semi-subterranean Temple in Tiwanaku. © *William M. Donato/Fortean Picture Library.*

The people of Tiwanaku believed in Viracocha, the creator god. According to Andean mythology, Viracocha initially arose from the depths of Lake Titicaca and created the stars and the sky, Earth, and all the animals and people on Earth. Viracocha was the god of civilization as well, and according to myth, this god actually spent time with the ancient Andean people, teaching them the arts, agriculture, astronomy and geometry, and morality. In ancient Andean arts, Viracocha is usually shown carrying a staff in one or both hands and often wears a headdress that looks like the rays of a rising sun. For the Tiwanaku people, Viracocha was also the weather god; in their artwork, Viracocha carries thunderbolts, and tears—probably a symbol for raindrops—run down the god's face. (For information on the Inca version of Viracocha, see Chapter 12.)

Arts and sciences

The Tiwanaku are considered the most skilled stone-masons (skilled builders who expertly lay cut or otherwise fitted units of stone in construction) and stone carvers of all the pre-Columbian groups. They were also highly skilled weavers and ceramists. They used remarkable precision in their stonework, and their city planning shows the same careful attention to detail. In addition, the Tiwanaku developed advanced sewage and canal systems that allowed their city to prosper for hundreds of years.

Decline

Sometime before 1000 C.E. a severe drought struck the southern Central Andes, lasting long enough to dry up the water sources for the fields and destroy the crops. By 1000 C.E. the once fertile fields had been abandoned. Even after it was abandoned, Tiwanaku remained sacred to Andean people, and the modern people of the Andes still revere the ancient city in the twenty-first century.

For More Information

Books

Davies, Nigel. *The Ancient Kingdoms of Peru*. London: Penguin, 1997.

Fagan, Brian. *Kingdoms of Gold, Kingdoms of Jade: The Americas before Columbus*. London and New York: Thames and Hudson, 1991.

Morris, Craig, and Adriana Von Hagen. *The Inka Empire and Its Andean Origins*. New York: Abbeville Press, 1993.

Moseley, Michael E. *The Incas and Their Ancestors: The Archaeology of Peru*. London and New York: Thames and Hudson, 1992.

Von Hagen, Adriana, and Craig Morris. *The Cities of the Ancient Andes*. London and New York: Thames and Hudson, 1998.

Periodicals

Straughan, Baird. "The Secrets of the Ancient Tiwanaku Are Benefiting Today's Bolivia." *Smithsonian* (February 1991): p. 38.

Web Sites

"Tiwanaku." *E-Museum @ Minnesota State University, Mankato.* http://www.mnsu.edu/emuseum/prehistory/latinamerica/south/cultures/tiwanaku.html (accessed on October 18, 2004).

Vranich, Alexei. "Tiwanaku History and Context." *Archaeology's Interactive Dig/Archaeology Magazine.* http://www.archaeology.org/interactive/tiwanaku/history.html (accessed on October 18, 2004).

Wari Culture

8

An empire is a vast, complex political unit extending across political boundaries and dominated by one central power. To varying degrees, the dominant power takes control of the economy, government, and culture in communities throughout its empire. The Wari (pronounced wah-REE) empire and the Tiwanaku (pronounced tee-wah-NAH-coo) empire influenced or governed much of the Central Andes from 700 c.e. to about 900 c.e. Many archaeologists consider this period to be the first empire-building era in the Americas.

At its height, beginning about 700 c.e., the Wari empire appears to have been larger and stronger than the Tiwanaku empire to the south. The Tiwanaku state unified Andean peoples through shared culture and trade. Scholars suspect that the Wari empire spread in a different way: They believe that Wari leaders used military force to subdue other cultures and that they forced the conquered peoples to conform to the Wari culture. These experts disagree, however, about how much power the Wari empire had over its outposts (remote settlements or headquarters through which a central government manages outlying areas).

Words to Know

Administrative center: The place in a region or state in which the day-to-day operations of business, government, and religion are carried out.

Authoritarian government: Strict rule by the elite; in this type of government, leaders are not constitutionally responsible to the people, and the people have little or no power.

Chicha: A kind of beer that Andean peoples made from maize or other grains.

Colony: A group of people living as a community in a land away from their home that is ruled by their distant home government.

Empire: A vast, complex political unit extending across political boundaries and dominated by one central power, which generally takes control of the economy, government, and culture in communities throughout its territory.

Hallucinogenic drug: A mind- and sense-altering drug that may create visions of things not physically present.

Outpost: A remote settlement or headquarters through which a central government manages outlying areas.

Propaganda: Ideas, information, or rumors spread for the purpose of helping or hurting a cause or a person.

Quipu: Also *khipu.* A set of multicolored cotton cords knotted at intervals, used for counting and record keeping.

Trophy head: The head of an enemy, carried as a token of victory in combat.

Archaeologists and historians know less about Wari civilization than about some of the other major pre-Inca (pronounced ING-kuh) civilizations. By the time the Spanish reached South America in the sixteenth century, the abandoned Wari centers had fallen into such disrepair that they were generally ignored. Many archaeologists assumed the Wari ruins were simply part of the Tiwanaku empire. Wari history remained overlooked, for the most part, until the 1940s. In that decade excavations turned up evidence that the two cultures were independent. Sixty years later, in the early twenty-first century, scholars are finding intriguing new information about the Wari empire, and their discoveries are overturning many of the old theories about the Wari.

The Inca empire (1438–1533) recognized the Tiwanaku empire as its predecessor, but it appears that the

Incas adopted at least as many customs and ideas from the Wari as they did from the Tiwanaku. The Incas used the Wari empire's extensive network of roads throughout the Central Andes as the basis for their own road systems. They adopted the Wari's distinctive system of sending settlers to new areas to create farming colonies (people living as a community in a land away from their home that is ruled by their distant home government) and they did their record keeping on *quipus* (pronounced KEE-poos), instruments used and possibly invented by the Wari. (A *quipu* is a device made of colored strings that are knotted at regular intervals; it was used for complex accounting calculations.) As scholars increase their understanding of the Wari empire, they are realizing that the Wari had tremendous influence on the Inca civilization and on the very idea of empire-building.

Dates of predominance
600–1000 C.E.

Name variations, pronunciation, and origins
Spelled Wari; Huari. Pronounced wah-REE. The word refers to the city, the empire, the people who lived within the empire, and the culture they developed.

Location
The city of Wari was in the highlands of the Ayacucho Valley of south-central Peru, on a hill overlooking the Mantaro River, about 16 miles (26 kilometers) north of the modern city of Ayacucho. It is about 430 miles (692 kilometers) northwest of Tiwanaku.

By the mid-700s the Wari empire extended 1,000 miles (1,609 kilometers) along the spine of the Andes, stretching 435 miles (700 kilometers) to the north of the city of Wari to Huamachuco, and south to the border of present-day Peru. The Wari empire encompassed many cities and communities throughout Peru. Some of the important outposts of the Wari empire were Pikillacta near Cuzco (pronounced KOO-sko), Cajamarquilla

near Lima, and Wilkawain near Huaraz. Viracochapampa in Huamachuco was at the northern Wari frontier, while Cerro Baúl, the only city set up to be defended from military attack, was at the southernmost outpost of the empire, in the heart of Tiwanaku territory.

Map showing the sites of the ancient Wari civilization in Peru. *Map by XNR Productions. The Gale Group.*

Important sites

Wari

The city of Wari, covering about 6 square miles (15.5 square kilometers), was built in the highlands at an elevation of about 9,100 feet (2,774 meters) above sea level. Estimates of the population during the city's most active years (600 to 900 C.E.) range from twenty thousand to one hundred thousand. The city had several sections—religious, residential, and administrative—separated by high walls. A few of these walls had precision-fitted stonework similar to Tiwanaku stonemasonry, but the stone buildings were held together with mud mortar. The religious section of the city was built first. Instead of mounds or pyramids, the Wari religious centers often had D-shaped temples that were not particularly attractive when viewed from the outside. The residences of Wari were multistory buildings arranged in large rectangular compounds. Each compound was built around a patio. The long narrow rooms in which people lived had doors leading out to the patios and to the surrounding streets. Artifacts found in the different residential sections of Wari make it clear that the city's social classes were sharply divided, with the elite living in one section and the common people in another. A system of underground tunnels ran beneath the city. As the Wari empire grew, the city served as its capital.

Pikillacta

Situated in the valley of Cuzco, Peru, Pikillacta is the second-largest known site of Wari ruins. Like the capital city

The ruins of Pikillacta, the second-largest known Wari site. © Brian A. Vikander/Corbis.

of Wari, it flourished between 600 and 900 C.E. One of several Wari centers in the Lucre basin (a depression in the earth, often with a body of water in it), Pikillacta is thought to have been the headquarters of religious operations for a wide area. It was a well-planned city, carefully laid out like a grid and surrounded by high walls that were built before any buildings were erected. The buildings of Pikillacta had multiple stories and plastered walls and floors. The exteriors of the buildings were plastered in white. Pikillacta was built in three stages. Mysteriously, during the last phase of construction—before the work was complete—Pikillacta was carefully prepared for abandonment (please see Decline in this chapter).

Archaeologist Gordon McEwan, who has worked at the Pikillacta site, believes that people who lived in the surrounding area built the city as a means of paying their taxes to the Wari empire. He also theorizes that people probably traveled to Pikillacta to participate in sacred ceremonies. The city had only a few long straight roads, and its buildings contained one identical room after another. There were few doors. This arrangement created a maze-like environment that was not designed for uninvited travelers. "You came here as a guest, perhaps of the local government," says McEwan in *National Geographic*. McEwan points out that the walls surrounding the city stood about 40 feet (12 meters) high and there were only seven roads going through the whole city. He concludes, "You didn't get into Pikillacta without an invitation and a guide. You couldn't have found your way around by yourself."

Azángaro

Azángaro in the Huanta Valley was another Wari outpost positioned fairly close to the capital. Its buildings were carefully arranged around a large rectangular compound. Azángaro functioned as a busy farming center from about 650 to 800 C.E. Archaeologists believe it was the administrative center (the place in a region or state in which the day-to-day operations of business, government, and religion are carried out) of the area's maize (corn) production.

Cerro Baúl

Around 600 C.E. the Wari built Cerro Baúl atop a high and nearly inaccessible mesa (a highland area with a flat top and steep sides) in the Moquegua Valley, which had long been the territory of the Tiwanaku. The position of Cerro Baúl made it easy to defend; it was a natural fortress. Like other Andean peoples, the Wari probably revered the surrounding mountains, and it is possible that Cerro Baúl itself was considered a sacred place. Priests, other elites, and artisans probably lived in the lofty city. Most of the people of Cerro Baúl lived below the city, where they farmed terraced (cut and dug out large steps in the hillside to create level ground for farming) slopes of the Andes. Within the city, life was difficult. The city dwellers probably developed systems for carrying food, water, and materials up the steep slopes, because there were no sources of these daily necessities available to them in the city. The people in the city raised guinea pigs for food and created jewelry and hunting points from stones and shells. It is likely that they traded some of their goods with farmers living below in exchange for crops.

Cerro Baúl was divided into two sections. One held ceremonial buildings made from cut stones. Archaeologists believe that at least one of these buildings was a temple where Wari priests performed sacrifice and other rituals. The priests, rulers, and administrators lived in this sacred center of the city. The other section of the city contained the more modest homes of the working people, particularly the workshops and homes of the artisans.

Scholars do not fully understand the relationship between the Wari and the Tiwanaku, but they have assumed that the two empires were rivals, mainly because the empires dominated neighboring portions of the Andes at the same time. However, if they were rivals or enemies, it would not have made sense for the Wari to create Cerro Baúl, a settlement in Tiwanaku territory. Instead it seems that the Wari and the Tiwanaku at Cerro Baúl cooperated with each other. From their high position on the mesa, the Wari had control of the main water source and shared it with the Tiwanaku

View of the high mountain slopes of the Wari outpost Cerro Baúl. *Courtesy of Dr. Ryan Williams.*

below. Goods passed back and forth between the two communities, and there is evidence that the Wari and the Tiwanaku even participated in ritual ceremonies together. The Wari may have been influenced by the extensive Tiwanaku religious system that prevailed in the region at the time (see Chapter 7 for more information on the Tiwanaku religion); perhaps this was why they placed a city in the area and lived there peacefully. It is also possible, according to some scholars, that the Wari were not as militant as experts once thought.

History

Before the city of Wari was established in the Ayacucho Valley, a group called the Huarpa lived in small farming villages throughout the valley. The Huarpa prospered from about 200 B.C.E. to 600 C.E. According to Michael Moseley in *The Incas and Their Ancestors* (1992), a severe drought (a long period of little or no rainfall) occurred in the Andes in the middle of the sixth century, probably causing the fall of many peoples, including the Moche (pronounced MO-chay; see Chapter 5). The Huarpa moved higher into the Ayacucho Valley, where they could find highland springs and rivers at their sources. This gave them an advantage: They could use as much water as they wanted before the people in the lower valley had any chance to diminish the supply.

The city of Wari was built sometime between 500 and 600 C.E. The artifacts found there show little in common with the Huarpa style of art, indicating that the Huarpa may have left and a group now called the Wari took the site over. Besides building monuments and residences, the people of Wari terraced the steep western slopes of the Andes around their city and dug irrigation canals around their highland water sources. These were simply ditches at the top of the water stream that diverted the water flow onto the farmed areas. Rather than moving down the valley to farm certain products, they used these techniques to grow maize and peppers in the steep highland country.

The Wari people began to spread their influence soon after their capital was established. They moved into areas in the Andean highlands and took over water sources in the upper valleys. By establishing colonies near these water sources, they were able to gain control throughout the high-

land valleys, and soon they had colonies stretching hundreds of miles north of the capital. Scholars believe that after the Wari established control over the water supply, they built administrative centers in local communities and dispatched small groups of Wari lords to rule over the valley.

Some experts think that the Wari may have ruled without much use of force. However, most scholars believe that the Wari conquered some or all of the members of their empire by using strong military force. They think that the Wari then imposed their own culture and religion on their outposts, forbidding the people to practice their own traditions. How much power the Wari exercised over faraway communities probably varied from one outpost to another.

Government

Many experts believe that the Wari empire was the first centrally ruled state in the Andes. From what scholars

The Wari created terraces, similar to those shown here, to improve irrigation and farming in the Andes slopes. *© Galen Rowell/Corbis.*

have learned about the Wari, it seems that an extreme authoritarian government (strict rule by the elite) was the key to their dominance. The imagery painted on Wari pottery suggests that the Wari focused heavily on warfare and exerting their power over their enemies. One of the common themes of their artwork was the depiction of prisoners of war being sacrificed (killed and offered as a gift to the gods). Wari leaders and warriors are frequently depicted wearing trophy heads—the heads of the sacrificed captives—as symbols of their triumph and power. Although no one knows exactly how the government operated, it is clear that the Wari had enormous central power that allowed them to order and organize massive amounts of labor. To build administrative centers, set up colonies, dig irrigation canals, and create a highway system through the Andes, the Wari must have commanded tens of thousands of workers on their projects. Wari leaders are known to have ordered large groups of people to pack up and move to a new location to start a new colony. Military force and the threat of violent death were large factors in retaining power in faraway places.

Besides military power, the Wari lords used a form of public relations (establishing and promoting a good relationship with the public) to persuade people in outposts to provide labor or to relocate to a faraway place. From time to time, Wari lords invited people living in a wide area surrounding the colony to a festival. In return they expected the labor and loyalty of their invited guests. The Wari may have found that kindness and gifts were more persuasive (and less costly) than the presence of soldiers or the use of military force, especially in faraway regions (see the box titled *"Chicha and the Reciprocity Ceremony"* on page 131).

Economy

The capital city of Wari was built upon a well-established Andean trade route, which brought rapid wealth to the developing city. Throughout its two hundred years of prosperity, the Wari empire placed all its outposts on major Andean trade routes, and many scholars believe that trade was one of the main reasons the Wari wanted to expand their empire. Having a variety of products and markets would im-

Chicha and the Reciprocity Ceremony

As the Wari empire expanded, Wari lords arrived in communities and religious centers throughout a large part of the Central Andes. In the new outposts, they were strangers, and fewer in number than the locals, although presumably backed by military force and in control of water supplies. What the Wari lords needed most from the people in these outposts was labor; in order to get it, they tried to create a feeling of obligation among the common workers. One of the ways they made people feel obligated to them was through a ritual that involved massive quantities of *chicha*, a kind of beer that is still popular in the Andes in the twenty-first century. The *chicha* ritual later became an important part of the rule of the Incas over their empire.

Several times a year, the Wari lords in command of the empire's cities and regional centers invited people from the surrounding areas to participate in a grand feast. The feast was a way of thanking and rewarding the people for their hard work. Each invited guest received a ceramic pot decorated specially for the occasion; using these pots, the people all drank their fill of *chicha*. In the words of archaeologist Patrick Ryan Williams, in a 2003 article in *In the Field:* "The drinking rituals were designed to cement relationships between inferiors and superiors within the empire by reducing all parties to a shared state of staggering intoxication." As the festivals got under way and the guests were filling themselves with food and drink, the rulers would make their demands for local labor for the coming months. Quite under the influence of the *chicha*, the people readily agreed to perform the proposed tasks, and they were then expected to fulfill their promise. Modern historians call this huge celebration, which usually ended with most people being very drunk, a reciprocity ceremony. The term "reciprocity" refers to an exchange that mutually benefits everyone involved in the exchange.

The Wari lords absorbed considerable expenses to put on these festivals. To make the *chicha* they needed great amounts of corn. The corn, of course, was grown and harvested by the guests, the working people, and was a significant portion of the labor requirement. The lords provided all the food for the guests as well as the ceramic drinking pots, which were ceremonially smashed at the end of the celebration. Besides this, the festivals interrupted the people's labors for a few days, decreasing their productivity. Though very costly to both lords and workers, these festivals successfully promoted loyalty to the Wari leaders, and they created a sense of community and purpose among the local people.

prove their ability to trade and thus increase their prosperity. Many archaeologists believe that the Wari ensured a supply of diverse products by relocating people—sometimes whole villages—to areas where new industries or crops could be established.

Religion

From the artifacts analyzed thus far, researchers cannot give a detailed description of the Wari religion. Experts generally think that Tiwanaku was the spiritual empire of the time, and the Wari worshiped many of the same gods as the Tiwanaku. The Wari had their own version of the Tiwanaku Gateway God (see Chapter 7 for more information). Theirs was an agricultural deity; instead of a sunburst headdress, the Wari deity had corncobs emanating from its head. The Wari generally painted the image of the Gateway God (also called the Staff God or Viracocha) on ceramics, while the Tiwanaku usually carved it in stone.

Like most pre-Columbian (existing before Spanish explorer Christopher Columbus arrived in the Americas in 1492) Andean peoples, the Wari practiced sacrifice rituals, killing animals or humans and offering the victims as a gift to the gods. (Archaeologists have found the remains of human and llama sacrifices at different Wari sites.) The Wari priests took hallucinogenic drugs (mind- and sense-altering drugs that may create visions of things not physically present), believing that these substances helped them communicate with the gods. Through a drug-induced vision, a priest might contact and influence one of the gods, asking the deity to send rain or to prevent drought, earthquakes, flooding, or other natural disasters.

The Wari participated in the common Andean tradition of ancestor worship, with the belief that deceased relatives actively took care of their living descendants. In Andean societies, family groupings or *ayllus* (pronounced EYE-yoos) were determined by ancestors, and ancestry often determined a person's rights to land or water. It was good to have an ancestor's remains handy in case proof was needed of one's bloodline. The bones of dead relatives or even whole preserved bodies (mummies) were kept around for many years. Like other Andean peoples, the Wari often prayed to the remains of their relatives or consulted them for advice.

Scholars believe that the Wari stole remains or mummies from the communities they conquered. Pikillacta probably served as a storage center for stolen bodies and mummies that were being held for ransom. According to archaeologist Gordon McEwan, as quoted by Virginia Morell in *National Geographic:* "They captured other peoples' mummies or ordered them to bring their ancestral bundles to places like Pikillacta for storage. The only access you then had to your ancestors—and so to your land and water—was through the state. If you didn't comply, the Wari destroyed your ancestors, which left you destitute."

Arts and sciences

The Wari were master ceramists. The themes that were painted on Wari pottery are limited in number, leading archaeologists to theorize that the central government permitted only certain images to be represented on ceramics. If this theory is true, the Wari lords were practicing an early form of government propaganda, controlling artistic expression by decree and thereby determining which ideas, beliefs, and traditions would be presented to the people. If the Wari rulers were like the later Inca rulers, as many experts now believe, they probably dictated the stories that storytellers could relate as well, so that all the people within the empire would know a single history that exalted the Wari lords and justified their power.

Some Wari ceramics have very detailed scenes on them. Archaeologists, using other evidence to corroborate their findings, have concluded that these scenes are representations of actual people and events of the Wari empire. Other Wari ceramics are decorated with religious symbols—half-human, half-animal figures and deities such as the Gateway or Staff God—and with shapes and figures that archaeologists cannot identify.

A Wari mummy's tunic. *The Art Archive/Museo de Arte Municipal Lima/Dagli Orti.*

A Wari ceremonial bowl.

The Art Archive/Archaeological Museum Lima/Dagli Orti.

Other crafts besides pottery were important in the Wari empire, particularly for the purpose of trade. The Wari fashioned jewelry, hunting points, and beads using imported materials such as gold, silver, copper, semiprecious stones, and the coveted Spondylus shell (a highly valued shell of a spiny, coral-colored oyster that could only be obtained off the coast of present-day Ecuador). The Wari were also excellent textile manufacturers and often put their religious imagery on cloth.

The Wari people are the first known users of the *quipu,* or *khipu,* a set of cotton cords of different colors, marked with intentionally placed knots that helped the Wari count, calculate, and keep records of goods and perhaps even labor. No one knows exactly how the *quipu* functioned.

Decline

Sometime between 700 and 800 C.E., the city of Wari built a set of massive walls. Scholars believe that plans were under way to build a new section of the city within the walls, but shortly after workers erected the walls, the city of Wari was abandoned. Around 850, the residents of Pikillacta sealed up some of their city's doorways and abandoned the place. Soon after 1000, the Wari abandoned Cerro Baúl, ceremonially burying some of the sacred buildings and burning others. At about the same time, the Tiwanaku abandoned the area as well. By 1100, most Wari and Tiwanaku cities had been abandoned. No one knows why these two cultures fell, but scholars have theorized that the demise of both empires was caused by long-term drought in the Andes, which probably reduced crops and caused widespread starvation. The circumstances surrounding the decline of the Wari remain mysterious, but the Wari culture did not completely disappear. The Wari influence was at work among a small highland group called the Incas, who were just beginning to expand. On the way to creating their own empire, the Incas would incorporate many lessons learned from the rule of the Wari.

For More Information

Books

Davies, Nigel. *The Ancient Kingdoms of Peru*. London: Penguin, 1997.

Fagan, Brian. *Kingdoms of Gold, Kingdoms of Jade: The Americas before Columbus*. London and New York: Thames and Hudson, 1991.

Morris, Craig, and Adriana Von Hagen. *The Inka Empire and Its Andean Origins*. New York: Abbeville Press, 1993.

Moseley, Michael E. *The Incas and Their Ancestors: The Archaeology of Peru*. London and New York: Thames and Hudson, 1992.

Von Hagen, Adriana, and Craig Morris. *The Cities of the Ancient Andes*. London and New York: Thames and Hudson, 1998.

Periodicals

Morell, Virginia. "Empires across the Andes." *National Geographic* (June 2002): p. 106.

Web Sites

Williams, Patrick Ryan, and Donna J. Nash. "Clash of the Andean Titans: Wari and Tiwanaku at Cerro Baúl." *In the Field*. Available at http://fm1.fmnh.org/aa/Files/rwilliams/WilliamsITF.pdf (accessed on September 29, 2004).

Williams, Patrick Ryan, Michael E. Moseley, and Donna J. Nash. "Empires of the Andes." *Scientific American: Discovering Archaeology,* March/April 2000. Available at http://www.aymara.org/biblio/baul.html (accessed on September 29, 2004).

Kingdom of Chimor

9

At its peak around 1400 C.E., the kingdom of Chimor (pronounced chee-MOR) had a larger empire than any of the other Andean civilizations that preceded the Incas (pronounced ING-kuhs); its capital city, Chan Chan, was the largest pre-Inca city. (An empire is a vast, complex political unit extending across political boundaries and dominated by one central power.) Chimor had a powerful government and a thriving economy that boasted a flourishing import (bringing goods from another region into one's home region) and export (sending or transporting goods produced or grown in one's home region to another region) trade system and large-scale crafts production. Information about the Chimú (pronounced chee-MOO) is more plentiful than what is available on most other early Andean civilizations. This is partly because archaeological excavations of Chimú sites have been highly productive. In addition, sixteenth-century Spanish explorers chronicled the oral traditions and memories of the Chimú, and a few of these written records—the first known written history of the ancient Andes—still survive.

Words to Know

Administrator: A person who manages or supervises the day-to-day operations of business, government, and religious organizations.

Adobe: Sun-dried earthen brick used for building.

Caravanserai: A place where caravans, or herds, of llamas brought their loads of goods and rested from their trip; the caravanserai was also the distribution point for the delivered goods.

Elite: A group of people within a society who are in a socially superior position and have more power and privileges than others.

Empire: A vast, complex political unit extending across political boundaries and dominated by one central power, which generally takes control of the economy, government, and culture in communities throughout its territory.

Export: To send or transport goods produced or grown in one's home region to another region in order to trade or sell them there.

Frieze: A band of decoration running around the top part of a wall, often a temple wall.

Import: To bring goods from another region into one's home region, where they can be acquired by trade or purchase.

Pre-Columbian: Existing before Spanish explorer Christopher Columbus arrived in the Americas in 1492.

Succession: The system of passing power within the ruling class, usually upon the death of the current ruler.

Tribute: A payment to a nation or its ruler, usually made by people from a conquered territory as a sign that they surrender to the imposed rule; payment could be made in goods or labor or both.

Dates of predominance
1150–1470 C.E.

Name variations and pronunciation
Chimú; Chimu; Chimor. Pronounced chee-MOO; chee-MOR. Chimú is the name of the people and their culture, while the state or kingdom is called Chimor.

Location
Chan Chan, the seat of power in the Chimor kingdom, was located about 2 miles (3.2 kilometers) from the pre-

sent-day city of Trujillo, in the Moche (pronounced MO-chay) Valley of northern coastal Peru. At its height, the Chimor empire extended about 600 miles (965 kilometers) along the coastline, from the Tumbes River at the northern border of Peru to the Chillón River in the south.

Important sites

Chan Chan

Chan Chan was the capital of the Chimor kingdom. The Chimú people who lived there are said to have called it "jang-jang," which means "sun-sun" or "the great sun" in Yunca, the now-extinct language of the Chimú. (Spanish explorers misunderstanding the word, changed the city's name to its present spelling.) Chan Chan was built in stages, beginning in about 850 C.E. and continuing through 1470. By its later years, it covered nearly 8 square miles (20.7 square kilometers), more area than any other pre-Columbian (existing before Spanish explorer Christopher Columbus arrived in the Americas in 1492) city in South America. Estimates of Chan Chan's population range from thirty-six thousand to seventy thousand people; it reached its maximum population in the later years of the empire. The entire city was made of adobe (sun-baked earthen bricks), and the walls of the city featured elaborate friezes (bands of decoration near the top part of the walls) and carvings.

Chan Chan was a unique Andean city. It had at least nine *ciudadelas,* or huge, rectangular palace compounds, making up a large part of what would normally be the central area. Many scholars believe that when a new king took power in Chimor, he would build a *ciudadela* in Chan Chan. Once the large compound was complete, it became the center of royal business. The king and his family, along with some government administrators (people who manage or su-

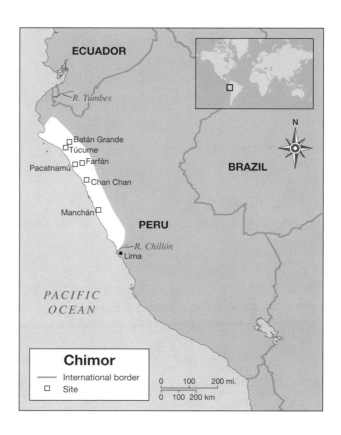

Map showing the sites of the ancient Kingdom of Chimor in Peru. *Map by XNR Productions. The Gale Group.*

Adobe walls with elaborate friezes surround Chan Chan. © *Charles & Josette Lenars/Corbis.*

pervise the day-to-day operations of business, government, and religious organizations), lived at the compound. When the king died, he was buried in a large T-shaped burial platform in the central part of the *ciudadela.* The burial chambers of the kings were never sealed, so that his attendants could continue to serve the mummified (preserved) body of the king. His family, servants, and nobles continued to live in the compound, retaining the king's wealth, while the successor—the next king—was forced to build another *ciudadela.* Scholars think the first *ciudadelas* served several generations of kings, but by about 1200, workers in Chan Chan were building a *ciudadela* for each king as he came into power.

Ciudadelas varied in size. The smaller ones were about 240,000 square feet (22,320 square meters); the large ones had a total area of 870,000 square feet (80,910 square meters). All were surrounded with high walls up to 30 feet (9.1 meters) tall. The streets between the compounds and other buildings were wide and connected to a well-developed road

system. Most *ciudadelas* had only one doorway for entry on their north side, where visitors were admitted to the public court. From corridors off this northern court there were *audiencias,* tiny structures often built as small additions to the compound. This is where the administrators and some nobility lived and worked. Inside the northern entry was the central area of the *ciudadela,* where the burial platform for the king took center stage. The central area also had storage space for food and goods—some *ciudadelas* had as many as two hundred storerooms—and sometimes builders squeezed a few *audiencias* into the area too. In this central area, the nobles and administrators of the kingdom accepted tribute (payment to a nation or its ruler, usually made by people from a conquered territory as a sign that they surrender to the imposed rule). Tribute was generally in the form of food, crafts, textiles, or other products. The southern part of most *ciudadelas* had a water well and residences for the servants and low-ranking nobility. Outside the *ciudadelas,* but close

Ruins of the administrative sector at Chan Chan, the capital of the Chimor Kingdom. *© Kevin Schafer/Corbis.*

by, were residential compounds for the elite (a group of people within a society who are in a socially superior position and have more power and privileges than others).

In areas between the compounds for the elite and around the edges of the city were the *barrios,* a series of smaller compounds with rooms for living and rooms for working at crafts. These were built of wattle and daub, woven cane and twigs covered with mud. Workers, servants, and artisans lived in this part of the city; by the end of the Chimor kingdom, the population of this sector was about twenty thousand.

Farfán

Around 1150 the Chimú gained control of the Jequetepeque Valley to the north of Chan Chan and established Farfán. This was the first round of Chimú expansion. At Farfán, archaeologists have found six rectangular compounds that look very much like Chan Chan's *ciudadelas.* The line of compounds is about 2 miles (3.2 kilometers) long. There is no evidence of neighborhoods with living quarters, so some experts believe Farfán was an administrative center only—a place where the Chimú could oversee the governing of the region. Farfán is the only city in the Chimú empire that was built to look like Chan Chan.

Túcume

Around 1300 the Chimú launched a second round of expansion, much bigger than the first. One of their conquests was the Lambayeque region in the north. There, the Chimú moved into the already thriving city of Túcume, where many excellent crafts were produced. The people who had founded Túcume had been elaborate in their city's design. It was the site of twenty-six terraced pyramids and had an advanced culture. The Chimú overhauled the economy and rebuilt the platform mounds of the city. As the Chimú lords created new business and trade, artisans and other workers moved to the city to work, and its population grew significantly. Under the Chimú the beautiful craftwork that was traditional to the city became an industry. The Chimú lords chose a few designs for each craft, and the artisans produced these over and over again for distribution around a wide area. Scholars believe that the Chimú ruled Túcume through local leaders and that the state-managed craft industry was their primary goal in this conquest. Túcume remained an important city after the decline of the Chimú empire and during the reign of the Incas, but was probably abandoned before or when the Spanish arrived in the area in 1531. It was then largely forgotten until 1988, when Norwegian explorer Thor Heyerdahl (1914–2002) became interested in the city and began extensive and successful excavations.

Manchán

During the second phase of their expansion, the Chimú took over an area in the Casma Valley, south of Chan Chan. According to Nigel Davies in *The Ancient Kingdoms of Peru* (1997), the Chimú established about ten administrative sites and occupied five villages in the Casma Valley. The center of this region was Manchán, a city with some of the features of Chan Chan. It appears that Manchán was ruled by local leaders. The city had nine compounds containing *audiencia* structures and wattle and daub residences. Manchán was a center of the metalwork and textile industries, so it was home to many workers involved in metal or textile crafts.

History

The Chimor kingdom originated in the Moche Valley, and its people were probably descendants of the Moche people, who ruled the valley and a small empire from about 100 C.E. to 800 C.E. No one knows what happened in the valley after the Moche culture collapsed, but most experts think the northern coastal area broke into small, independently ruled towns and regions. The Wari (pronounced wah-REE) empire (see Chapter 8 for more information) probably had significant influence in the area until about 900 C.E. Around that time, the people in the Moche Valley began building a center at Chan Chan, and they came to be known as the Chimú. By 1150 the Chimú had grown powerful, and they began to expand their empire. The first expansion was minor. The Chimú took the nearby Jequetepeque Valley, north of Chan Chan, and established the cities of Farfán, an administrative or trading center, and Pacatnamú, a ceremonial center

Chimú metalwork, such as this gold vase, was highly influenced by the Lambayeque culture. © *Charles & Josette Lenars/Corbis.*

(city-like centers usually run by priests and rulers, in which people from surrounding areas gather to practice the ceremonies of their religion, often at large temples and plazas built specifically for this purpose).

In the 1300s, the Chimú empire expanded again. This time, the Chimú conquered territory both north and south of Chan Chan. To their south they took over the Casma Valley. In the north they extended their rule into the Lambayeque Valley. At that time the Lambayeque culture dominated a large part of the northern coastal region, from the northern border of present-day Peru to the modern town of Trujillo in the south. This area included the ancient centers of Batán Grande and Sipán. The people of the Lambayeque region had a reputation for exquisite metalwork, and they were highly skilled in other crafts as well. By taking control of the Lambayeque Valley, the Chimú increased their territory, but more important, they greatly improved their empire's economy and prestige. They took control of the Lambayeque textile and metalwork industries and directed the production of other luxury goods for trade. They captured some of the most skilled artisans in the valley and placed them in other regional centers to build up production and trade throughout their empire. In places like Túcume the Chimú created a system of craft production directed by the government. Their motives for building such a large empire appear to have been largely economic. Many historians believe that the Chimú achieved some of their conquests without violence or the use of force. In these cases, the Chimú may have promised profitable trading deals to regions that submitted to their rule.

Oral tradition and Spanish chronicles

There are a few existing historical chronicles of the kingdom of Chimor. (A chronicle is a continuous historical account of events arranged in order of time without analysis or interpretation.) The information in these accounts is sketchy, and the successions (the passing of the position from one ruler, upon his or her death, to the next ruler) they outline are vague. However, they do provide some names and an idea of the way the Chimú people remembered their own past. Archaeologists look for artifacts and other evidence that might support these textual histories. Sometimes they are successful; sometimes not.

Anonymous History of Trujillo, **1604.** This badly damaged manuscript by an unknown author was found in the early twentieth century in Lima, Peru. Its first chapter is a brief history of the Chimor kingdom. The chronicler relates that the kingdom originated when a man called Taycanamo (or Tacaynamo) arrived in the area of Chan Chan on a wooden raft. Taycanamo told the Chimú people he had come from across the sea to govern them. He had brought with him some yellow powders, which he claimed had magic powers. In his first year in Chimor, Taycanamo built a temple, where he performed rituals with the powders. Soon, he earned the loyalty of the people and was accepted as the king of Chimor. According to this legend, nine descendants of Taycanamo succeeded him as king of Chimor. His grandson, Nancenpinco, was credited with accomplishing the first great expansion of the kingdom. More expansion and conquests occurred under later kings, but the document does not give many details. The last king in this line was Minchancaman, who was the reigning monarch when the Incas conquered the Chimú in 1470. When Spanish soldiers arrived in the area of Chan Chan in the sixteenth century, the local people told them that their king, Minchancaman, had been taken by the Incas to Cuzco (pronounced KOO-sko) at the time of conquest. This seems to corroborate that Minchancaman, at least, was an actual historical figure.

Chronicles of Cabello de Balboa, **c. 1581.** Spanish priest Miguel Cabello de Balboa (birth and death dates unknown) wrote this brief history of the Lambayeque Valley. He lived in Lambayeque and presumably learned the legends of the region from its residents. His account states that the first ruler of Lambayeque was a man from the south named Naylamp, who arrived in the valley in great splendor on a fleet of rafts.

With him were his favorite courtesans (sexual slaves or prostitutes of the elite), his servants, trumpeters, and cupbearers. One of his courtesans was in charge of throwing crushed Spondylus shells (highly valued shells of a spiny, coral-colored oyster that could only be obtained off the coast of present-day Ecuador) under Naylamp's feet as he walked. Naylamp brought with him an idol (a representation or symbol of an object of worship) called Yampellec, which was made of green stone; "Yampellec" is probably the source of the modern name "Lambayeque." Naylamp built a palace at Chot (later called Chotuna) and continued to rule in Lambayeque. Upon his death, his servants buried him and then spread the news that he had grown wings and soared away from his kingdom forever.

Naylamp's descendants ruled the region for nine successive reigns. According to Cabello de Balboa, the last descendant of Naylamp to rule was Fempellec, who made the disastrous decision to move the green idol Yampellec from its place in Chot. A terrible flood overwhelmed the Lambayeque Valley, and the people blamed Fempellec for the disaster. They rose up against him, tying up his hands and feet and throwing him into the ocean, killing him. Nearby, the Chimú were waiting, and when the Lambayeque people were busy with their uprising, the Chimú took over the valley. They installed Pongmassa, a Chimú governor, to rule the region. By the time the Incas conquered the Lambayeque area in the 1470s, Pongmassa's grandson, Oxa, was the Chimú ruler there.

Archaeological finds support the basic outline of Chimú history that these two documents provide. However, most experts have observed that trying to match the legends with the artifacts too precisely has not been very useful. Over the years, the people who passed these tales from generation to generation probably condensed some information or glossed over eras that lacked dramatic or heroic events.

Government

The kingdom of Chimor was ruled by a monarch (king), and the right to rule passed from father to son. The king ruled by divine right; that is, the Chimú people believed

that their king had been appointed by the gods to rule them. The king of Chimor ruled from the city of Chan Chan. Next in the line of political power in the empire was an elite group of nobles or lords who held powerful positions in the government and enjoyed great wealth. The nobles set themselves at a great distance from the common people and artisans. These Chimú lords wore elaborate feathered clothing and gold and silver jewelry made from highly valued materials that were skillfully crafted by the top artisans in the empire.

Scholars think that Chimú lords set up governments in some of the valleys close to Chan Chan as the empire began to grow, and archaeological evidence suggests that the Chimú rebuilt some conquered cities to serve as government seats. However, most experts believe that Chimú leaders allowed the majority of conquered cities to govern themselves, as long as they participated in the tribute and trade systems imposed by the empire (see Economy for more information on tribute and trade systems). For some cities, it may have

The Chimú lords wore elaborate gold and silver jewelry, such as these ear plugs, skillfully crafted by top artisans. © *Burnstein Collection/Corbis.*

been quite profitable to be part of such a large trading network, and the Chimú may have made some of their conquests without using much force. At its height, though, the Chimor kingdom had a powerful military and could dictate its terms to the cities it occupied.

Economy

In the early years of their empire, the Chimú improved upon the irrigation systems set in place by the Moche civilization before them. Initially, they were successful in farming the dry Moche Valley land. They even made an attempt to build an irrigation canal from the neighboring Chicama River to bring its water into the Moche Valley. Unfortunately, earthquakes and changes in climate caused great damage to their system. Most Chimú irrigation works were abandoned well before the Incas conquered the Chimú empire. By about 1200, the Chimú decided that farming in the desert was not the best plan; they could obtain better access to foods by conquering other, more fertile lands. In their capital city, Chan Chan, they replaced the business of agriculture with state-controlled production of textiles and metalwork. Each area throughout the empire created surpluses of its own specialized products and exported the surplus in exchange for goods from other regions within and outside the empire.

The crafts industry

By the last years of the Chimú empire, Chan Chan had developed an organized, high-output craft industry. An estimated one-quarter of the city's population were artisans (craftspeople) who lived and worked in the city's *barrio*. Many of the raw materials the Chan Chan craftspeople used were imported. Some may have been carried in from faraway places on large seagoing rafts that traveled along the Pacific Coast, though little is known about the Chimú's ocean trade network. These raw materials were then loaded on the backs of llamas (a South American mammal that originated in Peru and probably descended from the guanaco) and deposited at one of the city's two caravanserais (places where the caravans, or herds, of llamas brought their loads of goods and rested from their trip). The top industry in Chan Chan was metalwork, so bronze and copper ingots were two of the city's main imports (ingots are unfinished metal pieces or bars that have been liquefied and molded into a shape that can be easily stored or carried to a metalworker). Chan Chan also imported alpaca fur for textiles. (Alpacas are domesticated mammals related to the llama that originated in Peru.) When imported goods such as these arrived in the city, they were brought to skilled workers in the *barrios*. Scholars are not certain how trade was accomplished: Private artisans may have exchanged their materials from merchants who traded for their own profit. Alternatively, merchants may have worked with city administrators handling the exchanges of materials as part of a large-scale city operation.

The crafts industry was key to the Chimú economy, so it was important for the lords of Chimor to cultivate skilled artisans who could become part of a large specialized labor pool. In earlier times, parents passed their job skills on to their children. In the house of a textile weaver, for example, the children would begin working with their parents at a young age and were fully skilled at the trade by adulthood. Often the families were part of an extended family grouping that specialized in the craft, and together these families formed a kind of guild (an association of people with common interests). The nobility of Chimor wished to speed up this generational process in Chan Chan, using the expertise of the artisans to train new crafters. They also wished to produce finer goods in Chan Chan. When they conquered the Lambayeque region, they brought many of the region's most skilled metalworkers to work in Chan Chan's *barrios*. As a result, Chan Chan became the largest manufacturer of fine metal goods in the empire.

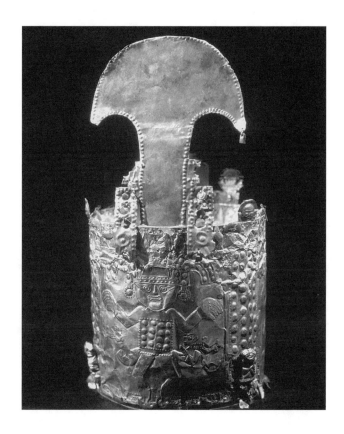

The Chimú excelled in creating exquisite objects from precious metals, such as this gold crown.
© *Gianni Dagli Orti/Corbis.*

Farming and fishing

Farming and fishing, although not as prevalent as the crafting industry, were also important in the Chimú economy. Farmers and peasants lived outside the capital city, in villages near their fields. They provided city dwellers with potatoes, maize (corn), squash, beans, and peppers. Fish was also a regular part of the Chimú diet, thanks to hardworking fishermen who lived in settlements near the ocean, away from the nobles and artisans (in Chimú society, most people considered fishermen to be inferior to these other groups). Although they did not live in Chan Chan, the fishermen and farmers were required to help build palace compounds and monuments in the city. Their labor on these projects was a form of tribute.

Religion

The Chimú worshiped the sea and a variety of ocean gods. Earlier Andean societies revered mountains and rain, which brought them water for their crops; the Chimú worshiped the ocean, which fed them with its abundant sea life and probably allowed them to travel and trade throughout their vast empire.

The Chimú also worshiped their ancestors. Ancestor worship is an ancient Andean religious tradition based on a belief that deceased people can exercise supernatural powers from beyond the grave to help their living descendants. Like many other Andean cultures, the Chimú often kept the mummified (preserved) bodies of the dead in an accessible chamber. When a Chimú king died, his *ciudadela* in Chan Chan became a kind of museum or shrine. The king's body was placed in a burial chamber inside the *ciudadela;* in the same chamber the Chimú placed hundreds of other bodies— the bodies of young men, young women, and llamas, all sacrificed (killed) to satisfy the gods and to accompany the king to the next world. The king's tomb also contained burial offerings: finely crafted gold masks and other metalwork; pottery; Spondylus shells, which were highly valued among Andean civilizations; and colorful textiles with vivid scenes or images woven into them. Experts believe that the family and staff of the king continued to run the *ciudadela* as if the king were alive, serving him and occasionally staging ceremonies and rituals. The king was sometimes brought out of the tomb to attend these events. Even though he was dead, his people believed that he still had divine powers, and it was the re-

sponsibility of the king's relatives and staff to maintain his image as an all-powerful ruler.

Chan Chan's adobe walls show an abundance of friezes and sculpted designs. © *Charles & Josette Lenars/Corbis.*

Arts and sciences

According to Davies, the greatest artistic achievement of the Chimú is their architecture. Their cities, particularly Chan Chan, were well planned, combining beauty with function. The desert environment provided few building materials, but the Chimú excelled at using the mud and clay that were available. Chan Chan, the largest all-adobe city ever built, features an abundance of friezes and sculpted designs—geometric patterns, animal figures, and sea imagery—molded right into the walls of the city's mud-colored buildings. Many of these designs are plated with gold or other precious metals. The reverence of the Chimú for the ocean is evident on the walls at Chan Chan, where there are many depictions of waves, sea life, seabirds, and even fishnets. The multiple *ciu-*

dadelas within the city were very functional. They had huge water wells that could be entered through chambers leading from the living areas—almost like having indoor plumbing. The city itself had underground canals for carrying water, and since it was a center of trade and production, it was equipped with hundreds of storage units for food and goods.

Metalwork was the main craft of the Chimú. Chimú artisans made jewelry, masks, ear spools, and other art objects, often from gold or bronze. Their artwork is still renowned for its beauty. Most of the metalworking skills of the Chimú culture originated in the Lambayeque Valley. When the Chimú conquered the Lambayeque region, they took control of its crafts and forced many of its most skilled metalworkers to relocate to Chan Chan.

Chimú pottery is easily recognized because of its characteristic dark black glazing; the Chimú also made red pottery. Chimú potters used many of the same techniques as Moche ceramists, but in general, the Chimú were not as artistic as the Moche in the field of ceramics. This was probably because the Chimú often mass-produced their crafts.

Decline

For about five hundred years the Chimú empire thrived and grew stronger. It spread to include about 600 miles (965 kilometers) of the northern coastal area. Well-planned cities and an advanced trade system united the different peoples living under Chimú rule. By the early fourteenth century, the Chimú empire had become the most powerful force in the Andes. To the south of the empire, small, independent states fought with one another for resources. There was little unity and nothing to threaten the power of the Chimú. Then, around 1350, the Incas, a small, little-known group from the city of Cuzco, began a series of military campaigns that would lead them to ever-expanding power. Inca conquests reached Chimú territory by about the middle of the 1400s. The Chimú fought vigorously and well against this fierce new enemy. Around 1470, the Incas surprised the Chimú by taking control of Chan Chan's water supply in the highlands above the city. Without water, the city could not function, and it surrendered to the Incas. The

Incas killed some of the Chimú nobility but took the king, Minchancaman, back to Cuzco to marry into the Inca royalty. They set up their own governments in the Chimú regions and transferred many of the most skilled artisans to Cuzco.

From 1470 on, Inca nobility ruled over the former Chimú people. There are records of a massive uprising of the Chimú people against the Inca rulers sometime after the conquest. The Incas put down the rebellion and relocated large groups of the rebels to other parts of the empire. The kingdom of Chimor was gone forever, but aspects of its culture would survive as part of the Inca empire.

For More Information

Books

Davies, Nigel. *The Ancient Kingdoms of Peru*. London: Penguin, 1997.

Fagan, Brian. *Kingdoms of Gold, Kingdoms of Jade: The Americas before Columbus*. London and New York: Thames and Hudson, 1991.

Morris, Craig, and Adriana Von Hagen. *The Inka Empire and Its Andean Origins*. New York: Abbeville Press, 1993.

Moseley, Michael E. *The Incas and Their Ancestors: The Archaeology of Peru*. London and New York: Thames and Hudson, 1992.

Von Hagen, Adriana, and Craig Morris. *The Cities of the Ancient Andes*. London and New York: Thames and Hudson, 1998.

Web Site

"Chan Chan Archaeological Zone, Peru." *HistoryChannel.com*. http://www.historychannel.com/classroom/unesco/chanchan/about_chimor.html (accessed on October 18, 2004).

The Rise of the Incas

While many people have never heard of the early cultures of the Andean region, like the Chavín (pronounced chah-VEEN), Moche (pronounced MO-chay), Tiwanaku (tee-wah-NAH-coo), Wari (wah-REE), and Chimú (chee-MOO), that existed before the Inca (ING-kuh) empire, most people know something about the Incas. That is at least partly because when the Spanish arrived in South America in the early 1530s, they found one wealthy and powerful empire, rather than many small states descending from the earlier cultures. (An empire is a vast, complex political unit extending across political boundaries and dominated by one central power, which generally takes control of the economy, government, and culture in communities throughout its territory.) In a mere ninety-five years between 1438 and 1533, the Incas spread their empire over almost 3,000 miles (4,827 kilometers) of western South America, unifying the highly diverse populations in the vast region under their control. In truth, the Incas were not the originators of many of the aspects of civilization for which they are often credited. Before the Inca empire was built, great innovations in farming, art,

Words to Know

Acllahuaci: A house where young women chosen by the Incas were isolated from daily Inca life; these women were trained in the arts of weaving fine cloth and making *chicha* and foods for festivals, and some went on to become religious workers.

Administrator: A person who manages or supervises the day-to-day operations of business, government, and religious organizations.

Ayllu: A group of extended families who live in the same area, share their land and work, and arrange for marriages and religious rituals as a group; the basic social unit of the Andean peoples.

Callanca: An Inca word meaning "great hall"; a place where people gathered for ceremonies and other events.

Chicha: A kind of beer that Andean peoples made from maize or other grains.

Chronicler: A person who writes down a record of historical events, arranged in the order of occurrence.

Colca: Storehouse for food and goods.

Conquistador: The Spanish word for "conqueror"; in English, the word usually refers to the leaders of the Spanish conquests of Mesoamerica and Peru in the sixteenth century.

Empire: A vast, complex political unit extending across political boundaries and dominated by one central power, which generally takes control of the economy, government, and culture in communities throughout its territory.

Hanan: The Quechua word for the upper half of a city or region.

architecture, and social organization were already in place throughout the Andes. The Inca government excelled at organizing all the various cultures and economies it had brought together. The incorporation of many diverse peoples into a unified system was probably the crowning accomplishment of the Incas.

Dates of predominance

1438–1533.

Name variations and pronunciation

Inca; Inka. Pronounced ING-kuh. Inca originally meant "ruler" and referred to the king or leader. It is also

Huaca: A sacred place, usually used for a temple, pyramid, or shrine.

Hurin: The Quechua word for the lower half of a city or region.

Inca: The word Inca originally meant "ruler" and referred to the king or leader. It is also used to mean the original group of Inca family clans that arose to prominence in the city of Cuzco. As the empire arose, the supreme ruler was called the "Sapa Inca" and members of the noble class were called "Incas."

Legend: A legend is a story handed down from earlier times, often believed to be historically true.

Missionary: A person, usually working for a religious organization, who tries to convert people, usually in a foreign land, to his or her religion.

Quechua: The Inca language, still spoken by Andean people today.

Sapa Inca: Supreme ruler of the Incas.

Stonemasonry: The work of a skilled builder who expertly lays cut or otherwise fitted units of stone in construction.

Suyo: A Quechua word for quarter, or portion.

Tribute: A payment to a nation or its ruler, usually made by people from a conquered territory as a sign that they surrender to the imposed rule; in the Inca empire, tribute was most often paid in labor, including farmwork, construction, and military service.

Ushnu: A large platform in a central part of a city plaza, where the king or noblemen stood to address the public or view public festivities.

used to mean the original group of Inca family clans that arose to prominence in the city of Cuzco (pronounced KOO-sko). As the empire arose, the supreme ruler was called the "Sapa Inca" and members of the noble class were called "Incas." The Incas called their empire Tawantinsuyu (also Tahuantinsuyu; pronounced tah-wahn-teen-SOO-yoo), which means "land of four quarters" in the Quechua (pronounced KECH-wah) language. Quechua is the Inca language, still spoken by Andean people today.

Location

The Inca homeland was in the area of Cuzco, a city in the highlands of southeast Peru, about 350 miles (563 kilo-

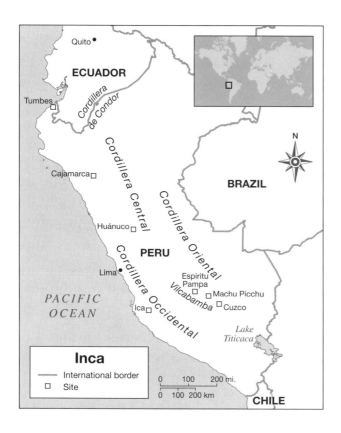

Inca

— International border
□ Site

| 0 | 100 | 200 mi. |
| 0 | 100 200 | km |

Map showing important sites in the Inca empire.
Map by XNR Productions. The Gale Group.

meters) southeast of Peru's present-day capital, Lima.

By the time of the Spanish conquest in 1533, Tawantinsuyu (the Inca empire) included a vast part of the Andean region between the mountains and the Pacific coast as well as some areas farther inland. The Incas controlled all of present-day Peru, most of present-day Ecuador and Bolivia, and northern parts of what is now Chile and Argentina. The Incas separated their empire into four *suyus,* or quarters, that radiated from Cuzco, their capital city. East of Cuzco was Antisuyu, which extended through the Andes to the tropical jungles in the Amazon basin (a depression in the earth, often with a body of water in it). West of Cuzco was Cuntisuyu, which included the coastal regions of Peru. South of Cuzco was Collasuyu, which included Lake Titicaca, other parts of Bolivia, and parts of Chile and Argentina. North of Cuzco was Chincasuyu, which included the northern highlands and Ecuador.

Important sites

The Inca nobility was firmly stationed in the capital city of Cuzco. It was the hub of the government and home to all Sapa Incas, alive or dead. There were other types of urban centers in the Inca empire, though. Surrounding Cuzco archaeologists have found significant smaller centers such as Machu Picchu and Sacsahuaman, probably built by the Sapa Incas as fortresses or retreats. Outside of the Cuzco region, the cities and towns that were conquered throughout the Andes region generally maintained their own governments, but the Incas built administrative centers to maintain control and keep records of their outlying territories. Though only a few Inca nobles and their staff of accountants, administrators, and servants, actually lived in these centers, they were built to accommodate huge festivals that were attended by the people from a large surrounding area.

Cuzco

Cuzco, the sacred city of the Incas and the capital of their empire, is the oldest city in the Americas that has been continuously inhabited by people. Cuzco is in the Andes Mountains, at an altitude of about 11,700 feet (3,566 meters). It was already an existing village or town when the Incas arrived sometime around 1200. The great Inca emperor Pachacutec (ruled 1438–1471) is believed to have thoroughly rebuilt the city during his reign. Before the Spanish conquest of 1533, Cuzco's population reached an estimated peak of forty thousand to one hundred thousand people.

Huge stone temples and fortresses occupied the ceremonial core of Cuzco, some of them covered in sheets of gold. There were two vast plazas in the ceremonial core of the city, where ceremonies and festivities took place. One of them was entirely filled with sand brought in from the Pacific Ocean. The city's holiest temple, the Coricancha, or Temple of the Sun, was located in the ceremonial core, at the meeting point of two rivers. Nearby were the palaces of living and dead kings. Also in the city's core was the *acllahuaci* ("house of chosen women"), where selected girls and women lived in isolation while they learned skills that would serve the empire such as weaving and making *chicha* (maize [corn] beer). The core of the city was also the site of *huacas* (sacred monuments), *callancas* (great halls), and *colcas* (storehouses for food and goods). The public buildings were made from large, precisely cut stones. In the middle of the city's paved streets, stone-lined channels of flowing water carried away waste and sewage. According to Brian M. Fagan, author of *Kingdoms of Gold, Kingdoms of Jade* (1991), the sanitation system in Cuzco was far better than that of fifteenth-century Europe.

Like most Inca cities, Cuzco was divided into upper and lower halves—*Hanan* (Upper) Cuzco and *Hurin* (Lower) Cuzco. It was then divided again, so that there were four quarters, or *suyos*. Cuzco was divided into even smaller sections by a system of *ceques*, lines that radiated from the Coricancha (Temple of the Sun) to the horizon. Along these lines were 328 *huacas*, usually comprised of a natural object, such

Ruins of Sacsahuaman near Cuzco, Peru. *The Library of Congress.*

as a cave, stream, or rock, or of something made by humans, such as a statue, monument, or fountain. Each *huaca* had its own special day of rituals.

Only the nobility and their servants and administrators (people who manage or supervise the day-to-day operations of business, government, and religious organizations) lived in the central part of Cuzco, which was surrounded by farmlands. Beyond these lands, according to Michael A. Malpass in *Daily Life in the Inca Empire* (1996), there were a variety of districts for the non-Inca people.

Sacsahuaman

Just north of Cuzco, perched on a hill, was a complex called Sacsahuaman (pronounced sox-ah-wah-MAHN), one of the amazing architectural accomplishments of the Inca world. The complex was built in the fifteenth century, probably under the orders of Pachacutec, the Inca emperor at that time.

Sacsahuaman was huge. Its walls stretched about a third of a mile in length. Three terraces, or giant stairs, led up the sides of the hill to the complex walls. The walls and buildings of Sacsahuaman were made of enormous stones. Some were the size of refrigerators, and others were much larger. In fact, archaeologists at the site found a stone block that measures 38 feet (11.6 meters) long, 18 feet (5.5 meters) high, and 6 feet (1.8 meters) thick. Some of the stones at the site weigh up to 100 tons (90.7 metric tons). How they were transported to the site from their source at a quarry remains a mystery; the wheel had not yet been discovered in the Americas. The stonemasonry (the cut and fit of the stones) at Sacsahuaman is remarkable. The blocks that form the walls were cut and sculpted so perfectly that they interlock at every point from front to back, fitting together like pieces of a jigsaw puzzle. Not even a piece of paper or blade of grass will fit between them. It is estimated that some thirty thousand people worked on building this complex (at different times) for a period of about seventy years. Sacsahuaman was probably built as a fortress, but it may have also functioned as a religious center.

Huánuco Pampa

Huánuco Pampa, which was built around 1460, was one of the largest of the Inca administrative centers, cities where Inca officials and their local representatives set up headquarters to oversee local and regional activities. Huánuco Pampa was situated in the Andean plains about 170 miles (273.5 kilometers) east of the present-day city of Lima in central Peru. It was perched in the mountains at an altitude of about 12,500 feet (3,810 meters) above sea level. It was built solely for the administration of that region, so it probably had only a very small permanent population of Incas and local administrators. In Huánuco Pampa, the Incas hosted large festivals, which often lasted for days. They gave the local people great quantities of food and *chicha* and then told them what labor would be expected from them in the months ahead. Local leaders brought their people's tribute (payment to a nation or its ruler; in this case probably harvested crops) to the five hundred storehouses just south of the city.

At the center of Huánuco Pampa lay a vast main plaza, where thousands of people from the region could as-

The impressive ruins of Machu Picchu, nestled among the peaks of the Andes Mountains.
Photograph by John M. Barth. Reproduced by permission.

semble. A large rectangular stone platform, called an *ushnu,* occupied the center of the plaza. Standing on this platform, the Inca emperor or Inca noblemen could address the people or view their festivities. In all, there were about four thousand buildings in Huánuco Pampa. Along with palaces and temples, there were many long rectangular buildings. Some of these probably served as temporary housing for the festival guests; others may have been used for preparing the festival food and *chicha.*

Machu Picchu

The magnificent Machu Picchu complex is perhaps the most famous of all Inca sites. It is nestled among soaring mountain peaks in the Urubamba River valley, which is just north of the Cuzco Valley. Machu Picchu was never a large center, but it has become one of South America's most popular tourist sites because of the beauty of its stone architecture.

Machu Picchu was made up of about two hundred buildings, and archaeologists estimate that its population was around one thousand people.

Historians believe that Machu Picchu was the private estate of Pachacutec, the great Inca emperor; it belonged to him personally and was probably used only by his relatives, chosen nobles, and servants. It is likely that Machu Picchu served as a kind of vacation home or religious retreat for Pachacutec. A small community of workers must have lived on the estate, growing food, cooking, tending gardens, and making *chicha* for the palace. Based on the sacred nature of relics that have been found at Machu Picchu, most experts agree that Machu Picchu probably had a religious significance that is no longer apparent.

Machu Picchu is surrounded on three sides by the Urubamba River gorge (a deep narrow passage with steep rocky sides, with a river running through it), and it is located

Aerial view of the narrow, winding road leading to Machu Picchu. © *Yann Arthus-Bertrand/Corbis.*

in a remote part of the lower river valley. It could only be reached by a dangerous climb up a 2,000-foot (610-meter) terraced cliff. When the Spanish invaded the Inca empire in the early 1500s, the Incas abandoned Machu Picchu. The Spanish never found the site, and it lay unobserved until 1911, when archaeologist Hiram Bingham (1875–1956) discovered it. Bingham also found numerous Inca sites along a narrow, paved road (now known as the Inca Trail) in the hills around the river. Bingham thought he had found Vilcabamba, the last capital city the Incas established after the Spanish conquest. This proved not to be the case.

Vilcabamba

The Incas fled Cuzco in 1533 to escape the Spanish conquistadores. (*Conquistador* is the Spanish word for "conqueror"; in English, the word usually refers to the leaders of the Spanish conquests of Mesoamerica and Peru in the sixteenth century.) They went to a region of Peru known as Vilcabamba, a remote, heavily forested, and mountainous area northwest of Cuzco. There, in exile, they reestablished their society and built a capital city. The Incas built new temples, palaces, and fortresses in this capital and probably built other settlements and ceremonial centers (city-like centers usually run by priests and rulers, in which people from surrounding areas gather to practice the ceremonies of their religion, often at large temples and plazas built specifically for this purpose) in the surrounding wilderness region. In Vilcabamba the Incas witnessed the succession (passing the position from one ruler, upon his death, to the next ruler) of three Inca emperors between 1533 and 1572. When the Spanish prepared to attack the Inca at Vilcabamba in 1571, the Inca people burned their capital city and fled, abandoning the ruins forever. For centuries, the location of the "lost city of Vilcabamba" remained unknown.

Archaeologists mistakenly thought they had found the Vilcabamba capital when the ruins at Machu Picchu were first discovered in 1911. By the end of the twentieth century, though, many archaeologists were convinced that the exiled Inca government had actually been centered at a site called Espiritu Pampa. The buildings and monuments that were found there fit the Spanish conquistadores' descriptions of the Inca capital in Vilcabamba.

In 1999 British explorer Peter Frost encountered ruins in the southern part of Vilcabamba, 22 miles (35.4 kilometers) southwest of Machu Picchu, on a mountain peak called Cerro Victoria. The site contains ruins of religious buildings and burial grounds and was clearly the scene of religious rituals (formal acts performed the same way each time, usually used as a means of religious worship). In 2001 American archaeologist Gary Ziegler and British writer and explorer Hugh Thomson assembled a crew and explored even deeper into Vilcabamba. They found another Inca site, Cota Coca, which is larger than the site at Cerro Victoria. Cota Coca was probably another place of refuge for the Incas after the Spanish invasion of Cuzco, their capital. The ongoing work at these sites and at other sites in the difficult Vilcabamba terrain seems likely to reveal much more than is currently known about the final period of the Inca empire. (See Chapter 14 for more information on Vilcabamba and the years of Inca exile.)

History

Like other Andean societies before them, the Incas had no system of writing; there are no written documents recording Inca history before the Spanish arrived in Peru in 1532. There are, however, many documents that were written in the first half-century after the Spanish conquest. A few of the Spanish conquistadores and missionaries (people, usually working for a religious organization, who try to convert others in a foreign land to their religion) recorded their own observations as well as the memories and oral traditions (history and stories passed from generation to generation through spoken accounts) of the Andean people they met. These people, for a variety of reasons, took on the role of chroniclers: They observed their new surroundings, interviewed people, and did other research to find out about Inca history—and then they wrote down what they learned. Because of the work of the Spanish chroniclers, modern people know a lot more about the Incas than they do about earlier Andean cultures. While the Inca empire flourished in prehistory (the period of time in any given region, beginning with the appearance of the first human beings there and ending with the occurrence of the first written records), there was still a substantial Inca population who remembered the days of the empire in the historical era (the period of human existence described by written records). These written records help bring the Inca empire to life.

How accurate are the chronicles?

The Spanish chroniclers provide rich details in the Inca story, details that archaeology generally cannot supply. For factual accuracy, however, the chronicles are not always reliable, and most historians try to verify these accounts through archaeological research and other sources of evidence. Historians have always noted problems in the Spanish chronicles. Even when the writers were genuinely interested in the culture and found good eyewitnesses, they tended to view the Inca story through biased European and Christian viewpoints. Some of their accounts attempt to justify Spain's conquest of Inca lands. Furthermore, most of the Spanish chroniclers arrived in the Americas long after other Andean civilizations were absorbed by the Inca empire; therefore, the Andean people they talked to had only vague memories of the Incas' rise to power.

The accuracy of Inca chroniclers has also come into question at times. After the Spanish conquest, Inca chroniclers wrote down what they knew of their people's history and oral traditions. Some of them tend to idealize the Inca past. All of them base their accounts on an oral history of the Andeans that was almost certainly revised by each Inca emperor for his own interests.

Public relations campaigns and political "spin" are not unique to the modern world. Looking back at the Inca world, it is clear that the emperor Pachacutec, who began his rule in 1438, was a master of persuasion and propaganda (ideas, information, or rumors spread for the purpose of helping or hurting a cause or person). Historians believe that Pachacutec had all the storytellers of the empire brought to him early in his reign. He provided them with an official "history" of the Inca empire that he wished them to tell from that day forward, instructing them to forget the older histories. Pachacutec's version of history depicted the pre-empire days as a time of sheer chaos, when there was no civilizing force in the world. According to Pachacutec's history, the Incas were created by one of the gods to bring people out of

this darkness and chaos. This "history" neglects to mention the great accomplishments of the Chavín, the Nazca (pronounced NAHZ-cah), the Moche, the Wari, and other Andean peoples, who introduced most of the advances that Inca civilization is known for. Pachacutec's revision of history was intended to unite the empire; he hoped to persuade the people that the gods had given the Incas the mission to rule over the vast Andean region.

Manco Capac, first king of the Incas, holding the sun god, Inti—his creator according to Inca legend.
The Art Archive/Museo Pedro de Osma Lima/Mireille Vautier.

Inca origins: Legends and traditions

The legends recorded by the chroniclers give credit to Manco Capac, the legendary first king of the Incas, for founding the city of Cuzco (the Inca capital) and establishing the Inca royal lineage. (A legend is a story handed down from earlier times, often believed to be historically true.) According to one of these legends, the sun god Inti created eight siblings, who emerged from a cave called Pacariqtambo, about 20

The Chroniclers of the Inca Empire

Spanish chroniclers: After Spanish soldiers defeated the Incas in 1533, the Spanish missionaries started trying to convert the Andean peoples to Christianity. They also tried to train the Incas to be more like Europeans. As part of the conversion process, the Spanish conquistadores tore down the temples, or *huacas,* and other cultural buildings and monuments throughout the empire. Some of the missionaries decided to learn as much as they could about the native religion and history, hoping that the more they knew about the Inca ways, the easier it would be to eliminate them.

These are some of the main Spanish chroniclers who recorded Inca history:

• Pedro Sarmiento de Gamboa (c. 1532–1592), a Spanish historian, mathematician, navigator, and astronomer, was hired by the Spanish government several decades after the Spanish conquest to write a history of the Incas. De Gamboa located people who had been alive at the time of the conquest and interviewed them. Spanish leaders had a definite purpose for assigning this project: They wanted to prove their right to Inca lands, and they hired de Gamboa to write a history that would support their claims. Because of this motive (and the amount of time that had elapsed since the conquest), de

Gamboa's 1572 report, *History of the Incas,* is considered biased (prejudiced or unfair).

• Father Bernabé Cobo (1580–1657) was a Jesuit missionary from Spain who arrived in Peru in 1599, more than sixty years after the Spanish conquest. Cobo did research and interviews near Cuzco and Lake Titicaca, seeking out people who remembered the pre-Spanish empire. His massive *Historia del Nuevo Mundo* (*History of the New World*) (c. 1653) provides many details of Inca life interpreted from a Christian viewpoint.

• Juan de Betanzos (birth and death dates unknown) was a Spanish subject who became the top Quechua language interpreter for the viceroyalty (Spanish state) of Peru. Betanzos married Inca noblewoman Doña Angelina Yupanque, who had been one of the Sapa Inca Atahuallpa's (pronounced AH-tah-WAHL-pahs) wives until his death at the hands of the Spanish in 1533. She was later mistress to the Spanish conqueror Francisco Pizarro (c. 1475–1541). Doña Angelina and her family probably provided much of the information that went into *Narrative of the Incas* (completed by Betanzos in 1557) a long and well-researched account of the Inca empire written by

Betanzos. Unfortunately, much of the manuscript of the book was lost for centuries. In the 1980s scholars discovered the entire text in Spain. Most of the standard histories of the Incas were written before this valuable source was available. The complete manuscript has reshaped the modern world's view of some parts of Inca history, and it will probably inspire new publications about the Inca past.

- Pedro Cieza de León (c. 1518–1560) was a Spanish soldier and explorer who arrived in Peru about 1548. Cieza was very interested in other cultures and provided a detailed and respected account of the Incas in *Chronicle of Peru* (1554).

Inca chroniclers: Two Inca writers, born after the Spanish conquest and educated by Spanish teachers, provided histories of the Inca empire:

- Garcilaso de la Vega (1539–1616), also known as "El Inca," was the son of a Spanish army captain and an Inca noblewoman. Reared by his mother, de la Vega learned the language, customs, and stories of the Incas, but later his father sent him to Spain to be educated as a nobleman. De la Vega wrote *Royal Commentaries of the Incas* (1609), which details the personalities, events, customs, and ceremonies of the Inca empire from its beginnings to the arrival of the Spanish conquerors. The book idealizes the Incas, presenting their world as a perfect civilization. It is considered one of the first great literary works of the Americas, and it also has value as a historical record, though it is probably inaccurate on many factual matters.

- Felipe Huaman Poma de Ayala (1535–c. 1615) was the son of a royal Inca mother and an Andean father who was probably the ruler of one of the outlying provinces. Poma wrote *La primer nueva corónica y buen gobierno* (*The First New Chronicle and Good Government,* 1615), a 1,200-page account of the Incas that included nearly four hundred drawings of Inca history and life before and after the Spanish conquest. He wrote the chronicle in the form of a letter and sent it to King Philip II of Spain (1527–1598), hoping to get help for the Andean people in colonial Peru. The king never saw the manuscript and it was lost for centuries. In 1908 it was found in the Royal Library of Copenhagen, and in the 1970s, Inca scholars gave it their attention. Most modern histories of the Incas feature the illustrations of Huamán Poma de Ayala as one of the most useful links to the Inca past.

Labels within image:
Manco Ccapac Ynga I. — Sinchiroca Ynga II. — Lloqui Yanqui Yupanqui Ynga III. — Mayta Ccapac Ynga IV. — Ccapac Yupanqui Ynga V. — Mama Huaco.

Yncaroca Ynga VI. — Yahuar Huacac Ynga VII. — Viracocha Ynga VIII. — Pachacutic Ynga IX. — Yncayupanqui Ynga X. — Tupacyupanqui Ynga XI.

FIGIES D LOS INGAS REIES D PERV

Genealogy of Inca rulers (from left): Manco Capac, Sinchi Roca, Lloque Yupanqui, Mayta Capac, Capac Yupanqui, Inca Roca, Yahuar Huaca, Viracocha, Pachacutec, Tupac Yupanqui. *The Art Archive/Museo Pedro de Osma Lima/Mireille Vautier.*

miles (32 kilometers) southeast of Cuzco. There were four brothers—Ayar (Lord) Uchu, Ayar Cachi, Ayar Anca, and Ayar Manco (who would soon be called Manco Capac)—and four sisters, who were also the wives of the brothers: Mama Ocllo, Mama Huaco, Mama Ipacura (or Mama Cura), and Mama Raua. The cave at Pacariqtambo had three windows, and according to the legend, Manco Capac and his brothers and sisters came through the middle window. Other groups of people emerged from the two side windows, and these people would become the ten Inca *ayllus* (pronounced EYE-yoos), or family groupings, that helped found and rule Cuzco.

Manco Capac, his brothers and sisters, and the ten *ayllus* immediately set out to locate a place where they could start a new civilization. As they traveled, the great strength of one brother, Ayar Cachi, filled the others with fear, so they lured him into a cave and then barred its door. Stuck in the cave, Ayar Cachi turned to stone, and his stone image became a *huaca* of the Inca people. Later during the journey, two more brothers turned to stone; like Ayar Cachi before them, the transformed brothers became sacred stone *huacas* that would be revered for many years to come. At this point, out of the original eight siblings, only Manco Capac and the four sisters remained. However, a new family member soon joined the trip: Mama Ocllo, Manco Capac's sister/wife, gave birth to a son, Sinchi Roca.

When Manco Capac and his band of travelers arrived in the area of Cuzco, they received a sign that they were to settle there. There were already people living in Cuzco, and the Inca travelers were few and weak. Conflicts ensued, but the Incas managed to remain in the location and soon began to build their center and temple there. Manco Capac ruled for many years, and all the Inca kings who succeeded him were his direct descendants.

In another version of this story of Inca origins, only Manco

The Inca Rulers

The Eight Legendary Kings

- Manco Capac, founder of the Incas
- Sinchi Roca, son of Manco Capac
- Lloque Yupanqui, son of Sinchi Roca
- Mayta Capac, son of Lloque Yupanqui
- Capac Yupanqui, son of Mayta Capac
- Inca Roca, son of Capac Yupanqui
- Yahuar Huaca, son of Inca Roca
- Viracocha, son of Yahuar Huaca

The Emperors

- Pachacutec or Pachacuti (ruled 1438–1471), son of Viracocha and first emperor of the Inca empire
- Tupac Inca Yupanqui (ruled 1471–1493), son of Pachacutec
- Huayna Capac (pronounced WHY-nuh CA-poc; ruled 1493–1525), son of Tupac Inca Yupanqui
- Huáscar (ruled 1525–1532), son of Huayna Capac
- Atahuallpa (ruled 1532–1533), son of Huayna Capac

Inca Kings after the Conquest

- Manco Inca (ruled 1533–1545), son of Huayna Capac
- Sayri Tupa Inca (ruled 1545–1558), son of Manco Inca
- Titu Cusi (ruled 1558–1571), son of Manco Inca
- Tupac Amarú (ruled 1571–1572), son of Manco Inca

Capac and his sister/wife emerge from a cave, and the cave is near Lake Titicaca, in the highlands of present-day Bolivia, where the Tiwanaku people had once lived. They travel to find a place to begin their civilization, and they have divine instructions about how to locate the right spot: They are to plant a gold staff in the ground; if the staff sinks deeply into the soil, they will know that they have arrived at their destination. According to the legend, the staff sank deeply into the ground at Cuzco.

Inca origins: Modern history's view

With few proven sources of accurate information, modern historians can present only a sketchy picture of the origins of the Incas. No one knows exactly where the Incas came from or when they arrived in the village of Cuzco. Between 1000 and 1470 C.E. the northern Andean highlands were united under Chimú rule (see Chapter 9 for more information). However, in the southern Andean region, where the Incas emerged, the population remained divided, existing in small independent groups that were often at war with their neighbors. By the thirteenth century, the diverse populations in the Cuzco Valley were slowly uniting and becoming more powerful. The Incas were a small group of farmers, apparently smaller and less powerful than some of the other groups in the area. Nevertheless, around 1200 they had begun to rise to prominence in Cuzco.

No one knows whether the first Inca king, Manco Capac, is a historical or mythical (imaginary) figure. The Spanish chroniclers' accounts of the first seven Inca kings are vague. Whoever actually ruled the Incas in the pre-empire years managed to gain and keep power over the immediate homeland area by making alliances with neighboring groups. The Incas probably did this through marriages and by making small military conquests near home. By the time Viracocha took power as the eighth Inca king (probably in the late 1300s), the Incas ruled over an area that extended about 25 miles (40.2 kilometers) around Cuzco.

In 1438, near the end of Viracocha's reign, the history of the Incas hit a turning point. At that time the Chancas, a group of powerful and warlike people, prepared to attack Cuzco. The aging Viracocha and Urco, his son and intended successor, fled from the city, believing there was no hope of prevailing against this strong enemy. In desperation, the nobles of the city sought out another of Viracocha's sons, Inca Yupanqui, and begged him to lead the upcoming battle. Before agreeing to fight, Inca Yupanqui obtained a promise from the nobles; they promised that, for the good of the kingdom, they would not allow the cowardly Urco to take the throne after Viracocha. Then Inca Yupanqui sent out a plea in the Cuzco region for warriors to come and help in the fight against the Chancas. However, legend has it that Inca Yupanqui still had far too few soldiers. He is said to have called upon the stones around Cuzco to come to his aid, and they miraculously arose and began fighting as soldiers. With the help of the stones and his allies, he was able to defeat the Chancas. According to the Inca legends, these stones were later collected and became Inca shrines.

Pachacutec and the great empire

After the defeat of the Chancas in 1438, Viracocha gave up his throne to his son, Inca Yupanqui, who then took the name Pachacutec (or Pachacuti; the name means "he who changed the world" or "earthquake"). Pachacutec became the ninth Inca king and the first Inca emperor. Pachacutec's reign marked the beginning of the Incas' greatest period, which lasted almost a hundred years. Pachacutec began expanding Inca territory and at the same time devised a rigorous government, economy, and way of life that would sustain the diverse peoples that eventually fell under Inca rule. Although some of the accomplishments attributed to Pachacutec actually may have been carried out by his son, Tupac Inca Yupanqui, or his grandson, Huayna Capac, many historians consider Pachacutec one of the most remarkable leaders of all time.

Soon after he took power, Pachacutec led an army into the Colloa area near Lake Titicaca. In battle after battle, he forced the surrender of regional armies and added great expanses to his empire. In other cases, the Incas used gifts and promises to persuade people to join the empire, and some regions surrendered to them without a fight. Generally, Inca rulers demanded that the conquered people work harder and produce more than they ever had before conquest in order to

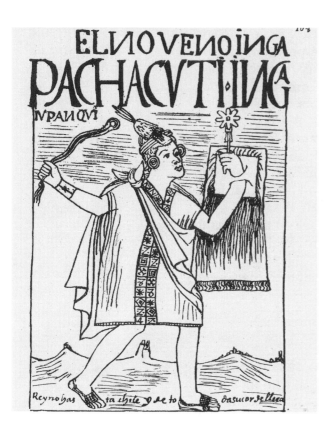

ELNOVENO INGA PACHACVTI INGA IVPANQVI

Reyno has ta chile y de to dasucoyse llesa

Illustration of Pachacutec, whose reign marked the beginning of the greatest period of the Inca empire.
The Art Archive/Archaeological Museum Lima/Dagli Orti.

meet the central government's heavy demands of crops and other goods and labor. However, they usually allowed the local people to govern themselves and retain their customs as long as they could produce goods or food required by the empire. The Incas did not force people to immediately adapt to a new culture, and that was one of the keys to their success.

After large military campaigns in the north, Pachacutec turned military affairs over to his son, Tupac (also Tupa or Topa) Inca Yupanqui in 1463. He then focused his attention on the capital city. During his military campaigns, Pachacutec had encountered the ruins of Tiwanaku (see Chapter 7 for more information). The ancient city impressed him so much that he decided to go home and rebuild Cuzco. On his return, Pachacutec evacuated (forced everyone to leave) Cuzco and then ordered workers to demolish parts of the town so that he could rebuild and reorganize it from top to bottom. He transformed the small town of Cuzco into the great capital city of Tawantinsuyu. In the city, he introduced new customs, a new religious program, and a new legal system.

Tupac Inca Yupanqui and the expansion of the empire

Experts believe that Pachacutec's son, Tupac Inca Yupanqui (ruled 1471–1493), was responsible for the tremendous expansion of the Inca empire, which stretched more than 2,000 miles (3,218 kilometers) down the western side of South America, from the northern part of Ecuador to central Chile. After his father's death, Tupac Inca Yupanqui became the new Inca ruler. He is said to have amassed an army of forty thousand men in the northern city of Cajamarca. Proceeding north, he conquered the city of Tumebamba in present-day Ecuador and made it an administrative center of the

Inca empire. Moving south, Tupac Inca Yupanqui conquered the Chimor kingdom, which had a population of about one million people and a highly advanced culture (see Chapter 9 for more information). From there he took control of the southern cities of Ica and Chincha. Continuing south, he fought battles with the peoples living near Lake Titicaca in present-day Bolivia. Then he headed into what is now Chile, where he took control of the Maule River area. After trying unsuccessfully to take lands in the tropical areas east of the Andes, Tupac Inca Yupanqui fell sick and returned to Cuzco. He continued some of the rebuilding work his father had begun in the city, and he oversaw the completion of Sacsahuaman, a giant complex north of Cuzco. As he grew old, Tupac Inca Yupanqui turned over the command of the army to his son, Huayna Capac. Worn out from years of military campaigns, Tupac Inca Yupanqui died in 1493, and Huayna Capac ascended the throne.

Portrait of Huayna Capac, Inca emperor. *The Art Archive/Museo Pedro de Osma Lima/Mireille Vautier.*

Huayna Capac continued the work of his father and grandfather, pushing deeper into present-day Chile and Bolivia. Later he turned his attention north, where he spent about ten years conquering the Quito kingdom (present-day Ecuador). In addition, throughout his reign he put down many small rebellions that broke out among the peoples who had been conquered. But Huayna Capac was different than the earlier emperors. He remained aloof from the Inca nobility in Cuzco and spent most of his time in the city of Tumebamba (in present-day Ecuador), where he built a second capital. This may have caused an early split within the empire, which would become much larger after Huayna Capac's death. During the later part of his reign, Inca expansion slowed down greatly, probably because there were no more nearby lands left to be conquered. As the battles of conquest slowed down, more uprisings began to occur. According to several accounts, Huayna Capac handled many of the uprisings with intelligence and grace.

Around 1524, Huayna Capac learned that there were strangers—European explorers—who had crossed the ocean and landed on the shores of the Americas. The Europeans brought smallpox (a severe contagious viral disease spread by particles emitted from the mouth when an infected person speaks, coughs, or sneezes) with them on their journey, and before they ever arrived in Peru, the disease began to spread, infecting the people of the Inca empire and starting a deadly epidemic (sudden spreading of an infectious disease, in which large proportions of the population become infected). Huayna Capac was one of many who were infected. The disease killed him in 1525; it also killed the son he had chosen to be heir to the throne.

The Inca empire was at its peak when Huayna Capac died. Its territory was vast, larger than at any other time in Inca history. Its population was somewhere between 9 million and 16 million people. The empire controlled great wealth, and it had abundant natural resources and a hardworking labor force. It also had a huge army. But Huayna Capac's death was the beginning of the end of the great Inca empire. Because the deceased emperor's chosen heir was dead, the Inca nobility had to choose someone else to be the next ruler. They chose Huayna Capac's son Huáscar. Huáscar was the legitimate heir to the throne, because his mother had been Huayna Capac's principal wife. Although Sapa Incas usually had many—even hundreds—of wives, they only had one principle wife, usually a sister. Only the offspring of the principle wife were usually considered legitimate heirs to the throne. However, another son of Huayna Capac, whose name was Atahuallpa, felt that he should have been named the new emperor. Atahuallpa's mother was a concubine from the kingdom of Quito, so he had the support of the vast Inca armies in that region. (A concubine is a woman who lives with and has a sexual relationship with a man but is not married to him.) Before long, the two sons began to fight each other for power, and their struggle initiated a three-year civil war. Atahuallpa's forces finally captured his brother. However, just as Atahuallpa prepared to take the throne in 1532, Spanish conquistadores arrived in Peru. The Spanish had heard that Cuzco contained great riches. They wanted gold and silver, but also the workers and the lands of the Inca empire. Devastated by the civil war and the smallpox epidemic, the powerful Inca empire was at its weakest as it faced its most dangerous enemy.

For More Information

Books

Adams, Richard E. W. *Ancient Civilizations of the New World.* Boulder, CO: Westview Press, 1997.

Davies, Nigel. *The Ancient Kingdoms of Peru.* London and New York: Penguin Books, 1997.

Fagan, Brian M. *Kingdoms of Gold, Kingdoms of Jade: The Americas before Columbus.* London and New York: Thames and Hudson, 1991.

Malpass, Michael A. *Daily Life in the Inca Empire.* Westport, CT: Greenwood Press, 1996.

Von Hagen, Adriana, and Craig Morris. *The Cities of the Ancient Andes.* London and New York: Thames and Hudson, 1998.

Web Site

Rostworowski, Maria. *The Incas.* http://incas.perucultural.org.pe/english/ hissurg4.htm (accessed on September 30, 2004).

Inca Government and Economy

W hen the Incas (pronounced ING-kuhs) began their rise to power in the Cuzco (pronounced KOO-sko) Valley in the fourteenth and fifteenth centuries, they were one small ethnic group among many. Then, in 1438, Inca king Pachacutec defeated a powerful enemy, the Chancas, and forced the defeated state to provide thousands of soldiers to expand his armies. With a much larger army, the Incas were able to conquer additional territories. From the Incas' conquest of the Chancas until the Spanish conquest of the Incas in 1533, the Inca empire grew into a vast and heavily populated state. (An empire is a vast, complex political unit extending across political boundaries and dominated by one central power, which generally takes control of the economy, government, and culture in communities throughout its territory; a state is a body of people living under a single independent government.) The empire had a complex system of government and a unique economy that continue to fascinate scholars and politicians in the twenty-first century.

The word "Inca" can be confusing. It can mean "ruler," referring to the Inca king or leader. The term is also sometimes used to describe members of the original Inca tribe or ethnic

Words to Know

Administration: The management and work (rather than the policy making or public relations) of running a public, religious, or business operation.

Ayllu: A group of extended families who live in the same area, share their land and work, and arrange for marriages and religious rituals as a group; the basic social unit of the Andean peoples.

Chasqui: A messenger who was trained to memorize and relay messages. *Chasqui* posts stood about a mile apart along the road system of the Inca empire. When a message was given to a *chasqui,* he would run to the next post and convey the message to the *chasqui* there, who would then run to the next post, and so on.

Coya: The Sapa Inca's sister/wife, also known as his principal wife, and queen of the Inca empire.

Curaca: A local leader of a region conquered by the Incas; after conquest, *curacas* were trained to serve their regions as representatives of the Inca government.

Empire: A vast, complex political unit extending across political boundaries and dominated by one central power, which generally takes control of the economy, government, and culture in communities throughout its territory.

Hierarchy: The ranking of a group of people according to their social, economic, or political position.

Inca: The word Inca originally meant "ruler" and referred to the king or leader. It is also used to mean the original group of Inca family clans that arose to prominence in the city of

group—ten Inca family clans that rose to prominence in the city of Cuzco. In this book, the supreme ruler of the Incas is referred to as Sapa Inca (an official title meaning "only" or "unique" ruler), and the nobility of Inca origin are referred to as the Incas. Some writers have used the word "Inca" to describe all the people of the Inca empire. However, this usage is not really accurate: The people in conquered regions had to live under Inca rule, but they did not consider themselves Incas and were certainly not accepted as Incas by the ruling nobility.

Running an empire

Many of the regions the Incas conquered in the fifteenth century, such as the vast Chimor kingdom in the

Cuzco. As the empire arose, the supreme ruler was called the "Sapa Inca" and members of the noble class were called "Incas."

Mit'a: A tax imposed on the common people by the Inca government; the tax was a labor requirement rather than a monetary sum—the head of every household was obliged to work on public projects (building monuments, repairing roads or bridges, transporting goods) for a set period each year.

Mitima: An Inca resettlement policy that required potential rebels in newly conquered regions to leave their villages and settle in distant regions where the majority of people were loyal to the Inca empire; this policy helped the Incas prevent many uprisings.

Mummy: A body that has been preserved, either by human technique or unusual environmental conditions, such as extreme cold or dryness.

Pantheon: All of the gods that a particular group of people worship.

Quipu: Also *khipu*. A set of multicolored cotton cords knotted at intervals, used for counting and record keeping.

Sapa Inca: Supreme ruler of the Incas.

Terrace: One of a series of large horizontal ridges, like stairs, made on a mountain or hillside to create a level space for farming.

Villac Umu: Inca term for chief priest.

Welfare state: A state or government that assumes responsibility for the welfare of its citizens.

northern coastal Peru had highly developed cultures with efficient governments and economies and advanced systems of agriculture, trade, and manufacturing. The Inca empire has always been noted for its sophistication in these areas. This sophistication was mainly due to the advanced state of development of the cultures the Incas brought into their empire.

The Incas had a give-and-take philosophy about governing their empire: They generally allowed conquered territories to operate in the same way they had before conquest, as long as the people living there fulfilled certain requirements, particularly by providing extensive labor to the empire. Though the Incas imposed their religion on the conquered states, they also adopted the gods of the defeated

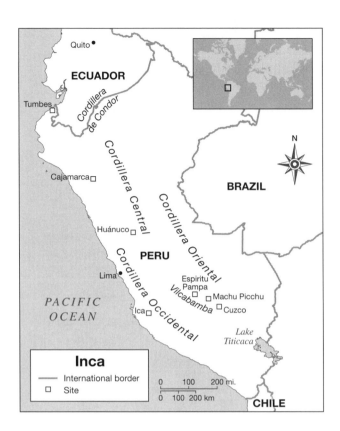

people into the empire's pantheon (all of the gods that a particular group of people worship). They ensured that every farmer had enough land to farm, and they provided craftspeople with materials for their arts. But life for the peoples conquered by the Incas was far from free. In order to maintain control over such a vast area and over millions of people, the Incas created an incredibly complex administrative system. Officials representing the empire carefully managed the work of the conquered people, demanding the maximum amount of work out of every individual.

Map showing important sites in the Inca empire.
Map by XNR Productions. The Gale Group.

The Sapa Inca

The head of all Inca rule was the Sapa Inca. During the golden years of the empire, 1438 to 1533, there were only three Great Sapa Incas: Pachacutec (also called Pachacuti), who ruled from 1438 to 1471; Tupac Inca Yupanqui, who ruled from 1471 to 1493; and Huayna Capac (pronounced WHY-nuh CA-poc), who ruled from 1493 to 1525. The warring half brothers Huáscar and Atahuallpa (pronounced AH-tah-WAHL-pah) were also Sapa Incas who ruled, though briefly, before the Spanish conquest in 1533.

The Sapa Inca was considered a descendant of Inti, the sun god, and therefore was regarded as a semidivine (godlike) being. He held authority over all things. Upon taking power, the Sapa Inca married one of his sisters to keep the royal bloodline purely Inca. The Sapa Inca's sister/wife, also known as his principal wife, was called the *coya,* or queen. Sapa Incas had many other wives as well, and sometimes Sapa Incas had hundreds of children. However, only the sons of the principal wife were eligible to inherit the Sapa Inca's position. The Sapa Inca considered the worthiness of each of these sons before choosing a successor; succession to the throne was not a matter of birth order.

During the years of Inca dominance, the position of Sapa Inca was surrounded by symbols and rituals. The Sapa Inca wore a braided headband with red tassels wrapped several times around his brow and carried a special gold club. When he traveled, he was carried upon an immense litter (an enclosed platform, usually borne on the shoulders of servants), accompanied by a multitude of servants and attendants. Also in this large traveling group were the many wives of the Sapa Inca and some of their children. The wives walked closest to the Sapa Inca and provided a buffer between him and all the other people.

Everyone treated the Sapa Inca with extreme ceremonial reverence. When people needed to speak to the Sapa Inca, they would approach him barefoot and with a heavy load on their back as a sign of humility. They were required to look at their feet—never into his eyes—and often one of his wives would hold a cloth screen across his face so that it was impossible for anyone to look upon the Sapa Inca directly. No one except his wives was allowed to touch any clothing he had worn, and his wives periodically burned his used clothing to ensure this. The leftovers of the Sapa Inca's meals were also burned. If the Sapa Inca wished to spit, one of his wives would hold out her hand so he could spit into it. If a hair fell from his head, a wife would quickly eat it so that no one would ever be able to touch it. The Incas feared that if others had access to articles that had been close to, or part of, the Sapa Inca, such items could be used to put an evil spell on him.

The divine role of the Sapa Inca continued after his death, and so did his reverential treatment. His relatives had the body mummified (treated with preservative herbs so that it would not decay), and then all of them except for the successor to the throne continued to live in the Sapa Inca's palace, using his vast stores of wealth; the household of the dead Sapa Inca was called the *panaca*. Meanwhile, the Sapa Inca's successor had to go out and build a new palace and find new sources of food and goods to supply it. Even after the new Sapa Inca ascended the throne in his own palace, the deceased Sapa Inca was treated as if he were still alive and ruling the empire. During festivals and ceremonies the various *panacas* of all the deceased Sapa Incas brought out the sacred mummies and sat them together on a platform. They

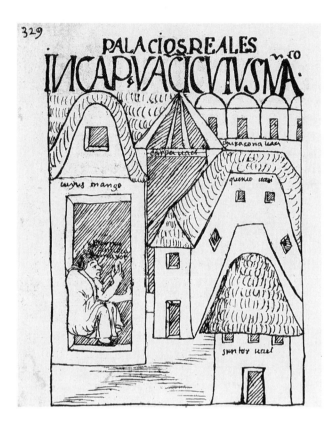

Illustration of a royal palace and residence of the Sapa Inca. *The Art Archive/Archaeological Museum Lima/Dagli Orti.*

even fed the mummies and gave them *chicha* (beer made from maize [corn]) to drink.

Incas and Incas-by-privilege

In the Inca homeland, the people next in line to the Sapa Inca were the other Incas, who had the top privileges of the kingdom. They were entitled to live in the center of Cuzco with their servants, and they sent their children to special schools. Incas were later called *orejones,* meaning "big ears" in Spanish, because only Incas were entitled to wear prestigious earplugs, large, ornamental tube-shaped studs that were fitted into a hole in their earlobes.

There was a distinct hierarchy (ranking of a group of people according to their social position) among the Incas. The most powerful people were those closely related to the Sapa Inca. Next in line were the Incas who were not closely related to the Sapa Inca. (Though it was believed that all Inca nobility stemmed from the same families, over the years some of the blood relations had become distant.) As the Incas acquired more territory, they found it necessary to give noble ranking to a third group of non-Inca people. Members of the third group were known as Incas-by-privilege. Though they were not Incas by birth, they were Quechua-speaking (pronounced KECH-wah) people who had lived in the Cuzco area for a long time. The Incas added this group to their elite because even though an Inca man could have many wives, the Incas could not produce enough offspring (Incas by blood) to manage the entire empire by themselves.

Terms of conquest

When the Incas conquered a territory, all the land and many of the resources in the area (such as mines or livestock) became the property of the empire. All the land in a conquered territory was divided into thirds: One-third belonged to the Inca state, one-third belonged to the Inca state religion, and one-third was left to the peasants. The peasants used this land to grow crops and raise animals for their own use; they were also responsible for farming the other two-thirds of the territory—for the benefit of the Inca government and state religion, with its thousands of higher and lower priests, attendants, monuments, and festivities.

The Incas did not wish to impose their rule through force, partly because it would be inefficient to place a large military force in each region. Instead, they often gave gifts and privileges to the local leaders of the regions they conquered. Frequently they brought these leaders, called *curacas,* to Cuzco with their families, providing them with feasts and entertainment and teaching them about the culture. They then sent the *curacas* back to rule their regions as representatives of the Inca empire. The *curacas'* sons, though, were kept in Cuzco, where they were educated in the ways of the empire. Acting as representatives of the Incas, *curacas* ruled in most of the conquered territories of the empire.

Management of government-owned land

After conquering a territory, the Incas sent in administrators to take a census to evaluate how many people lived in the region. Then they assessed the land to determine how much work could be done there. Once the administrators had figured how much land each household could cultivate, they distributed the land among family groups, or *ayllus* (pronounced EYE-yoos). *Ayllus* were the most common social unit of the Andes and had existed there long before the rise of the Incas. In *The Incas and Their Ancestors* (2001, revised) Michael E. Moseley describes *ayllus* as "kin collectives" or "a group of related individuals and couples who exchange labor and cooperate in the management of land and herds." The *ayllu* usually consisted of several extended families who lived near one another within a village or farming community. The *ayllu* organized the labor for farming projects among all its members and determined how much land each household would receive each year. The *ayllu* also arranged marriages among its members and staged religious rituals and ceremonies for the group.

Members of conquered states performed various *mit'a* duties for the Inca government, including building roads and bridges, such as those shown here.
© *Enzo & Paolo Ragazzini/Corbis.*

The administration (management and work [rather than the policy making or public relations]) of running a public, religious, or business operation) of the empire would have been impossible without some form of record keeping. The Incas did not have a writing system, but they used *quipus* (or *khipus*; pronounced KEE-poos) for counting and calculations. The *quipu* was a set of multicolored cotton cords that were knotted at intervals. The knots and colors signified different items being counted (people, gold and silver, or units of time, for example) or different positions in the decimal system, such as tens, hundreds, and thousands. *Quipus* could record an amazing amount of detail, and some scholars believe that the Incas used *quipus* to record stories as well as numerical accounts. *Quipu camayocs, quipu* keepers, were important empire officials who functioned like modern accountants recording the number of people in a region, the tributes they owed, and the amount of goods stored in the area. (See Chapter 12 for more information on the *quipu*.)

The Administrative Hierarchy

Directly under the Sapa Inca, there were four *apos,* or officials, who each directed one-quarter of the empire. (The Incas divided their empire into four *suyus,* or quarters, that radiated from Cuzco, the capital city.) The *apos* were Inca men, usually directly related to the Sapa Inca. The four quarters they ruled were divided into provinces. In all, there were eighty provinces, and each province had about twenty thousand households. A governor oversaw each province and reported to the *apo* of his quarter.

There was mathematical order to the administration of the provinces under the *curacas.* There were two top-level *curacas* in each province; each of them oversaw 10,000 households and reported to the provincial governor who was responsible for all 20,000. These two *curacas* were each in charge of ten *curacas,* each of whom oversaw 1,000 households. Under each of these ten *curacas* were two more, each in charge of 500 households. Under each of them there were five *curacas* who were each in charge of 100 households. At the lowest level, an official oversaw the work of ten people. The conquered workers were the lowest people in the Inca hierarchy. It is estimated that for every 10,000 workers in the Inca empire there were about 1,300 officials overseeing them.

In *Daily Life in the Inca Empire* (1996) Michael A. Malpass provides an excellent model of the way this administrative system worked. In his example, the Sapa Inca wanted a bridge built in a particular province, and 600 laborers were needed for the job. The king made it known that he wanted 600 laborers, and his administrators did the rest:

> The governor of the province summoned the two curacas *of 10,000 households and told them they needed to call up 300 men each. Each* curaca *then ordered his two* curacas *of 5,000 households to provide 150 men. In turn, each of these called his five* curacas *of 1,000 households and ordered 30 men from each. These officials each called two* curacas *of 500 to present 15 men each. The five* curacas *below them were ordered to call up 3 men from their 100 households! These 600 men worked for a period of time, fulfilling the* mit'a *rotation, and then returned home. Next the process was repeated to find another 600 men to work. This continued for 18 months until the bridge was complete.*

Mit'a: Working for the empire

Rather than forcing the members of conquered states to pay monetary taxes to the Inca government, the Incas required every household to provide one person who could perform a set amount of labor for the government each year; this labor obligation was called *mit'a,* which means "rotation." *Mit'a* obligations were over and above the farming requirements for the state. A *mit'a* project might involve serving in the military, working in gold mines, or building monuments, public buildings, bridges, or roads. When the designated person left to work on a government project, other members of his *ayllu* would take over his work. The *curacas* determined who would provide labor for any given project, taking special care not to strain the workforce of any particular community by taking too many people away or by interrupting seasonal farmwork.

Ayni: The reciprocity principle

One of the reasons the Incas conquered territories was to obtain labor from the people who lived in the conquered lands. By imposing the *mit'a* labor obligation on new members of the empire, the Incas could afford to maintain a huge army, feed the elderly and sick, build cities, put more land to agricultural use, and employ artists and scientists. Inca rulers made very heavy labor demands on the people they conquered, and hard work was the rule for everyone.

Like the leaders of many Andean states before them, the Inca rulers believed in *ayni,* or reciprocity—a give-and-take system between themselves and the conquered states. In return for the labor it demanded, the Inca government promised to provide the people with protection from their enemies and freedom from want. The Incas also provided conquered territories with religious monuments, roads, irrigation systems, arts, and an abundance of raw materials from all regions. For example, they distributed llama wool (for weaving) throughout the empire. They also gave llama herds to villages that had not had them before. The *ayni* principle was the motivation behind lavish festivals and ceremonies put on by the Inca state on a regular basis. At these events, which went on throughout the empire, the workers were given great quantities of food and *chicha* and allowed to celebrate for many days. This was an ancient Andean custom that was used to cement the bonds between the ruler and the people. (See the box on page 131 for information on the *chicha* reciprocity ceremony.)

Preventing rebellion

Even though the Incas offered gifts and protection to their conquests, many people who lived in the conquered territories were unhappy to be forced to work for the empire. Some surely despised their rulers; after all, before the gift giving, the Incas had defeated them in war and taken away their independence. These hard feelings led to many uprisings against Inca rule during the short span of the empire. The Inca rulers used several strategies to stifle rebellion. They hoped to keep the local leaders of the states happy with special privileges and gifts. But they had a backup plan too: They required the sons of local leaders to attend special schools in Cuzco. There the sons received an education, but they were also in effect being held hostage; local leaders would think twice before rebelling, for fear that harm might come to their sons in the Inca capital. Among the common people, the Incas used religion as a unifying and controlling force: They promoted their own religion throughout newly conquered territories, but they honored the gods of the conquered peoples too. The Incas cleverly invited people from conquered states to bring the images or holy statues of their gods to Cuzco. There, the Incas could hold the sacred images hostage and threaten to harm them if the people rebelled.

Relocating rebellious people—or *mitimas* was the Incas' key method for preventing rebellion in the empire. The *mitima* relocation policy forced large groups of potential or actual rebels in a recently conquered village to move to a distant land where people loyal to the Incas were already living. People who had been living in the empire longer and were known to be loyal were then moved into the village to replace the *mitimas*. The *mitimas* were not allowed to visit their old homes. Living among people they did not know, they had no strength to rebel. They were thrown into a new culture and often forced to learn the Quechua language and participate in the religious rituals of a new community. By moving people around the empire in this way, the Incas did more than simply prevent rebellion; they gradually minimized the cultural differences among the diverse Andean ethnic groups. The *mitima* system also had a second advantage. If a village was located in a climate that was not conducive to the growth of maize, for example, the Incas could send off some members of the population to establish a colony in a good maize-growing region. Then the colonists could transport maize to their old home territory in exchange for the goods they needed in the colony. This kind of

Depiction of Inca warriors armed with clubs and spears. © *Bettmann/Corbis.*

government-arranged exchange was essential to life in the extreme environment of the Andes, and it also prevented rebellion. The leaders of the home territory were receiving what they needed in order to thrive economically because of the exchange system with the new *mitima* colony, and therefore they were much less likely to revolt.

Military

The Incas acquired their vast empire through an extraordinary series of military successes. Some experts believe that the Incas began their empire-building era right after they conquered the Chancas, who attacked them in 1438. Upon defeating their enemy, the Incas immediately demanded that the Chanca soldiers join their forces. With this powerful new army, they were able to defeat neighboring states, each time building a greater force of soldiers from the armies of the conquered territories. But there were several obvious problems with this system: How could the Inca government create a loyal force out of enemy soldiers? How could it feed such a huge army? With such a vast expanse of territory, how could the central government keep track of its forces?

The Incas sought the loyalty of defeated soldiers through persuasion. After battles, the Incas usually killed only the leaders of a defeated army, returning other prisoners of war to their homes. The defeated soldiers were asked to serve in the Inca military and were promised land, goods, and special privileges in return. In addition, knowing that deep-seated hostilities often existed between neighboring tribes, the Incas would try to pit newly recruited forces against a nearby enemy tribe whenever possible.

There were few trained soldiers in the Inca army. The Incas relied on their great numbers rather than military skills. The soldiers fought in hand-to-hand combat with clubs, swords, and spear-throwers, most made of either copper or stone. It was not expensive to maintain such a large army. The soldiers were, for the most part, peasants who only served for a short time under the *mit'a* system and then returned home to work their crops. The *ayllus* back home took care of the soldiers' work while they were gone. To feed its troops, the Inca government developed huge stores of food from their share of the crops grown in newly conquered lands. In order to get the food to the soldiers, the Incas improved their already extensive road system, which also served to facilitate communications between the capital city and remote areas of warfare.

Inca roads

Although the Incas did not use the wheel for transportation, they had one of the largest road systems of all ancient world empires, with over 14,000 miles (22,526 kilometers) of road crossing through the most remote parts of the mountains and down to the sea. Bridges spanned water and heights on the roads. Alongside the roads there were temporary lodges and storehouses approximately one day's walk apart. The local people were in charge of keeping these storehouses stocked with food (and sometimes with weapons and clothing and other necessities for soldiers). Travel on the roads was mostly restricted to government-ordered projects and military operations. The roads were also used to transport goods from lowlands to high-

Remains of a temporary lodge on an Inca road.
© Dave G. Houser/Corbis.

lands. It was not legal for the common worker in the Inca empire to travel without government authorization.

Chasqui posts stood at regular intervals along the roads. *Chasquis* were runners who had been trained to memorize and relay messages to troops and to central headquarters. When a message was given to a *chasqui,* he would run to the next *chasqui* post (about a mile away) and convey the message. The *chasqui* at that post would run on to the next post and do the same. If the message was being delivered to someone 100 miles (160.9 kilometers) away, there might be one hundred *chasquis,* and the time it took to deliver the message was surprisingly short.

Law and order

The Incas had laws to regulate almost every aspect of the daily life of the common people; nobles had a different set of laws to live by but were by no means exempt. There were laws about what kinds of crops people could grow and what kind of clothes to wear. Everyone had to learn the Quechua language that was spoken at Cuzco. Women were held responsible for the cleanliness of their homes, and there were inspections to ensure that they met a certain standard. If a household had not been kept up properly, the woman who lived there was forced to eat dirt from her house with the whole village watching. The man of the household was often included in the punishment as well, probably for not having managed his wife better.

There were apparently no prisons in the Inca empire. Few people committed crimes, partly because the punishments were extremely stiff and also because the rigid Inca government allowed few opportunities for its overworked people to get into trouble. For the most part, the local *curacas* were in charge of enforcing the laws that had been established by the Incas. The government imposed a physical punishment for some crimes. For example, if the crime was damaging government property or rape, law enforcement officials would drop a large rock on the guilty party's back from a height of 3 feet (.91 meters). Stealing was punishable by whipping for a first offense, but repeat offenders were sometimes hung by their feet until they died. Murderers were often thrown over a cliff or stoned to death. Adultery (sexual relations between a married person and someone who is not the person's spouse) between common people was punishable by torture; if nobles committed adultery, they were hung naked over a cliff to be eaten by birds. A person who had committed treason (betrayal of one's people or country, especially by giving aid to an enemy or waging war against it) was thrown into a pit full of snakes and ferocious wild animals. Fortunately, these grisly punishments were not carried out very often. The Inca labor system allowed little time for com-

Chasquis, **or Inca messengers, were trained to memorize and deliver messages throughout the Inca empire.** *The Art Archive/Archaeological Museum Lima/Dagli Orti.*

mitting crimes and the consequences may have seemed too terrible. There was apparently little crime in the Inca empire.

Only a provincial governor or the Sapa Inca himself could condemn someone to death. People accused of crimes had a right to defend themselves. *Curacas* delivered punishments other than the death penalty. They also resolved quarrels and grievances among their people. If the common people had a complaint about a *curaca,* they could go to the provincial governor and were entitled to a hearing and an investigation of their charges.

Marriage was required by the Inca government. Common men had to marry by about the age of twenty-five and women by the age of sixteen. Marriages were handled by local *ayllus,* but about once a year, Inca officials would arrive in a town to marry the remaining single people. On these days, single males would line up, and then single females would form a line facing them. Sometimes a happy couple would choose each other and be married. In other cases, though, when there was no willing partner for an individual, the Inca officials would force two people into marriage. For common people, monogamy (marriage to only one spouse) was the rule. There was no divorce. Nobles were married for life to one woman, their principal wife, but they could take "secondary wives" as well.

Economy

The main industry of the Inca empire was farming—a very difficult endeavor on the cold, steep slopes of the Andes Mountains and on the desertlike coastal plains of Peru. Many of the peoples conquered by the Incas already had terraces (a series of large horizontal ridges, like stairs, made on a mountain or hillside to create a level space for farming) and systems for irrigation, and the Incas made extensive additions to these agricultural advances. Using *mit'a* labor to construct irrigation canals and carve terraces from steep mountainsides, they ensured that all arable land (land fit for farming) was put to use. The Incas also delivered llamas to regions that had not had them before; these animals were raised for their wool and meat and served as pack animals too. Many scholars agree that the Incas put more land to use for farming and animal-raising than any society since.

The Incas farmed the steep slopes of the Andes by creating a series of level steps, called terraces, depicted here. © *Chris Rainier/Corbis.*

The Inca empire encompassed a variety of extreme climates, and farmers had to specialize in whatever crops they could grow in a particular area. Some crops, such as potatoes, would grow in high-altitude cool climates, while others, such as maize, grew in the hot, irrigated lowland areas. For thousands of years, Andean peoples had survived by trading their products with one another, exchanging crops from one climate zone for items from a different zone. Rather than allow a free trade system (trade based on the unrestricted exchange of goods) that would have competed with their own power and control, the Incas encouraged each region to set up colonies in a variety of climate zones—highland, lowland, coastal—so that each region could be mostly self-sufficient.

An economy without money

The Inca economy was not based on a money system, and it did not have commerce (the buying and selling of goods, especially on a large scale) or free trade. The govern-

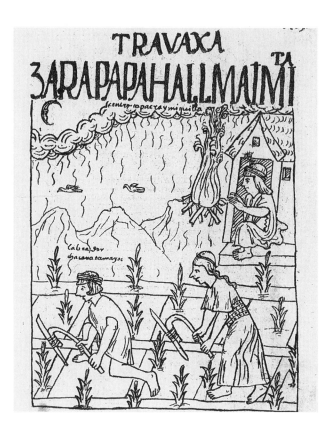

TRAVAXA
3ARAPAPAHALLMAIMI

Illustration of Incas planting maize seedlings. *The Art Archive/Archaeological Museum Lima/Dagli Orti.*

ment made sure that everyone had enough land or goods to survive, and it managed the exchange of goods between faraway regions. There were no merchants acting on their own behalf. The government promised to take care of the old and the sick, using the large supply of surplus goods produced by *mit'a* labor. In times of famine, the government storehouses were opened to the public so that no one would starve. Instead of money, the Incas invested *mit'a* labor: They directed terracing and irrigation projects that enabled peasants to grow more food. Once surplus food was stored away, some of the people were able to quit farming and pursue other activities. The Incas' investment paid off in cultural advances: A large group of full-time artisans began to produce pottery, metalwork, and other crafts. Cloth, one of the most treasured products among the Andean peoples, was produced in huge quantities in the homes of almost all people of the empire. When rewards beyond land and food were needed, the Incas usually bestowed fine cloth upon their people.

The workings of the Inca economy have prompted some scholars to call the empire a welfare state (a state or government that assumes responsibility for the welfare of its citizens). Others consider the Inca economy a socialist system (a system characterized by government ownership of the means of production and government-controlled distribution of goods). The Inca economy was unique among the world's ancient civilizations in that the government maintained control of almost all exchanges and took over all aspects of trade. Because the government had such a vast labor supply, it was able to put away huge amounts of stored goods, reserving the surplus and then providing goods when and where they were most needed. Most people living in the empire prospered more under Inca rule than they had under their former governments.

Some writers in the nineteenth century considered the Inca empire a Utopia (an ideal or perfect society), but the empire was far from perfect by most twenty-first-century standards. The economic system was not effective in all parts of the empire, and some of the conquered states lost more than they gained by joining the empire. Equality among people was never a goal of the Inca empire: The nobility and privileged ranks were exempt from the labor requirements and owned their land outright. In a few cases, common people were able to rise above the peasant lifestyle (particularly through military accomplishments), but most never had any opportunity to advance. Further, common people were not able to exercise free will over the most important aspects of their lives. Still, the concern of the Inca government for its people is noteworthy. They were basically free from the fear of hunger. The government supported the elderly and sick. There was little crime. Unlike many other ancient civilizations, in the Inca empire if common people performed their obligation to the government, they were usually assured of a certain standard of life. In *The Ancient American Civilizations* (1972) Friedrich Katz remarks that "there is no other state in pre-Spanish America, in the ancient East or in European antiquity in which trade was so uniquely controlled by the state that not a single general article of barter served as currency.... Hardly any state of comparable size in antiquity ... allowed the peasantry such far-reaching social rights as did the Inca state."

For More Information

Books

Adams, Richard E.W. *Ancient Civilizations of the New World*. Boulder, CO: Westview Press, 1997.

Davies, Nigel. *The Ancient Kingdoms of Peru*. London and New York: Penguin Books, 1997.

Fagan, Brian M. *Kingdoms of Gold, Kingdoms of Jade: The Americas before Columbus*. London and New York: Thames and Hudson, 1991.

Katz, Friedrich. *The Ancient American Civilizations*. London: Phoenix Press, 1972.

Malpass, Michael A. *Daily Life in the Inca Empire*. Westport, CT: Greenwood Press, 1996.

Moseley, Michael E. *The Incas and Their Ancestors: The Archaeology of Peru,* revised ed. New York: Thames and Hudson, 2001.

Time-Life Books. *Incas: Lords of Gold and Glory.* Alexandria, VA: Time-Life Books, 1992.

Web Site

Rostworowski, Maria. *The Incas.* http://incas.perucultural.org.pe/english/ hissurg4.htm (accessed on September 30, 2004).

Inca Religion, Arts, and Sciences

12

The Incas (pronounced ING-kuhs) had a culture of their own well before the empire began its expansion in 1438, but this culture changed and grew significantly in the ninety-five years that followed—the era of the Inca empire. (An empire is a vast, complex political unit extending across political boundaries and dominated by one central power, which generally takes control of the economy, government, and culture in communities throughout its territory.) The Incas adopted and incorporated the important gods as well as the arts and the sciences of the people they had conquered. The Inca government created a system that skillfully organized the various cultures it had brought together. It brought unity to the people it controlled by providing a set of traditions that were familiar and acceptable to the entire empire.

Religion

The different Andean cultures conquered by the Incas all had their own set of religious beliefs, practices, and major deities. However, rather than switching to the Inca state reli-

Words to Know

Acllahuaci: A house where young women chosen by the Incas were isolated from daily Inca life; these women were trained in the arts of weaving fine cloth and making *chicha* and foods for festivals, and some went on to become religious workers.

Ayllu: A group of extended families who live in the same area, share their land and work, and arrange for marriages and religious rituals as a group; the basic social unit of the Andean peoples.

Ceque: A Quechua word meaning "border"; *ceques* were imaginary lines that divided Cuzco into sections, creating distinct districts that determined a person's social, economic, and religious duties.

Empire: A vast, complex political unit extending across political boundaries and dominated by one central power, which generally takes control of the economy, government, and culture in communities throughout its territory.

Idol: A likeness or image of an object of worship.

Mummy: A body that has been preserved, either by human technique or unusual environmental conditions, such as extreme cold or dryness.

Myth: A traditional, often imaginary story dealing with ancestors, heroes, or supernatural beings, and usually making an attempt to explain a belief, practice, or natural phenomenon.

Quechua: The Inca language, still spoken by Andean people today.

Quipu: Also *khipu.* A set of multicolored cotton cords knotted at intervals, used for counting and record keeping.

Ritual: A formal act performed the same way each time, usually used as a means of religious worship by a particular group.

Sacrifice: To make an offering to the gods, through personal possessions like cloth or jewels, or by killing an animal or human as the ultimate gift.

Stonemasonry: The work of a skilled builder who expertly lays cut or otherwise fitted units of stone in construction.

Villac Umu: Inca term for chief priest.

gion after they were conquered, most of the Andean peoples simply added the Inca gods to their own set of gods and spirits. The Incas in turn adopted the gods of the people they conquered, hoping to unify their empire through shared religious beliefs. As the Inca empire expanded, religious practices in the Andes grew and changed.

Religion dominated every aspect of the Inca world. The importance of religion to the Incas is demonstrated by the way they divided up the lands they conquered: one-third for the Inca government, one-third for the peasants who worked as farmers, and a full third for the support of Inca religious institutions.

Origin myths

In the myth of Inca origins, the first Inca king, Manco Capac, and his seven siblings emerged from the caves of Pacariqtambo, or from Lake Titicaca, in another version. (A myth is a traditional, often imaginary story dealing with ancestors, heroes, or supernatural beings, and usually making an attempt to explain a belief, practice, or natural phenomenon. It should be noted whenever discussing the cultures of other peoples, that what is viewed as myth to an observer may be interpreted as an absolute truth to a believer.) These first Incas were created by the sun god Inti, and their mission was to bring civilization to the world. According to many scholars, Inti was the primary god of the Incas.

Map showing important sites in the Inca empire.
Map by XNR Productions. The Gale Group.

Another Inca myth describes the creation of the earth. According to this myth, the god Viracocha created the world first and then made people out of stone or clay at Tiwanaku (pronounced tee-wah-NAH-coo; see Chapter 7 for more information). (Andean peoples had worshiped Viracocha for thousands of years prior to the rise of the Incas; Viracocha is generally portrayed as neither man nor woman, but in this Inca myth, the god appears in human form.) Viracocha then led the people he had created from stone and clay to Cuzco (pronounced KOO-sko). Eventually Viracocha left the world to reign invisibly from the heavens. After leaving the earth, Viracocha apparently gave other deities control over the daily lives of human beings. While many scholars

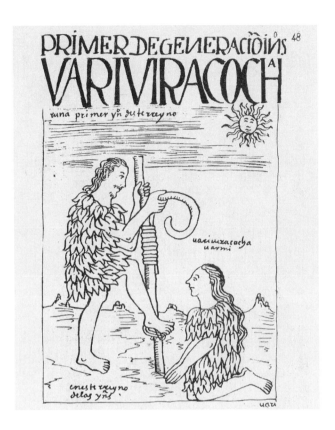

PRIMER DEGENERACIOŋS 48
VARIVIRACOCH A

runa primer yñ guterreyno

uariuxacocha
uarmi

enest reyno
delas yñs.

uau

Illustration depicting a man and a woman created by the god Viracocha. *The Art Archive/Archaeological Museum Lima/Dagli Orti.*

consider Viracocha the supreme god of the Incas, others put Inti in the number one position. The majority of Inca temples are dedicated to Inti.

Worshipping the Inca gods

Almost all religion in the ancient Andes was deeply connected to the forces of nature and to the success of farming. The Inca religion was no exception. Inti was the source of warmth, light, and healthy crops. Inti ruled over the earth with Illapa, the thunder god who brought the necessary rains, and Mama-Quilla, the moon goddess and wife of Inti. Inti was represented as a golden disk with a face, surrounded by radiating sunbeams. Other important Inca gods include Pacha-Mama, the earth goddess, and Mama-Cocha, the goddess of the sea.

When they conquered new lands, the Incas required the conquered people to worship Inti. Temples dedicated to Inti were built in every region. Each temple had its own priests, and local people had to support the temples and the priests with their labor. Although the Incas demanded that conquered people accept the Inca gods, they also accepted the conquered people's gods into the Inca pantheon (the officially recognized set of Inca gods). They invited the defeated states to bring the idols (representations or likenesses) of their gods to Cuzco and promised to place the idols in the Temple of the Sun, or Coricancha, the highest place of honor for an Inca god. Though it was a seemingly benevolent gesture, the Incas had a sinister motive. In *Inca Religion and Customs,* first published in 1653, Spanish chronicler Father Bernabé Cobo describes what the Incas did with these visiting idols:

> When some province rebelled against them, the Incas ordered the protective native gods [the idols] of the rebellious province to be brought out and put in public, where they were whipped ignominiously [in a humiliating way] every day until such province was

made to serve the Incas again. After the rebels were subdued, their gods were restored to their places and honored with sacrifices [offerings to the gods, through personal possessions like cloth or jewels, or by killing an animal or human as the ultimate gift].The rebelling province, presumably horrified by the base treatment of their gods, were forced into submission.

The curved Inca wall, a remnant of an Inca sun temple, stands adjoined to this Spanish-style church in Cuzco. © Michael Freeman/Corbis.

Huaca worship

Quite separate from the official Inca religion was the everyday worship practiced by the peasants in conquered Andean villages. Almost every Andean community worshiped the forces of nature, such as thunder and lightning, rain, or the rising of the sun each day. They also revered the earth's natural features, such as mountains, rivers, jaguars, and snakes. This type of worship had been practiced among the *ayllus* for thousands of years. *Ayllus* (pronounced EYE-yoos) were groups of extended families that formed a self-sufficient community, farming cooperatively, arranging marriages within their group, and practicing religious rites together. The members of each *ayllu* believed that their ancestors sprang from a specific point or an object, such as a tree or a stream or even an herb. The *ayllus* worshiped these points or objects of their origin as *huacas,* or sacred places.

Huacas were the basis of the sacred landscape of the Incas in Cuzco. A series of forty-one imaginary lines, or *ceques,* radiated from Coricancha, the main religious center of the Incas (*ceque* is a Quechua word that means border). The *ceques* divided the city into distinct districts that required certain social, economic, and religious duties from the people who lived within them. Along the *ceques* there were 328 *huacas,* both natural and human-made places (such as springs, piles of rocks, or fountains) that were considered sacred. These places were believed to have supernatural powers, or to be the homes of supernatural spirits. Some scholars think that the *huacas* may have marked the days of the year and that there may have been a *huaca* for every calendar day. The *huacas* also may have marked water sources.

Ancestor worship was extremely important to everyone within the Inca empire, and it had been important for centuries before the Incas came into power. The bodies of the dead were considered *huacas* and treated with the utmost dignity and reverence. When the Sapa Inca (supreme ruler of the Incas) died, his body was mummified (preserved) by a complex procedure that involved taking out the organs, filling the body cavity with preservative substances, and then drying out the body to prevent decay. The mummy was sometimes brought out of the burial chamber to attend ceremonies. At festivals, servants and relatives of the dead ruler even fed the mummy and gave it *chicha* (beer made from maize [corn]) to drink.

Appeasing the gods

The Incas and indeed most or all early Andean cultures believed that the gods of nature controlled their world and their lives. The only way they felt they could gain control of natural forces such as rain or earthquakes was by appeasing the gods—that is, making the gods happy. Hoping to please the gods, they carefully fulfilled every detail of their traditional rituals (formal acts performed the same way each time as a means of religious worship) and ceremonies. The Incas and their subjects practiced sacrifices as one way to make the gods happy. In most Inca sacrifices, the offerings were llamas (South American mammals with soft, fleecy wool), fine textiles, and even *chicha*. Human sacrifice was also an Inca tradition, but not on a large scale.

Certain important occasions and ceremonies called for the sacrifice of humans—the installation of a new Sapa Inca, earthquakes, or victory in battle, to name a few. Usually the victims were children between ten and fifteen years old. Only children of particular beauty were chosen, and it was considered an honor to be selected. When children were selected from conquered territories, they were often brought to Cuzco to participate in ceremonies before they were sacrificed. Then they were taken home, where they were often given a feast and *chicha* to drink. During the sacrifice, some were buried alive. Others had their hearts cut out, and the hearts, still beating, were immediately presented to the gods.

Depiction of Incas performing a sacrifice, hoping to please the gods. © *Bettmann/Corbis.*

The Incas had a concept of afterlife similar to Christian notions of heaven and hell. They believed that people who led good lives would be rewarded after death by eternal life in a place beyond the sun. People who were bad during their lives went to a dark place in the center of the earth after they died. But only common people had to worry about their destiny in the afterlife. Inca nobles went to the place beyond the sun and did not have to fear the dark underworld no matter how they lived their lives.

Priests and chosen women

The most powerful person in the Inca religion and the second most powerful person in the empire was the *Vil-*

lac Umu, or chief priest. He was generally a brother or close relative of the Sapa Inca and was in charge of every priest in the Inca empire. The chief priest chose ten bishops (high-ranking officials who oversaw regional priests)—one for each of the religious districts in the empire; all the bishops were Incas. Within the districts, the priests were generally family members of the local leaders, or *curacas.* In Cuzco the *Villac Umu* had a staff of about four thousand religious officials to help him run the state religion.

Every region had its own temple of the sun, and each temple had its own priest or group of priests. Within each of these temples, every major god the Incas worshiped was represented by a *huaca.* All *huacas* needed maintenance—that is, prescribed rituals and ceremonies to properly honor the gods they represented—and the priests were responsible for performing this work. Priests and their attendants had many other job responsibilities too, including changing the weather, curing illnesses, and seeing into the future. Priests also led the many ceremonial festivals held throughout the year. They heard people's confessions and helped them atone for the wrongs they had done. In addition, they were the chief educators of the Inca boys. To fulfill all these duties, the Inca state religion required many priests.

Women also took part in the religion of the empire, as *acllas,* or "chosen women." Girls between the ages of eight and nine were selected by judges who traveled the empire for this purpose. The young girls were brought to local houses, where they were secluded from the public and trained by *mamaconas,* or older chosen women. They learned how to spin and weave fine cloth and how to make *chicha* and prepare food for religious ceremonies. At the age of fourteen, some of the chosen girls were sent to a festival in Cuzco; at this festival the Sapa Inca would select wives for himself and for noblemen he wished to reward. Those who were not selected to marry the nobles became *mamaconas* and were married symbolically to the Inca sun god, Inti, or to other gods. These women, called "Virgins of the Sun" by the Spanish, became priestesses and worked at ceremonies and in temples throughout the empire. (They are often compared to the nuns of the Roman Catholic Church, but some of the similarities may well have been exaggerated by Spanish chroniclers who were Catholics themselves.) Some *acllas* were chosen to be sacrificed to the sun god. According to estimates, the empire had about fifteen thousand women serving as *acllas* at any one time during the years of Inca dominance.

The *acllahuaci* ("house of the chosen women"), situated right next to the Coricancha in the main section of Cuzco, was the residence of about fifteen hundred chosen women. There they were completely isolated from the public. The only nonreligious people who visited them were the *coya* (the sister/wife of the Sapa Inca) and her daughters. The chosen women were sworn to chastity (abstaining from sexual relations), and the punishment for having sexual relations with them was death. However, the Sapa Inca was apparently above this law and was known to occasionally have sexual relations with the chosen women.

An Inca *aclla,* or "chosen woman." The Spanish called *acllas* "Virgins of the Sun." *The Art Archive/Bibliothèque des Arts Décoratifs Paris/Dagli Orti (A).*

Ceremonies and rituals

For thousands of years, Andean peoples carefully carried out rituals and ceremonies to honor the gods, believing that this was the way to ensure abundant crops, maintain good health, and prevent disasters. By the time the Incas came to power, ceremonies had become dramatic events. There were still some simple daily sacrifices, with bits of wood or thread burned as offerings to the gods. But other ceremonies were magnificent week-long festivals attended by thousands. Some major ceremonies took place only when a particular event occurred, such as a natural disaster, a military battle, or the illness of a Sapa Inca. However, there were many ceremonies that occurred regularly. In fact, the Incas held at least one official state ceremony every month of the year (see the box on page 209).

The three main Inca ceremonies were Capac Raymi (Great Festival), Aymoray (which means both "corn harvest" and "May"), and Inti Raymi (festival of the sun). Capac Raymi

Remains of an *acllahuaci,*
where the Inca "chosen
women" lived in seclusion.
The Art Archive/Dagli Orti.

was celebrated in December at the beginning of the rainy season. This festival celebrated the puberty or initiation into manhood of fourteen-year-old Inca boys. In Cuzco, the festival lasted
about three weeks. First the boys climbed a tall mountain peak,
where they sacrificed llamas and sought the approval of the spirit of the mountain. When they returned to Cuzco, the boys participated in a dance during which their relatives whipped the
boys' legs. Then the boys went back up the mountain and began
an extremely dangerous race down a steep mountainside. After
twenty-one days of repeating these and other ordeals and rituals, the boys attended a ceremony and received large earplugs,
which were then inserted into their split earlobes. At this ceremony the Inca boys formally became warriors and *orejones*
(Spanish for "big ears"), or men of the royal Inca line. Boys who
were not Incas went through similar puberty rituals.

The biggest Inca festival was Inti Raymi, the festival of
the sun, which is still held annually in Cuzco. It was celebrated throughout the Inca empire, but the biggest and most elab-

Inca State Ceremonies

Month	Andean month	Festival
December	Capac Raymi	Great Festival
January	Hutu Pacify	Small ripening
February	Human Poky	Great ripening
March	Paccar Ware	Garment of flowers
April	Airway	Dance of the young maize
May	Aymoray	Corn harvest
June	Inti Raymi	Festival of the sun
July	Anta Situate	Earthly purification
August	Capac Situate	General purification sacrifice
September	Cay Raymi	Festival of the coya
October	Yuma Raymi	Festival of the water
November	Ayamarca	Procession of the dead

orate ceremony was in Cuzco. The festivities went on for nine days on a hill near the city. They began at sunrise on the day of the winter solstice, which takes place in June in the Southern Hemisphere. This is the time of year when the sun is at its greatest distance from the equator, marking the beginning of the sun's new year. The festival connected the new year to the Inca myth of creation. It provided recognition to the sun god Inti as the source of all life and the father of the first Incas.

In Cuzco, the royal Incas all participated in Inti Raymi. Even the mummies of the deceased former kings were brought out daily to "participate" in the festivities. The event began as the sun rose. The *orejones* (Inca nobles) chanted together in prayer. The Sapa Inca himself also chanted. Hundreds of llamas as well as other offerings were sacrificed to please Inti (the sun god) and other gods such as Viracocha and Illapa. Dancing, feasting, and drinking accompanied the sacrifice rituals. Each day as the sun went down, everyone grew very quiet and raised their hands in prayer. Then the festivities ceased for the day,

Incas participate in Inti Raymi, the festival of the sun. © *Bettmann/Corbis.*

and everyone went home silently, to start up anew with the rising of the sun the next day. After nine days of this, the Sapa Inca performed a special ceremony, taking a hand plow and breaking the earth; the other Incas then did the same. They believed that the lands of the empire would not grow crops unless the Sapa Inca led the way.

Arts

The Incas are generally considered less skilled in most arts than many of the Andean peoples who preceded them. Most of the best art forms of the Inca empire were developed and perfected by other cultures before the Incas conquered them. For example, in the Chimor kingdom of northern coastal Peru, metalwork was a key industry. Most of the metalworking skills of the Chimú (pronounced chee-MOO) culture originated in even earlier civilizations in the Lambayeque Valley. When the Incas conquered the Chimor kingdom, they took control of its crafts industry, bringing the best Chimú metalworkers to Cuzco to begin large-scale production of their crafts. However, experts believe that large-scale production probably compromised the artisans' ability to achieve the intricate beauty that earlier Chimú pieces were known for. Unfortunately, there is not much evidence to prove or disprove this theory, because few Inca metalwork artifacts are still in existence. Gold, silver, and bronze artifacts were stolen and destroyed by the Spanish conquerors and later by local looters who sold the artifacts to illegal dealers in ancient Peruvian arts.

Some historians theorize that the rigid government structure and work ethic of the Incas stifled artistic expression in the empire. However, the artisans of the Inca empire usually achieved technical perfection in whatever they produced. They especially excelled at stonemasonry and textile arts.

Stonemasonry

Along with metalwork, the Incas are known for their stonemasonry (work of a skilled builder who expertly lays cut or otherwise fitted units of stone in construction). The most elegant Inca architecture is simple and, for the most part, undecorated on the outside. Temples and palaces were constructed of precisely cut limestone or granite blocks, some of which were immense. They were pieced together like an intricate and three-dimensional jigsaw puzzle. They needed no mortar to cement them together because the fit was so perfect. These buildings are still standing five centuries later, while earthquakes and the ravages of time have crumbled more-modern structures. The Incas are renowned for creating buildings that blended in beautifully with the surrounding landscape.

Inca buildings demanded precise planning. Projects generally began with a small clay model of the proposed building. Then, blocks of stone had to be broken out of the earth and transported to the building site. The Incas probably placed wedges of wood into the cracks of rocks at a quarry (a large dug-out area of earth used as a source of stones) and then soaked the wood with water. Expanded by the water, the wood would split the rocks, and a team of men could then cut and dig out a large and very heavy block. The Incas did not have wheels to help them transport the massive rocks. The blocks were probably put on a large board or frame that was pulled by hundreds of laborers. In fact, leading up to one of the major Inca construction sites that remained unfinished after the Spanish conquest of 1533, there are many huge boulders that never made it all the way to the building site. The Spanish called these boulders *piedras cansadas* (tired stones).

The Incas had no iron tools for cutting the stones. Once a block of stone arrived at the work site, a group of workers would begin the long process of cutting the stone to fit into the wall, probably using hard stone instruments to chip, rub, and sculpt the blocks. Copper and bronze—the metals the Incas normally used—are too soft to have helped much in this process. Because there are no written records documenting the construction process, no one knows exactly how the Inca builders created such perfectly fitting stones (though there are many theories on how it could have been done). Whatever their technique, the result was a simple and unadorned architecture. The stone buildings of the Incas have a stark beauty that remains unparalleled in history.

Textiles

The creation of beautiful cloth with vivid designs and intricate weaves has a history dating back to about 3000 B.C.E. in the Andes. For the Incas, weaving was the ultimate visual artistic expression; it was universally appreciated, in the way that painting is appreciated by many modern civilizations. Making colorful textiles was extremely time-consuming for the Incas, and it required a wide variety of skilled laborers. The two most common types of cloth were woven from cotton or from alpaca or llama wool. There were different natural colors of cotton, ranging from brown to white; llama wool was either brown or white. To begin making

This Inca stone wall, still standing in Cuzco, shows the precision with which the Incas cut and fit each stone. © *Nevada Wier/Corbis.*

cloth, spinners used a spindle (a stick with tapered ends that twists the thread in hand spinning) and whorl (a ball or drum-shaped section that attaches to the spindle to keep it rotating evenly) to spin the raw cotton or wool into fine threads of various colors. Inca women throughout the empire would spin thread with a spindle and whorl even while they did other tasks. These threads were given to dyers, who were experts in preparing mineral and vegetable pigments, natural substances that gave vibrant color to the threads. After dyeing, the spun threads were sent on to the weavers. Most often, young girls and women did the weaving as part of their household tasks. Some of the finest cloth, called *cumbi* cloth, was produced by well-trained women in the *acllahuaci,* or house of the chosen women. Even women in the upper ranks of society were expected to spin and weave. Thanks to the labor of all these women, the Inca empire was filled with exquisite textiles in a bright array of colors, decorated with geometric shapes and vivid depictions of animals and humans.

Cloth was used for clothing of all sorts, but it had other uses as well. In the Inca empire, cloth was valued more highly than gold. The Incas held labor in very high esteem, and cloth took many hours of labor to make. Because it was so highly valued, it was often used as a reward for people's efforts, almost like money. For example, soldiers were given cloth as a reward for their military service, and conquered rulers were given *cumbi* cloth when they agreed to accept the rule of the Inca empire. Cloth made by Inca noblewomen was given to local temples or to the Inca empire. The finest *cumbi* cloth, which sometimes took thousands of hours to produce, was burned daily as a sacrificial offering to the gods.

Incas were highly skilled in weaving textiles, such as this cacao bag with a llama pattern. *The Art Archive/Archaeological Museum Lima/Dagli Orti.*

Music and literature

Music and dance were important to the Incas and were prominently featured at Inca festivals. At these celebrations groups of men chanted out songs in perfect unison. For musical instruments, they used drums, whistles, flutes, and panpipes (wind instruments with several pipes attached to a mouthpiece) made from wood, bone, and ceramics. During the large ceremonies, such as Inti Raymi, a band of musicians would march, almost like a modern marching band, playing music all day. Others would begin a ritual form of religious dancing with repetitive rhythms and almost trance-like movements. Although many other aspects of Inca culture have been lost, the music from pre-Spanish times lives on in the Andes and has been incorporated into the region's modern music.

Although the Incas had no writing system, their empire had a great deal of oral literature in the form of religious poems, drama, story songs, and tales of royal heroism and history. These were passed on by word of mouth from generation to generation. Most of the Inca myths and legends were

Runasimi: The Quechua Language

When the Incas built their empire, it included many diverse populations that spoke about twenty different languages. The Incas demanded that the conquered peoples learn to speak the Inca language—*Runasimi,* or Quechua (pronounced KESCH-wah). They were very successful in spreading their language; it was the primary language of the Andean region by the time the Spanish arrived in the early 1500s. The Spanish decided that it might be easier to convert the local people to Christianity if they were taught in their own language. Therefore, the Spanish adapted the Roman alphabet to the Quechua language and developed a written version. Quechua was then used as a trade and missionary language, and it spread to parts of Colombia, Brazil, and Argentina that were not part of the Inca empire.

The Quechua language is an agglutinative language, meaning that new words can be formed by adding special syllables onto a root. The following example of how the words are built from their root is provided in the *Viva el perú!* Web site "Quechua: Language of the Incas." The sentence "Runasimita rimankichu?" means "Do you speak Quechua?" There are two root words in the sentence: *Runasimi* (Quechua) and *rimay* (to speak). *Runasimi* is a compound word in Quechua, coming from the words *runa* (people) and *simi* (mouth). The suffix *ta* is added to the root *Runasimi* to indicate that it is the object of the sentence. In the second word of this sentence, two suffixes are added to the root word *rima* from the verb *rimay.* The suffix *-nki* indicates that the word is in the present tense and the subject is second person singular. The suffix *-chu* indicates that this sentence is a question. Because of this system, some Quechua words

carefully memorized by storytellers and recited to the public during ceremonies and other gatherings. The Inca method of retaining important songs and stories is described by Father Bernabé Cobo in *Inca Religion and Customs* (c. 1653). Father Cobo witnessed the art of memorization within the temples:

> *The most notable aspect of this religion is how they had nothing written down to learn and keep. They made up for this shortcoming by memorizing everything so exactly that it seems as if these things were carved into the Incas' bones. For this purpose alone the Incas had more than a thousand men in the city of Cuzco who did nothing but remember these things. Along with these men others were raised from youth by them, and these youngsters were trained so that these things would not be forgotten. I certainly do not believe myself that such care in preserving their religion and remembering their opinions and shrines was taken by the ancient pagans nor any other people.*

are quite long; however, the numerous syllables can express many subtle shades of meaning.

Between eight million and ten million people in the Andes area still speak Quechua. Many Quechua words have been incorporated into the English language, including condor, jerky, llama, *pampa*, puma, and quinine. Many more Quechua words have made their way into the Spanish language. The following table presents a few Quechua words and phrases. Spellings and pronunciations differ by region.

Quechua Word/Phrase	Meaning
Tata	Father
Mama	Mother
Allillanchu? (ahl-yee-LYANCH-oo)	How are you?
Allillanmi. (ahl-yee-LYAN-mee)	I am fine.
Ima sutiyki? (ee-mah soo-TEE-kee)	What is your name?
Sutiyqa Joe. (soo-TEE-kah Joe)	My name is Joe.
Yusulpayki. (yoo-sool-PIE-kee)	Thank you.
Imamanta. (ee-mah-MAHN-tah)	You're welcome.
Juq ratukama. (shook rah-too-KAH-mah)	See you later.
Ama suwa, ama llulla, ama q'ella. (ah-mah soo-wah, ah-mah lyoo-yah, am-mah ay-yah)	Do not steal; do not lie; do not be lazy.

After the Spanish conquered the Inca empire in 1533, missionaries from Spain arrived to convert the Andean peoples to Christianity. They strove to eliminate all memory of Inca literature so that the people would be more receptive to the teachings of the Christian Bible. Within a generation, there was no one left who had carefully memorized the Inca legends and history, so these stories were lost after hundreds of years in existence. However, some poetry and songs of prayer that were recited within people's homes continued to be transmitted through the generations and were eventually written down for future generations to ponder.

One form of literature was the *jailli* (pronounced whay-lyi), a hymn or poem that was usually set to music. As the sun rose in the morning, Inca priests sang sacred *jaillis,* asking the gods to bring happiness, health, and prosperity to the people of the empire. Some *jaillis* celebrated the deeds of warriors. There were also *jaillis* for the harvest, which were sung by the members of the *ayllus* as they worked in their fields; usually the men would sing out a line and the women would respond by singing the next line. Most of the poetry from Inca times was not very fancy, but stated its message briefly and directly. The Inca poets did not use poetic structures, such as rhyme, specific rhythm sequences, or meter.

Two Quechua dramas are still performed in Peru in the twenty-first century, and they are said to have their origins in Inca times. The plays, *Ollantay* and *The Tragedy of the End of Atahuallpa,* are performed in and around Cuzco, generally in the Spanish language. These dramas were written down after the Spanish conquest, and historians suspect that Spanish priests wrote at least some parts because they reflect strong Christian and European themes. No one knows whether the priests added sections to existing Inca plays or wrote entire plays on their own.

Science

In sciences, as in the arts, the Incas tended to adapt the special skills of the states they had conquered and improve upon them. Most of the Incas' accomplishments were highly practical. They were outstanding engineers. Through irrigation systems and terracing (making large horizontal ridges, like stairs, on mountain slopes to create level spaces for farming), the Incas put almost all the arable land (suitable for farming) in their empire to use. The Incas inherited a road system from previous Andean societies, particularly the Wari, and built it up to traverse (run across) the entire empire—about 14,000 miles (22,526 kilometers) of roadway in all (see Chapter 11 for more information). They built excellent bridges, mainly of rope and fiber, providing access to remote areas. They also had advanced skills in medicine. Although they did not have a writing system, they did have an instrument for recording information: the *quipu.* Without this device, none of their other accomplishments would have been possible.

The *quipu*

A *quipu* (or *khipu*) is a long cord with a set of about one hundred strings hanging from it. Each string is knotted at intervals along its length. The placement of the knots indicates units of ten and multiples of ten—1, 10, 100, 1,000, 10,000, and so on. There is also a knot for zero. The knot closest to the top represented the highest number on the string. Detailed information was recorded on the threads, probably by using different colors or different knots. The color of the strings defined what kind of item was being counted. For example, purple strings might represent pieces of cloth, while yellow strings might represent gold bars. The Incas used *quipus* (pronounced KEE-poos) to record inventory, such as how much grain was in a storehouse. They also used the device to count the number of people in a given area and to keep track of labor obligations owed by the provinces.

A *quipu,* or Inca accounting device. © *Werner Forman/Corbis.*

People who kept records with the *quipu, quipu camayocs,* were professionals with extensive training in memorization. Each *quipu camayoc* had his own system of recording data and kept that system secret from everyone else. *Quipu camayocs* had access to information that was vital to the empire and unknown to anyone else. The penalties for errors among *quipu camayocs* were harsh, but in general these officials had very high status within the empire. Storytellers also used *quipus*. Historians believe that storytellers who used *quipus* thoroughly memorized the tale, but kept certain key facts recorded on the knotted strings to jog their memory. *Quipus* were used only to count and record numbers; they could not be used to calculate arithmetic functions—adding, subtracting, multiplying, or dividing; the Incas had special counting boards for these functions.

Inca Medicine

When people got sick in the Inca empire, priests usually performed healing ceremonies over them. The Incas also had a fairly sophisticated understanding of the medicinal properties of herbs and plants. The bark of one tree, for example, produced quinine, which the Incas used to cure cramps, chills, and many other ailments. The Incas used the leaves of the coca plant to numb people who were in pain. (Cocaine, which is derived from the same plant, was later prescribed by modern doctors for the same purpose.) Inca hunters dipped their arrows in a drug called curare that they extracted from a tropical vine; the substance instantly paralyzed the muscles of their prey. With the animal paralyzed, hunters could easily get their arrows back. (Modern doctors use curare as an anesthetic (a drug that causes a patient to temporarily lose feeling in a particular part of the body or to temporarily lose consciousness). Inca surgeons apparently performed amputations for medical purposes, and their patients survived in good health.

Archaeologists have made the surprising discovery that the Incas practiced brain surgery on living patients who apparently survived the ordeal. The Inca surgeons used bronze or copper knives, hammers, tweezers, and chisels to drill into the skull. They cut out a rectangular or circular hole, lifted out the hole,

Quipus were essential to the running of the empire and most historians believe they were a substitute for writing in the ancient Inca civilization. They provided records of all the goods and stock of the empire, of the population, of the amounts of labor owed to the government from every individual and province, of the justice system, and much more. Without *quipus,* it is unlikely that the Incas could have organized such a vast empire.

The Spanish destroyed all the Inca *quipus* they could find, superstitiously believing them to contain "evil" information because they did not understand them. A number of modern scholars believe that they understand the method *quipu* keepers might have used to record things, but their theories are controversial. Exactly how *quipus* recorded numbers remains a mystery, and because each *quipu camayoc* had a unique system of recording, it is difficult to make generalizations about *quipu* use.

Incas cultivating medicinal herbs.
© Bettmann/Corbis.

and went to work on the brain. Archaeologists have found hundreds of skulls with incisions that show the remarkable precision of Inca brain surgeons. Some of the skulls were operated on more than once, and one skull appears to have undergone five different surgeries. Experts believe that the Incas performed brain surgery to repair injuries to the head and to cure ailments such as chronic headaches and even epilepsy (a disorder of the nervous system that usually includes convulsions). How successful they were in curing the ailments is not known, but it is certain that the Incas were far ahead of all other ancient civilizations in the field of brain surgery.

Calendar and astronomy

Scholars have many theories about Inca calendars, but because the Incas did not keep written records, no one really knows how they recorded time. It is apparent that some form of calendar based on the movements of the stars and planets was used. The Incas' monthly ceremonies and rituals attest to their careful observance of the sun and the seasons.

Like other Inca arts and sciences, Inca astronomy (the study of the stars, planets, and other objects outside Earth's atmosphere) was highly practical; astronomical information was mainly used to time planting and harvesting. The Incas built observatories to watch the heavens. They also tracked the movement of the sun by erecting carefully oriented pillars on hilltops. By keeping track of the sun's position between the pillars when it rose and set the Incas could determine the right times to plant crops at different altitudes. To date, there are no records that suggest the Incas had any further astronomical knowledge.

For More Information

Books

Adams, Richard E. W. *Ancient Civilizations of the New World*. Boulder, CO: Westview Press, 1997.

Cobo, Bernabé. *Inca Religion and Customs*. Originally written c. 1653. Translated by Roland Hamilton. Austin: University of Texas Press, 1990.

Davies, Nigel. *The Ancient Kingdoms of Peru*. London and New York: Penguin Books, 1997.

Katz, Friedrich. *The Ancient American Civilizations*. London: Phoenix Press, 1972.

Malpass, Michael A. *Daily Life in the Inca Empire*. Westport, CT: Greenwood Press, 1996.

Time-Life Books. *Incas: Lords of Gold and Glory*. Alexandria, VA: Time-Life Books, 1992.

Web Site

"Quechua: Language of the Incas." *Viva el Perú!* http://www.geocities.com/TheTropics/4458/runasimi.html (accessed on October 7, 2004).

Daily Life in the Inca Empire

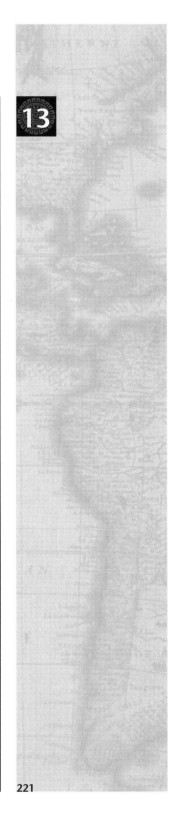

13

Of the estimated ten million people living in the Inca (pronounced ING-kuh) empire at the time of the Spanish conquest in 1533, the vast majority were working people whose lives were filled from dawn till dusk with hard work. In many ways, the Inca rulers were keen psychologists (people who study human thinking and behavior) who created a system to ensure that their people had neither the time nor the energy to rebel, commit crimes, or avoid their duties to the empire, their religion, their families, or their *ayllus* (pronounced EYE-yoos; extended families who lived in the same area, shared their land and work, and arranged for marriages and religious rituals as a group). Beyond obliging people to work very hard, the Inca government invited everyone to participate in lengthy festivals and other ceremonial activities directed by the empire. At these festivities—perhaps the only break from their toil that common workers ever received—the commoners often indulged in heavy drinking with nobles. Many experts believe the festivals provided the cement that held the empire together. (An empire is a vast, complex political unit extending across political boundaries

Words to Know

Aclla: A young woman chosen by the Incas to live in isolation from daily Inca life while learning how to weave and how to make *chicha* and foods for festivals; some *acllas* were eventually married to nobles, and others became religious workers.

Ayllu: A group of extended families who live in the same area, share their land and work, and arrange for marriages and religious rituals as a group; the basic social unit of the Andean peoples.

Coya: The Sapa Inca's sister/wife, also known as his principal wife, and queen of the Inca empire.

Curaca: A local leader of a region conquered by the Incas; after conquest, *curacas* were trained to serve their regions as representatives of the Inca government.

Empire: A vast, complex political unit extending across political boundaries and dominated by one central power, which generally takes control of the economy, government, and culture in communities throughout its territory.

Hierarchy: The ranking of a group of people according to their social, economic, or political position.

Mit'a: A tax imposed on the common people by the Inca government; the tax was a labor requirement rather than a monetary sum—the head of every household was obliged to work on public projects (building monuments, repairing roads or bridges, transporting goods) for a set period each year.

Monogamy: Marriage to one partner only.

Mummification: Preservation of a body through a complex procedure that involves taking out the organs, filling the body cavity with preservative substances, and then drying out the body to prevent decay; mummification can also occur naturally when environmental conditions, such as extreme cold or dryness, preserve the body.

Polygamy: Marriage in which spouses can have more than one partner; in Inca society, some men had multiple wives, but women could not take multiple husbands.

Quinoa: A high-protein grain grown in the Andes.

Quipu: Also *khipu*. A set of multicolored cotton cords knotted at intervals, used for counting and record keeping.

Yanacona: A commoner who was selected and trained in childhood to serve the Inca nobility, priests, or the empire in general; the position was a form of slavery.

and dominated by one central power, which generally takes control of the economy, government, and culture in communities throughout its territory.)

The Inca class system

The Incas ruled their empire with an almost mathematical precision, and the hierarchy (the ranking of people according to their social, economic, or political position) in Inca society was no less structured. At the top of the society, of course, was the Sapa Inca (supreme leader). Number two in the empire was the *Villac Umu,* or chief priest, always a close relative of the Sapa Inca. Next in line were the other blood relatives of the Sapa Inca. They received the high-ranking positions in the empire. The *coya,* or queen, the *apos,* or directors of the four quarters of the empire, and the head of the army were all closely related to the Sapa Inca (sometimes the Sapa Inca led the army himself). Next in line after the blood relatives came all other Incas—people who descended from the original ten *ayllus* (extended family groups that share common ancestors) that founded the Inca settlement in Cuzco (pronounced KOO-sko). This group of Incas became the empire's priests, commanders, and governors. Next in the hierarchy were a group known as the Incas-by-privilege. As the empire grew, there were not enough Incas to manage all the territory and people within it, so the Incas created a new class of Incas—the Incas-by-privilege—people who had lived in the Cuzco area for a long time and spoke the Quechua (pronounced KECH-wah) language. The Incas-by-privilege were generally put in charge of outlying peoples and colonies. Even with this addition to the hierarchy, the Incas were a small group. In an empire with a population of roughly ten million people, there were only a few thousand Incas at the time of the Spanish conquest in 1533.

Under the Inca class, there was a large class of public administrators (people who manage or supervise the day-to-day operations of business, government, and religious organizations) and local leaders. The former leaders of conquered

Map showing important sites in the Inca empire.
Map by XNR Productions. The Gale Group.

states, the *curacas,* were usually the governors of their people, but they answered to the Incas in all important matters. Other administrators called *quipu camayocs,* or *quipu* keepers, kept detailed records of the empire's stored goods, the *mit'a* labor obligations of each province (instead of collecting taxes in the form of money, the government required conquered states to send workers for various public projects), the population counts, and much more. Most architects, city planners, and engineers also belonged to this class, although some people in these professions were probably Incas.

Next in the hierarchy was a large class of artisans, or craftspeople. The Incas had plenty of food reserves and other supplies to support their artisans, and they encouraged the development of skilled specialists in many fields. Artisans had a somewhat easier life than farmers, though they were expected to work very hard. They usually worked full time for the Incas, the temple, or a *curaca* (local leader). The raw materials they needed were supplied to them, and they were paid for their work with food and other necessities. Craftspeople were not subject to the *mit'a* obligation.

Artisans in the Inca empire may have felt a little bit like factory workers. The Incas favored mass production (using the same design and method of production over and over to create a large quantity of identical or nearly identical items), and historians believe that Inca administrators controlled exactly what the artisans made and which designs were used. Potters in the Inca empire, for example, usually repeated the same geometric patterns on their ceramics. They used molds to make their ceramics, so each new item had the same shape as the last one. By the later days of the empire, artisans had become so specialized that there were entire communities dedicated to producing one type of craft—a village of potters in one place, for example, and a community of gold workers in another. On the outskirts of the capital city of Cuzco, craftspeople from all the different regions of the empire worked in small neighborhoods dedicated to special crafts.

Farmers were by far the largest and most important group of people in the Inca empire, but they were very near the bottom of the social hierarchy. Most farmers were poor and uneducated. They did not live in the cities, though they sometimes went there for ceremonies. They lived in rural areas in windowless huts and worked most of their waking hours. But everything in the Inca empire depended on them. They provided the tremendous surplus of goods that kept the empire and the state religion operating. Most of the prayers and sacrifices offered by the Incas were entreaties to the gods to make these farmers successful. In Inca times, the farmers were extremely good at what they did, and they were well organized for maximum production.

Daily life among the farmers and common people

A common Inca proverb was "Don't steal; don't lie; don't be lazy." There was little opportunity for dishonesty in the Inca empire, and laziness was simply not allowed among the hardworking farmers. People in the harsh environment of the Andes had probably been hard workers long before the Incas began to build an empire. All able-bodied people, from children to grandparents, were expected to work hard—very hard—at something, and they did.

The *ayllu*

The *ayllu* was the basic social unit in the Andean region before and after the rise of the Inca empire. *Ayllus* were groups of extended families who lived near each other in small villages, towns, or farming settlements. They worked together and shared their land and animals as well as the goods they produced by farming. Everyone in the Inca empire, commoner and noble alike, was born into an *ayllu*, married within the *ayllu*, and died in the same *ayllu*.

When the Incas took ownership of a newly conquered state, they took all of its land, livestock, and mines. (See Chapter 11 for more information about land ownership.) One-third of the land was to be worked for the empire, and one-third was for the upkeep of the state religion. The last third was distributed to the *ayllus,* and members of the *ayllu* divided the land among themselves according to their needs. Both the empire and the *ayllu* reassessed the needs of the people on a regular basis and would reapportion the land accordingly. At the *ayllu* level, land was distributed according to a local measure, depending on how much the land was capable of producing. For example, in the foothills of the mountain two acres might produce enough food for a family, but in the highlands it might take four acres, and in the coastal areas it might take three acres to produce a crop to sustain a family. When a couple married, they received a *topo,* an allotment of land deemed just the right size to support two people. Their *topo* was increased by another full allotment for each son they had, and by a much smaller piece of land for each daughter. Land was not distributed to single men; this was one way of ensuring that everyone married.

The family was not free to work its own land until the state and temple lands had been worked. The obligation to the Inca empire was probably carried out at the *ayllu* level in many places, with the male members of the *ayllu* working a section of lands together to provide the requirements. The head of the household, usually the male, was responsible for working the state and temple lands. Men might also be called away to fulfill the *mit'a* obligation, labor required by the Inca government. When this happened, other members of the *ayllu* would care for the absent man's crops or herds until he returned. The *ayllu* also worked together to build houses for newly married couples.

Work

After the Incas conquered new territories and redistributed the land, they set out heavy work requirements. Farmers suddenly had to work first for the state, next for the state religion, and then finally for themselves and their families, so they had little time for rest. But, according to the Inca principle of *ayni,* or give-and-take, the farmers did receive something in exchange for all their efforts. For one thing, the Incas ensured that everyone had some land to farm. In addition, the Incas kept storehouses full of food in every region. The old and the sick were entitled to food, and in case of a natural disaster or crop failure, the storehouses were open to the public. The Incas also greatly expanded the amount of available farmland by improving irrigation systems (bringing water to the crops) and creating terraces (large steps cut into the mountain slopes to create a level space for farming). The Inca management ensured that more foods were available to the farmers, too. An amazing network of roads that traversed the Inca empire enhanced the existing exchange system by providing easy travel between different regions.

The farmers of the Inca empire planted such a wide variety of crops that there were different crops coming in all year round. In *The Ancient Sun Kingdoms of the Americas* (1957), Inca expert V. W. Von Hagen describes the agricultural achievements of these farmers:

> Under the guidance of the Inca's "professionals," the whole of the realm—which included Andes, desert, and Upper Amazon—became a great center of plant domestication. More than half of the foods that the world eats today were developed by these Andean farmers; *it has been estimated that more kinds of food and medicinal plants were systematically cultivated here than in any other sizable area of the world!* One has only to mention the obvious: corn—that is, maize—(20 varieties); potatoes (40 varieties); sweet potatoes, squash, beans of infinite variety; manioc (from which come our farina and tapioca); peanuts, cashews, pineapples, chocolate, avocados, tomatoes, peppers, papaya, strawberries, mulberries; so many and so varied the plants, and so long domesticated in the Old World, one forgets that all of these originated in the Americas.

The members of an *ayllu* often worked together. At a spring planting, the men and women chanted out a working song as they went about their tasks. The men broke up the soil with foot plows, which were long poles with a footrest near the bottom and a wooden or bronze point. The women worked behind them, breaking apart the clods of dirt with bronze-bladed hoes.

Mit'a **work.** Instead of imposing a monetary tax on conquered territories, the Inca government required all households in the empire to provide labor for public projects for a certain amount of time every year (see Chapter 11 for more information on *mit'a*). A man from each household fulfilled this labor obligation by accepting whatever assignment the local leader gave him. Some workers were sent off to transport goods to other regions; others built roads or hauled stone blocks for construction projects; some men were assigned to military service. Empire officials coordinated *mit'a* assign-

Mines located throughout the Inca empire contained an abundance of precious metals for production of figures such as this one.
© Werner Forman/Corbis.

ments so that farmwork was disrupted as little as possible. The local *curacas* made sure that not too many people from one *ayllu* were drawn away at the same time; that way, the other members of the *ayllu* could easily cover for the temporary shortage of workers.

Mit'a workers played a role in the extensive mining that went on in the Inca empire. Mines located throughout the empire produced abundant gold, silver, and copper. Gold was found in its pure form in streams, and it was also dug out of hillsides. Silver was found in the form of silver ore (silver mixed with rock), both in the ground and in hillsides. After removing the ore, mine workers heated it to a very high temperature to separate the metal and rock. The *mit'a* laborers were called upon to do this work in the summertime. However, because mining was so physically difficult, miners worked for only a few hours a day. Only Incas were allowed to own silver and gold, so government representatives kept a careful watch over mining projects. The places where the metals were found were considered sacred and often became the sites of rituals (formal acts performed the same way each time as a means of religious worship).

Women did not leave their *ayllus* to do *mit'a* labor, but they were required to do a set amount of weaving and perhaps spinning for the empire. They had to accomplish this work whenever they could, in between their regular farmwork and household chores. This was a central task in their lives and central to the Inca economy.

Yanaconas and *acllas.* Few common people escaped the farming life. The *yanaconas* were one group that did change their way of life, for better or for worse. *Yanaconas* were men who served the Inca nobility as personal attendants or who served the empire in general by working as street sweepers, gardeners, sun temple attendants, and so on. *Yanaconas* were chosen at a young age, usually from a community of newly conquered people. Those chosen were often special young boys noted for their intelligence. After a period of training, they entered into the service of the empire. Though *yanaconas* were basically slaves who had no choice in their fate, some of them had a more comfortable life than the farm life they had left behind. For example, a *yanacona* who was lucky enough to work for the Sapa Inca's household would remain with the Sapa Inca after the ruler's death, tending to the mummy and living a fairly elegant life in the palace. On the other hand, an unlucky *yanacona* could become the personal slave of ill-natured people and be subjected to abuse and hard labor.

Like the *yanaconas,* the *acllas,* or chosen women, were taken from their homes in childhood to be trained for service to the empire or its religious institutions. Many spent long days weaving fine cloth for the Incas, but there was a wide range of fates in store for the *acllas* in training. Some were given to nobles as rewards, and the nobles took them as secondary wives. Their treatment depended on the nature of the noble. As secondary wives, they took a position within the household, usually working as a kind of nanny to the noble's sons. Other *acllas* were sacrificed to the sun god. Some *acllas* became *mamaconas,* or "Virgins of the Sun." These women did not take husbands (although they were symbolically married to the sun god or one of the other Inca gods), and they did not serve in any household. Instead, they took part in religious ceremonies and helped maintain the *huacas* and temples of the empire. *Mamaconas* commanded great respect.

Marriage, family, and child rearing

Marriage and family were central to the Inca culture, and the Incas required everyone to marry. Although Inca noblemen were allowed to practice polygamy (the men could have more than one wife), monogamy (marriage to one partner only) was the rule among the common people of the empire. When young couples decided to marry, they often entered into a trial marriage, to see if it would work. If it failed, both partners could go on to enter a new marriage without shame. Unlike the Christian Europeans of that time, the Andean peoples in the Inca empire placed no extra value on the virginity of a bride. However, Inca law stated that once a couple was formally married, they had to remain together for life. Even if divorces had been allowed, it would have been almost impossible to support oneself outside of marriage, because the Inca government distributed land only to married couples.

Before the Incas came to power, the division of labor between husbands and wives in Andean regions was more or less equal. In *Daily Life in the Inca Empire* (1996) Michael A. Malpass notes that the *mit'a* system of labor changed this. When men were called away to become warriors and to do the work of the empire, they gained status and became figures of authority; in comparison, the work that women did around the house and in the fields seemed ordinary and tedious. However, since everyone worked most of the time, the division of labor was fairly balanced. Both husband and wife worked the fields. Though men provided the *mit'a* service, women were responsible for a large amount of weaving for the empire. Women generally prepared food and kept the home clean. Men made sandals and helped with the weaving.

The birth of a child was a very welcome event in the Inca empire. There were rituals for both parents to perform to ensure the safe delivery of an infant. But pregnant mothers were expected to keep working right up to the day they gave birth, and they often gave birth without help. After giving birth, the mother either carried the baby around with her while she worked, tied in a pack across her chest, or she placed the baby in a cradle. The parents did not immediately name the baby; the naming occurred later, during a ceremony called *rutichikoy,* which accompanied the baby's weaning from breast-feeding. At the *rutichikoy* ceremony, the child received a haircut, a fingernail trim, and a name. A ceremony called *huarachicoy* marked a boy's puberty and passage into adulthood. In this ceremony the boy received a loincloth woven by his mother. For girls, small, family ceremonies called *quichicoy* marked the beginning of menstruation. At these puberty ceremonies, the boys and girls received new, adult names.

The children of nobles and *curacas* went to schools, but the children of common people received no formal education. Instead they watched their parents to learn their

trade. The children of workers were expected to begin working at a very early age. From age five to nine, boys and girls were expected to help watch younger siblings (brothers and sisters). They were also supposed to scare birds and other animals away from the crops, collect firewood, spin threads from wool, gather wild plants, and help out with cooking and cleaning. From age nine to twelve, they took on additional responsibilities: Boys herded animals and hunted birds; girls collected materials for dyeing cloth.

Houses

Peasants' houses varied from region to region, but overall they were not places where families spent much time, except to sleep or to escape wet weather. Most houses consisted of one dark, rectangular room with no windows. On the coast, houses were made of adobe or cane and reed. In the colder climates in the mountains, houses were generally

An Inca house with a thatched roof near Cuzco, Peru. © *Jeremy Horner/Corbis.*

Maize, or corn, was a main staple of the Inca diet, and it was also used to make *chicha.* © *Kevin Schafer/Corbis.*

made of stone and often had a stove made of stones cemented to the floor with mud in the middle of the room. Since there was no vent, the smoke from the stove simply passed through the thatching of the roof. There was no furniture in the houses in any region. Families slept together on the floor; those in the highlands used a llama fur as a mattress and blanket, and people on the coast used a lighter, woven blanket and floor covering. There was no need for chairs. When Inca people sat down, they got into a squatting position, with their feet together on the ground and their knees up close to their chins. Then they would pull their tunics (long blouses) over their knees and down over their legs. The tunic actually supported them in the squatting position.

Keeping the house clean was a matter of tradition, but in the time of the Inca empire it was also a matter of law. Twice a year, officials of the empire inspected households in conquered communities to make sure that people were properly caring for their homes. There was little privacy in homes in the

Inca empire. Doors had to be left open at mealtimes so that Inca officials could see whether all Inca rules were being followed.

Food

The common people of the Inca empire usually ate two meals each day—one in the morning and one in the late afternoon. They usually ate outside. Their diet included far more vegetables than meat. The only meat they were likely to eat was guinea pig, dog, or duck meat. Occasionally the peasants ate llama (a South American mammal with soft, fleecy wool) meat, but the few llamas that they owned were far too precious as pack animals to be slaughtered for food. People living on the coast or near Lake Titicaca ate fish. Most often, the common people cooked stews and other main dishes in ceramic pots over crude stoves made of stone and mud and roasted meats and vegetables on an open flame. Maize (corn), quinoa (pronounced KEEN-wah; a high-protein grain), and potatoes were the main staples of their diet, and chili peppers were a popular way to spice up the food. (A common Inca stew was made from corn kernels boiled with chilies and herbs until the corn popped open.) Bread was made by adding water to cornmeal or potato flour and placing the loaf in the hot ashes of a fire to bake. Guinea pig meat was often cooked in a soup thickened with flour made from potatoes.

By far the most common drink in the empire was *chicha,* an alcoholic beverage made from maize, quinoa, or other grains. People usually drank *chicha* after a meal. Making *chicha* was usually a job for the elderly or for people who were disabled or sick. If they used old maize or grains, they had to chew the kernels or seeds first, so that their saliva could break them down. Then they spit the pulp into jars of warm water, sealed the jars, buried them in the ground, and allowed them to sit for a few days. At that point, the *chicha* had fermented (process in which yeasts convert sugar to alcohol and carbon dioxide) and was ready to drink.

The farmers of the Inca empire produced many surplus crops, and fortunately, they knew how to preserve this extra food. They preserved maize and quinoa by pounding them out into flour. Women generally did this work, using a long, crescent-shaped stone to roll and grind

The History of the Potato

The world's first potatoes were grown in the Andes. Long before the Incas existed, in the earliest days of human life in the Andes, the hunters and gatherers in the highland plains of the Andes Mountains found root plants called tubers—the forerunners of the modern potato—and added them to their diet. It was too cold in the Andean highlands for grains to grow, so the tubers became a staple food source. They were nutritious, easy to store, and lasted a long time. By about 4500 B.C.E. Andean people had begun to plant and grow the earliest forms of *papas,* a Quechua (pronounced KECH-wah) word for potatoes.

The Moche (pronounced MO-chay), the Chimú (pronounced chee-MOO), and various other societies developed strong potato plants that resisted the mountain frosts. The Incas learned that if they rotated their potato fields regularly, they had healthier crops. Throughout the high-altitude areas of their empire where maize and quinoa would not grow, potatoes were the main crop.

The Incas revered the gifts of nature, including the potato. The Quechua language has hundreds of words for the potato. Inca art often depicts potatoes, and the people of the empire worshiped potato gods and performed potato ritu-

the grain on a stone slab. The flour could then be stored in large pots or jars. Other foods were stored in bins made from cornstalks and mud or in pits dug into the floor of the house.

The peasants of the Inca empire also preserved food by a method of freeze-drying. Freeze-dried potatoes were called *chuños.* They were made at high altitudes in the Andes, usually during the month of June, when it is warm in the sun during the day and freezes during the night. Women laid out the potatoes before evening, and the potatoes froze during the night. Then they were allowed to thaw in the morning sun. By about noon the potatoes were ready to be processed. The women walked on them repeatedly with bare feet, mashing them up thoroughly and getting all the juices out. Then they rinsed the mashed-up potato pulp and spread it out to dry in the sun. When the pulp was completely dry, they stored it in jars or bins in the home. *Chuños* were used to make bread and stews.

Incas harvesting potatoes. © *Bettmann/Corbis.*

als. They also used potatoes for medicine. When the Spanish conquistadores (the Spanish word for "conquerors") arrived in the Andean region in the early 1500s, they began to use potatoes for their own purposes. Because they lasted well, potatoes were particularly useful as food on ocean voyages, and Spanish sailors grew accustomed to eating them. Back in Spain the potato was initially viewed with fear or disgust, and it was used only for the poor or for prisons and hospitals. It was not until the eighteenth century that the potato became a widespread European crop.

Clothing

According to Inca law, members of each ethnic group or conquered state in the empire were required to wear their own distinctive native clothing. This made it possible for Inca officials to determine an individual's origins upon sight and to make sure that no one wandered into forbidden new territory. (Travel was not legal for common people in the empire.) Headbands and headdresses, belts, and woven bags were often the distinguishing differences in native attire.

The standard apparel for common men in the Inca empire was a knee-length sleeveless tunic made of cotton or wool, which was worn over a loincloth. Men also wore large capes over their shoulders. Women wore floor-length tunics with a sash at the waist. They wore shawls over their shoulders, pinning the ends together with a copper pin. In the cool climate of the highlands, clothing was usually made from llama wool, while in the warmer lowlands it was made from cotton. On their feet, both men and women wore sandals with leather soles; woven straps tied around the foot and ankle.

Play

Oddly, for such a busy and hardworking society, farming families had a great deal of time off each year—but only so that they could attend state-sponsored festivals. The Sapa Inca and his administrators put on many festivals for the workers throughout the year. These were held in the provincial or city plazas and included religious spectacles, dancing, music, and massive quantities of food and *chicha*. The celebrations often lasted for several days. Historians estimate that people in the Inca empire spent about 120 days each year at these festivals. The cost to the empire must have been enormous: The government paid for all the *chicha* and food, and it also had to absorb the cost of reduced productivity (for every day they were celebrating, the workers were not producing crops or other goods for the empire). These festivals were not invented by the Incas. The Wari (pronounced wah-REE) and the Tiwanaku (pronounced tee-wah-NAH-coo) used similar festivities to create a bond between themselves and their workers (see Chapters 7 and 8 for more information). Without newspapers or other written communications, the Incas had to convey their messages to the people by staging public events. There, the Inca nobility could tell the farmers about all the benefits they were receiving by being part of the great empire. They could relate the latest Inca military conquests and the heroic feats of the Sapa Inca. The rules of the kingdom and the work requirements for the year were also conveyed during these festivals. Announcements about the upcoming workload reached the people at the height of the celebration. As they danced and drank their free *chicha*, these labor obligations seemed like a fair tradeoff for the fun they were having at the moment. After the festival the people generally returned to their work feeling grateful to the Incas and ready to fulfill the tremendous labor obligations imposed by the Inca government.

Daily life among the nobility

When sixteenth-century Spanish explorers decided to invade the area that makes up present-day Peru, it was because they had heard that gold, silver, and other riches lined the streets of Cuzco. The stories they had heard were true. Cuzco was home to the Inca nobility, who had accumulated great fortunes as they created their empire. The central part of the city was home only to the wealthy elite. It was full of palaces, *panacas* (palaces of the deceased Sapa Incas), and temples, and some of these buildings were actually covered in gold.

Marriage, family, and child rearing among the nobility

Inca noblemen were allowed to have more than one wife. However, a nobleman had only one primary wife, to whom he remained married for life. His other, secondary wives lived in the house and took care of his sons. Noblewomen were expected to weave for the empire. But according to Andean elders who were interviewed about the life of the Incas, the Inca nobility did very little work. Stuart Stirling quotes one of these elders in *The Last Conquistador* (1999):

> The Incas of the eleven ayllu *never laboured for any one, for they were served by the Indians of all Peru.... For none of their caste [social class] and tribe, poor or rich, nor any other who was a descendant of the Incas of the eleven* ayllu *were servitors [servants] in any manner, for they were served in all the four provinces of this realm ... their sole office being to assist in the court of the Inca [Sapa Inca] where he resided, to eat and walk and to accompany him, and to discharge his commissions in war and peace, and to inspect the lands as great lords with their many servants.*

The Incas trained their boys in formal schools, where *amautas,* usually priests, taught them language, history, religion, and the use of the *quipu.* Upon reaching puberty, Inca boys in Cuzco underwent a three-week ritual during the Capac Raymi festival (festival of the sun). During this ritual, the boys climbed up a high mountain peak—twice. There, llamas were sacrificed, and sacred dances were performed. The boys were given beatings to test their bravery and endurance. At separate ceremonies they were given weapons and loincloths. At the end of this complex ritual, the boys' earlobes were split, and special earplugs were inserted in the lobes. The earplugs were the mark of Inca nobility.

Costume of an Inca man and his wife. *© Gianni Dagli Orti/Corbis.*

Clothing of nobles

The dress of the nobles was similar to that of the common people. Men wore knee-length tunics, loincloths, and capes. Women wore floor-length tunics with shawls. The material was much finer than the material used for farmers' clothes, and the designs that were woven or dyed into the nobles' clothing were more ornate. Inca women did not wear a lot of jewelry; a pin (to hold a shawl in place) and a necklace were common. Inca men, on the other hand, adorned themselves greatly, particularly for special occasions. The huge earplugs they wore in their earlobes were nearly two inches in diameter. Top-ranking Incas wore gold earplugs, while Incas-by-privilege wore silver or copper. Men also wore large metal bracelets made from medals they had won for bravery in battle. Former warriors also wore necklaces made from the teeth of their fallen enemies. When high-ranking Inca nobility appeared at festivals, they were usually decked out in vividly colored parrot feathers, woven gold tunics, and massive headdresses.

An Inca mummy.
© Bettmann/Corbis.

Burial practices of the Inca people

Burial practices in the Inca empire varied from region to region. Often, the deceased person, whether commoner or noble, was placed in a fetal position (lying on one side with knees curled up to the chest) with some of his or her belongings and wrapped in a special cloth or mat. The nobility, however, were often buried with many more belongings and dressed in elaborate clothing.

Archaeologists have found human remains throughout the area encompassed by the Inca empire, and in many cases, they discovered Inca bodies that were mummified—preserved by other human beings or by unusual environmental conditions, such as extreme cold or dryness. The Incas always mummified the Sapa Inca and revered his body as a *huaca,* or shrine. In *Narrative of the Incas* (1996; originally completed in 1557) Spanish chronicler Juan de Betanzos briefly describes the mummification process used for Sapa Inca Huayna Capac (pronounced WHY-nuh CA-poc), who ruled the empire from 1493 to 1525:

When he died, the nobles who were with him had him opened and took out all his entrails [internal organs], preparing him so that no damage would be done to him and without breaking any bone. They prepared and dried him in the Sun and the air. After he was dried and cured [prepared, preserved, or finished by a chemical or physical process] they dressed him in costly clothes and placed him on an ornate litter well adorned with feathers and gold.

The very dry climate of the Andes region, along with the high salt content in the soil, aided in the preservation of the Inca mummies. In the high elevations of the Andes frigid temperatures preserved bodies buried in the ground. These were mainly the bodies of children who were sacrificed on the mountaintops and then buried there.

The Spanish explorers thoroughly raided Inca graves in their pursuit of gold and silver, so until recently, archaeologists had few Inca burials to study. Then, in 2002, archaeologists found two thousand Inca mummies and tens of thousands of artifacts buried with them in the earth beneath a poor, temporary neighborhood in Lima, Peru. The bodies were extremely well preserved; many still had hair and skin. Archaeologists expect this finding to improve their knowledge and understanding of the daily life of the Inca people.

For More Information

Books

Betanzos, Juan de. *Narrative of the Incas.* Original manuscript completed in 1557. Translated by Roland Hamilton. Austin: University of Texas Press, 1996.

Malpass, Michael A. *Daily Life in the Inca Empire.* Westport, CT: Greenwood Press, 1996.

Stirling, Stuart. *The Last Conquistador: Mansio Serra de Leguizamón and the Conquest of the Incas.* Phoenix Mill, Stroud, Gloucestershire, UK: Sutton Publishing, 1999.

Time-Life Books. *Incas: Lords of Gold and Glory.* Alexandria, VA: Time-Life Books, 1992.

Von Hagen, V. W. *The Ancient Sun Kingdoms of the Americas.* Cleveland, OH: World Publishing Company, 1957.

Web Site

Harris, Eric R. "The Costume of the Inca." *World History Archives.* http://www.hartford-hwp.com/archives/41/414.html (accessed on October 12, 2004).

The Conquest of the Incas

14

The reign of the mighty Inca (pronounced ING-kuh) empire was remarkable but short. In 1438 the Incas were merely a group of related families residing in Cuzco (pronounced KOO-sko), without any aspirations of building an empire. Within the next ninety-five years, they had created the largest native empire that ever existed in the Americas; it stretched over almost 3,000 miles (4,827 kilometers) of western South America and had an estimated population of about ten million people. The empire was wealthy and powerful, and Inca leaders had massive military forces at their command. However, in the 1520s, illness, uprisings, and other social and political problems plagued the Incas. Then, in November 1532, a small army of Spanish conquistadores (Spanish word for "conquerors") marched into their territory. The Incas, weakened and disorganized by their previous problems, were in no condition to defend themselves. The empire was suddenly in jeopardy, and the Incas were about to take an abrupt fall.

Words to Know

Chronicler: A person who writes down a record of historical events, arranged in order of occurrence.

Conquistador: The Spanish word for "conqueror"; in English, the word usually refers to the leaders of the Spanish conquests of Mesoamerica and Peru in the sixteenth century.

Empire: A vast, complex political unit extending across political boundaries and dominated by one central power, which generally takes control of the economy, government, and culture in communities throughout its territory.

Epidemic: A sudden spreading of a contagious disease among a population, a community, or a region.

Harquebus: A heavy portable gun invented during the fifteenth century.

Mestizo: A person having mixed ancestry, specifically European and Amerindian.

Mummy: A body that has been preserved, either by human technique or unusual environmental conditions, such as extreme cold or dryness.

Panaca: The household of a dead Sapa Inca.

Pre-Columbian: Existing before Spanish explorer Christopher Columbus arrived in the Americas in 1492.

Quechua: The Inca language, still spoken by Andean people today.

Huayna Capac and the takeover of Quito

The last great Sapa Inca was Huayna (pronounced WHY-nuh) Capac, the eleventh Inca king, who ruled from 1493 to 1525. During Huayna Capac's reign, the empire's continuous expansion into new territories slowed down significantly. There were few lands left to conquer. The tropical areas east of the Andes were within reach, but battle in the jungle proved to be a futile pursuit. The slowdown in expansion was an early sign of trouble for the empire.

The constant growth of the empire was fueled by the *panaca* system, which allowed the relatives of a dead Sapa Inca to retain his palace and all his wealth. This forced the next Sapa Inca in line to find new sources of wealth, which usually meant conquering new territories and taking their wealth. Obtaining new territories was also important to the armies and the citizens of the empire, because it brought them rewards and more goods. With fewer new territories to conquer, the large Inca armies became restless. Because Inca armies were made up of soldiers from conquered lands, there was real danger of rebellion if the troops were not constantly winning battles. The new recruits had nothing to show for their efforts for the empire and, with time on their hands, found ways to make trouble. The common people in many areas were also restless for a variety of reasons, particularly because some areas received better treatment by the empire than others. Eventually, frustration with Inca rule led to multiple and sometimes violent uprisings.

Sometime in the middle of Huayna Capac's reign, major uprisings broke out in the north. The Sapa Inca began to focus his full attention on fighting in the Quito kingdom, which occupied the area that is now called Ecuador. He is said to have brought with him to the north Atahuallpa (pronounced AH-tah-WAHL-pah), his thirteen-year-old son by a secondary wife. For several years the Sapa Inca and Atahuallpa led large Inca armies in heavy battles in the north. They succeeded in defeating the armies of the Quito kingdom, and once again the empire expanded. After the battles were won, Huayna Capac chose to live in Quito rather than returning to his home in Cuzco. He built a magnificent new city in Quito, beginning what was meant to become a second Inca capital. Atahuallpa and a large number of Inca troops remained with him in Quito. Back in Cuzco, the ten *panacas* (households) of dead Sapa Incas retained their great power and continued to live in privilege and wealth. An individual *panaca* sometimes included nearly a thousand relatives and servants.

Map showing important sites in the Inca empire.
Map by XNR Productions. The Gale Group.

Around the empire, Inca control varied greatly from place to place. Some people reaped benefits from being part of the empire, while others were stifled by the requirements of labor and the loss of self-rule. The large-scale program of *mitima,* the relocation of rebellious people to far-off places, reinforced feelings of resentment toward the Incas. Thus, when the Spanish conquistadores arrived, they found many native Andeans who were willing to help them fight against the Incas.

The death of the Sapa Inca; civil war erupts

By about 1524 Huayna Capac began hearing of strange, bearded, white-skinned visitors who had arrived in

The Smallpox Epidemic

Smallpox is a severe contagious viral disease spread by particles emitted from the mouth when an infected person speaks, coughs, or sneezes. The disease begins with a high fever; then the skin erupts in pus-filled pimples over the face, back, chest, and limbs. Smallpox probably originated among humans more than ten thousand years ago in Egypt and Mesopotamia; it was often fatal. It had been around for many years in Europe by the time the Spanish began their voyages to the Americas in the early sixteenth century. In fact, the disease was so common in Europe that many people there developed immunity (resistance) to it. That meant that Europeans were able to carry the disease without starting an epidemic among themselves. The natives of the Americas, however, had no immunity to the disease. Smallpox was extremely deadly to them, and it spread rapidly after the arrival of the Spanish.

The first American smallpox epidemic occurred in 1518 on Hispaniola (a Caribbean island that is now divided into two nations: Haiti and the Dominican Republic). This outbreak killed about half of the native population there. Two years later the virus reached Mexico and was responsible for millions of deaths there—perhaps about one-third of the population. The disease is believed to have hit the Inca empire around 1525, and thousands of people died from it. By some estimates, smallpox may have killed 75 percent of the

huge ships on the coast to the north of the empire. The Sapa Inca is said to have had a premonition (a feeling, without basis in fact or reason, that something is going to happen) that these strangers would bring trouble to the Inca empire, but he probably did not realize how soon this would prove to be true. The Europeans brought smallpox with them (see box "The Smallpox Epidemic"), and the disease was probably carried down the coast by infected native people before the Spanish ever arrived in the Inca region. Soon, the people in the northern empire were falling ill and dying in great numbers. According to chronicler (a person who writes down a record of historical events arranged in order of occurrence) Juan de Betanzos in *Narrative of the Incas* (1996, originally completed in 1557), the Sapa Inca was one of the people infected: Huayna Capac "fell ill and the illness took his reason and understanding and gave him a skin irritation like leprosy

Inca empire population by the time the epidemics were over.

The smallpox epidemic changed history wherever it went, and the Incas are a prime example. The epidemic killed their ruler and the son he had chosen to be heir to the throne. Two of his other sons then attempted to claim the throne, and their conflict set off a deadly civil war that left the empire disorganized and divided. Grief over the widespread death broke the spirit of the people in the Inca empire. Many of them believed that the Europeans were using supernatural forces against them, and thus they lost their will to fight.

Some historians are currently questioning the influence of smallpox in the Inca defeat. A few recent investigators do not believe the disease arrived in the empire early enough to have been responsible for Huayna Capac's death. Sixteenth-century chroniclers observed that a plague had come to the northern part of the empire at the time of Huayna Capac's death, reaching down as far as Cuzco. For years historians have assumed that the plague must have been smallpox, which killed millions of natives throughout the two American continents. Hoping to finally confirm or disprove this assumption, archaeologists (scientists who dig up and examine artifacts, remains, and monuments of past human life) are currently searching for the mummy of Huayna Capac, which—if it exists—would be the best source of clues about the cause of his death.

[another deadly and deforming disease] that greatly weakened him." Huayna Capac and his chosen successor, a son named Ninancuyoci, both died of the disease in 1525.

After the death of the Sapa Inca and his heir, it was up to the Inca nobles in Cuzco to choose the next Sapa Inca from Huayna Capac's huge group of sons. Out of hundreds of sons, they chose Huáscar, who was the son of Huayna Capac's primary sister-wife, or *coya*. Like the Inca nobles who chose him, Huáscar lived in Cuzco. De Betanzos and some other chroniclers paint a vicious portrait of Huáscar, but others portray Huáscar as reform-oriented, wishing to change the way things were done to create better conditions in the empire. Whether out of contempt or the desire to reform, when Huáscar took the throne, he proclaimed the *panaca* system to be finished forever, saying that he would add the *panaca* lands of Inca ancestors to his own administration as

Portrait of Atahuallpa, Sapa Inca. © *Bettmann/Corbis.*

Sapa Inca. This, of course, outraged the Cuzco nobility who lived on the wealth of the *panacas*. Huáscar is said to have ordered the massacre of a large group of Incas at that time, probably to stop them from rebelling.

Meanwhile, Huáscar's half brother Atahuallpa, who according to some accounts had been his father's second choice for the throne, was still in command of a fifty-thousand-man army in Quito. Atahuallpa knew that he was likely to be killed if he returned to Cuzco, because he was considered a rival to the throne. To avoid this fate, he stayed in Quito with his father's armies for five years, despite Huáscar's constant requests that he return to Cuzco. Finally, Atahuallpa sent two army generals to speak to Huáscar on his behalf. Huáscar responded by torturing and killing the generals and sending his own army up to Quito in pursuit of Atahuallpa. Atahuallpa then gathered his own fearsome army, and the two Inca armies met in battle. It was the start of a violent civil war in the Inca empire.

For three years terrible warfare raged between the armies of the two half brothers. Tens of thousands of deaths occurred, and the people of the empire were divided in their loyalties. Finally, Atahuallpa's troops captured Huáscar. Atahuallpa showed his brother no mercy. Huáscar was tied up and forced to watch the brutal slaughter of his wives, children, friends, and relatives. Atahuallpa put his brother in prison and proclaimed himself Sapa Inca. But he never made it to Cuzco to take the throne. He was still resting with his soldiers after battle, camped out in the northern city of Cajamarca, when he learned that a group of about 160 Spaniards was marching toward Cajamarca.

It was a terrible time for the Inca empire to have an enemy approach. The civil war had killed thousands and divided the loyalties of the armies. The empire had also suffered from a smallpox epidemic that killed thousands and left the survivors grieving and dispirited. The new Sapa Inca had not had time to rally the empire under his rule, and many of the conquered peoples saw an opportunity to strike out at the empire. The Inca empire was at its weakest point ever and was about to face a frightening challenge.

Francisco Pizarro and the conquest

Francisco Pizarro (c. 1475–1541) was a Spanish soldier with no formal education. After taking part in military campaigns in Italy and Spain, he joined an expedition heading for the Americas in 1502. His first stop was Santo Domingo (a city in the present-day Dominican Republic). In 1509 he sailed on to Colombia, and from there he moved on to Panama. In 1513 he accompanied Vasco Núñez de Balboa (1475–1519) on his trip across the Isthmus of Darien to the Pacific Ocean. In the chronicle of the expedition, Pizarro is listed as the second European to see the Pacific Ocean.

Portrait of Francisco Pizarro, Spanish conquistador.

As soon as they arrived in Panama, the Spanish heard rumors of a rich land to the south called Birú. (The word was later corrupted to Peru.) Pizarro set up a partnership with two other men in Panama, Diego de Almagro (1475–1538) and a priest named Hernando de Luque (dates unknown); the three agreed to search for this land together. They set out in November 1524 and got as far south as Buenaventura on the coast of Colombia. Suffering from hunger and facing hostility from the native people, they turned back, but not before they had collected some gold and heard more tantalizing tales of a rich kingdom to the south.

Pizarro, Almagro, and Luque put together another expedition in 1526. Sailing from Panama with 160 men, they once again reached the bay at Buenaventura. They sent the

Francisco Pizarro leading his troops through the Andes on his way to Cajamarca.
© Bettmann/Corbis.

ship's pilot ahead to see what he could find. He was the first European to see Peru, and he returned to the ship with stories about a heavily populated land, rich with gold and silver. The entire expedition then sailed southward to the city of Tumbes, which stands on the southern shore of the Gulf of Guayaquil (on the border between present-day Ecuador and Peru). At this large and beautiful seaport, the inhabitants came out to greet them in boats made from balsa wood. (A balsa is a tropical tree with wood that is lightweight and often used for rafts and floats.) The natives brought them a wide variety of exotic foods and presented them with llamas (South American mammals with soft, fleecy wool), which the Europeans had never seen before. Pizarro then sent two of his men 200 miles (322 kilometers) south, where they heard about a great city further inland, the capital of a rich and powerful kingdom. The city was Cuzco. Lacking the resources to continue, they returned to Panama.

Pizarro returned to Spain in 1529 to get funding and permission to conquer the rich kingdom in Peru. The Spanish crown appointed him governor of the as yet unknown province. He then returned to Panama accompanied by his four half brothers, his partner Almagro, 180 other men, and 27 horses.

Pizarro and his men left Panama in early January 1531 to conquer Peru. The group traveled once again to Tumbes, which they found destroyed. Pizarro learned of the civil war among the Incas and heard that Atahuallpa was camped at the city of Cajamarca, which was much closer to Tumbes than the distant Inca capital of Cuzco. Before leaving Tumbes, Pizarro received some reinforcements (more men). In September 1532 his expedition set off, traveling across cold and mountainous terrain. They reached Cajamarca in November.

The meeting of Incas and Spaniards

Atahuallpa had learned that the Spanish were coming, but his messenger had told him that they were not warriors and that there were less than two hundred men. The Inca troops stationed at Cajamarca numbered about forty thousand, so Atahuallpa probably felt secure. As Pizarro and his men marched into the city, they were surrounded by warriors on all sides, and the chroniclers write of the Spaniards' terrible fear as they gazed about them. But the Inca soldiers had reason to fear as well. The Spaniards rode in on horses, and none of the Inca soldiers had ever seen a horse before. The Spaniards also had cannons and other advanced weapons, and they did not show their fear as they marched into the city's main square.

Pizarro sent two of his men—his brother Hernando (c. 1475–1578) and Spanish explorer Hernando de Soto (1500–1542)—with an interpreter to ask for a meeting with Atahuallpa. (On one of their earlier expeditions, the Spaniards had kidnapped two Incas and taught them Spanish so they could act as interpreters.) When the two messengers were brought to Atahuallpa, one of the emperor's wives held a screen before his face so the visitors could not look upon him, as was customary. De Soto, unhappy at being treated as an inferior, aggressively rushed his horse at Atahuallpa in an effort to scare him, but the Sapa Inca did not flinch. After discussion, he agreed to meet with Pizarro in the Cajamarca plaza the next day. Most historians believe that Atahuallpa never suspected the outnumbered strangers would try to attack; he let his guard down, and he would soon pay for that mistake.

The next day, November 16, 1532, the Spaniards stationed themselves in groups within the buildings surrounding the Cajamarca plaza, in preparation for an attack. Atahuallpa, on the other hand, put together an elaborate ceremonial procession for the meeting. Arriving in the plaza on a litter (an enclosed platform, usually borne on the shoulders of servants) carried by eighty Inca lords dressed in blue tunics, Atahuallpa was adorned in gold, emeralds, silver, and parrot feathers. The Incas accompanying him numbered in the thousands, but they were unarmed. Upon reaching the plaza, the Sapa Inca found only an interpreter and a Spanish missionary to greet him. Before launching an attack, the

Spanish customarily gave native peoples a chance to convert to Catholicism. The Spanish missionary handed Atahuallpa a Bible and spoke to him briefly about the Christian religion. The Sapa Inca was curious and looked at the Bible. Finding it altogether unsatisfactory as a sacred object, he threw it contemptuously to the ground. The Spaniards then attacked. Though they were instructed not to kill Atahuallpa, Pizarro's troops slaughtered an estimated six thousand unarmed Incas on the plaza that day. Atahuallpa was taken prisoner. The Inca troops posted outside Cajamarca fled when they heard what had happened.

The death of Atahuallpa

As a prisoner of war, Atahuallpa impressed his captors greatly. He quickly learned Spanish and even learned to play chess and to read. Realizing that the Spaniards were obsessed with gold, he offered to pay them for his freedom. Atahuallpa promised to fill the room where he was being held prisoner up to the ceiling with gold and to give the Spaniards twice as much silver. His aides then began collecting gold and silver, mainly from Cuzco, and made good on his promise. Load after load of gold and silver began to stream into Cajamarca from Cuzco. While this was going on, Atahuallpa ordered the murder of his brother, who was still being held prisoner by Atahuallpa's army. Atahuallpa probably feared that Huáscar might bribe the Spaniards with gold and silver and enlist their help in a war against Atahuallpa.

None of Atahuallpa's actions did him any good. The Spaniards took the gold but did not fulfill their end of the bargain. Instead they put Atahuallpa on trial for plots against the Spanish crown and for killing his brother. They sentenced him to death. Atahuallpa quickly accepted that his captors were going to kill him. However, when he realized that they planned to burn him alive, he became visibly upset for the first time. For an Inca, eternal life could only be achieved if the body was left intact. Burning was far worse than other kinds of death. He agreed to convert to Christianity if the Spaniards would agree to kill him in another way and give his body to his people to be mummified (preserved through a complex procedure that involves taking out the organs, filling the body cavity with preservative substances, and then drying out the body to prevent decay). The Spanish agreed, and on August 29, 1533, they killed him by strangulation. But cruelly, they burned part of his body after his death and then buried him.

The conquistadores in Cuzco

Pizarro received reinforcements and proceeded to Cuzco. He brought with him Manco Inca, a half brother of Atahuallpa and Huáscar, who had agreed to serve as a ruler under Spanish command. The Spaniards wanted to have a royal Inca in office—one they could fully control—to gain authority over the Inca populations. At first this plan worked. The Incas in Cuzco welcomed the Spanish and accepted Manco Inca as the Sapa Inca. They hoped that this would be the end of a turbulent time and that life could return to normal. But it was soon clear that this was not to be. The Spanish under Pizarro ruled Cuzco with cruelty, violence, and disrespect. They raped, tortured, and enslaved its people.

Illustration of Francisco Pizarro imprisoning the Inca ruler Atahuallpa.
© Bettmann/Corbis.

When he saw how the Spanish treated his people, Manco Inca was no longer easy to control. After a time, the Spanish imprisoned him. Recognizing that the Spanish would destroy the Inca culture, Manco Inca managed to make an escape from Cuzco in 1536. He hid in the wilderness and sent word throughout the empire that he would lead a rebellion against the Spanish. He asked for Andean peoples in surrounding areas to join him in the fight. Rejoicing in this plan for revolt, Andean people rushed to the Cuzco area by the thousands to fight the hated Spanish.

The revolt of Manco Inca

Manco Inca spearheaded a brilliant attack on the Spanish-occupied city of Cuzco. The native forces began by

Atahuallpa in manacles awaiting his death by strangulation. © *Bettmann/Corbis.*

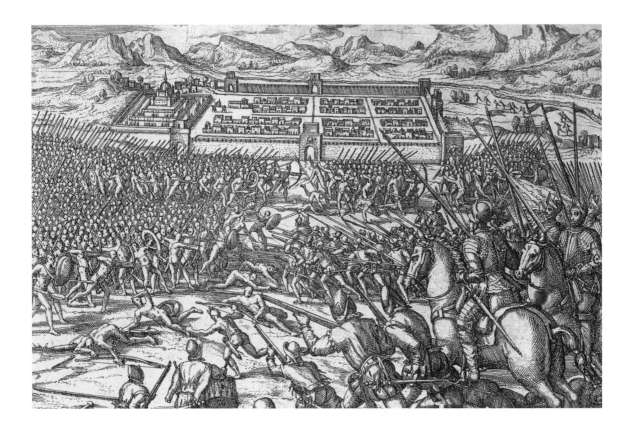

Engraving showing the
**Spanish and Andean battle
for Cuzco.** *The Art
Archive/Biblioteca Nazionale
Marciana Venice/Dagli Orti.*

shooting red-hot stones from their slings, setting the capital on fire. The two hundred Spanish soldiers occupying Cuzco retreated to Sacsahuaman (pronounced sox-ah-wah-MAHN), the stone fortress perched on a hill just north of the city. Using cannons and harquebuses (heavy matchlock guns invented during the fifteenth century), the small force was able to hold out against an army of about forty thousand Andean warriors led by Manco Inca. The Spanish were held in the fortress for nearly a year, cut off from supplies, and would have perished if they had not received help from some Incas within the city who had joined forces with the conquerors. Finally, Manco Inca's soldiers grew weary and began to leave; they needed to go home to tend their crops. Spain sent reinforcements, and the siege (takeover) of Cuzco failed. By that time, an estimated six million Incas had perished from smallpox and war.

The Spanish conquistadors and the priests and missionaries who accompanied them settled into their new home in Peru. Some of their initial acts included the complete destruction of the remains of the great Inca civilization. All the gold and silver they could find—the gold covering the sacred buildings, the intricate metalwork found in burial chambers and graves, and the beautiful gold jewelry and figurines found in the palaces of the Incas—was stolen, melted down, and sent back to Spain. The Spaniards destroyed Inca temples and burned the mummies of the Sapa Incas. Spanish priests went to work converting the Andean people to Christianity.

The rebel kingdom

After the failure of the siege of Cuzco, Manco Inca retreated to a remote, heavily forested, and mountainous area known as Vilcabamba, northwest of Cuzco. There, with a small force of about twenty thousand rebels, the Sapa Inca continued to launch occasional raids against the Spanish. In Vilcabamba, the Incas built new temples and fortresses, creating an Inca capital in isolation. Archaeologists are still trying to penetrate the harsh lands of Vilcabamba to learn more about the last days of the Inca empire in exile. In the first decade of the twenty-first century, they discovered new Inca-era sites in Vilcabamba, and more information about this mysterious last kingdom should become available in the decades to come.

Though the Incas were in hiding, the Spanish were still struggling in Cuzco. Greed and power struggles undermined the Spaniards' attempts to set up their own empire. A longtime conflict between Pizarro and Almagro eventually resulted in the assassination of Almagro. Factions faithful to Almagro then killed Pizarro in 1541. The killers of Pizarro were forced to flee from Cuzco and ended up in Vilcabamba, where they asked Manco Inca for refuge. This was readily granted; Manco Inca and all his subjects hated Pizarro and welcomed his killers. These Spaniards lived in Vilcabamba for three years with the Incas, but in 1545 they decided to return to Cuzco. They stabbed the Sapa Inca to death before they left.

After the Spaniards killed Manco Inca, the rule of the rebel kingdom in Vilcabamba fell to his three sons: Sayri Tupa Inca; Titu Cusi; and Tupac Amarú. Sayri Tupa Inca was only five years old when his reign as Sapa Inca began. In 1552 the king of Spain made attempts to communicate with

The Last Words of the Last Conquistador

Mansio Serra de Leguizamón (1512–1590) was a young Spanish conquistador who arrived in the Inca empire with Francisco Pizarro's expedition at the age of twenty and took part in the bloody conquest of the Incas. He remained in Peru for the rest of his life, and by the time of his death at the age of seventy-eight, he was believed to be the last living Spanish conquistador. The following is an excerpt from his last will and testament, addressed to the Spanish king and written in 1589 in Cuzco:

> It should be known to His Most Catholic Majesty that we found these [the Inca] realms in such order that there was not a thief, nor a vicious man, nor an adulteress, nor were there fallen women admitted among them, nor were they an immoral people, being content and honest in their labour. And that their lands, forests, mines, pastures, dwellings and all kinds of produce were regulated and distributed among them in such a manner that each person possessed his own property without any other seizing or occupying it.... All things, from the greatest to the smallest, had their place and order. And that the Incas were feared, obeyed and respected by their subjects as being very capable and skilled in their rule, as were their governors....
>
> But now they have come to such a pass in offence of God, owing to the bad example we have set them in all things, that these natives from doing no evil have changed into people who now do no good, or very little.... For now those who were once obeyed as kings and lords of these realms, as Incas with power and riches, have fallen to such poverty and necessity that they are the poorest of this kingdom and forced to perform the lowest and most menial of tasks, as porters of our goods and servants of our houses and as sweepers of our streets.

Sayri Tupa Inca, hoping to end the rebellion and bring the Inca kings back to Cuzco. The Sapa Inca's brothers sent him off to meet with the Spanish officials in Cuzco, remaining in Vilcabamba to see what would become of him. Sayri Tupa Inca remained in Cuzco, where the Spanish converted him to Christianity. Then, in 1558, Sayri Tupa Inca was poisoned by an unknown assassin.

When Titu Cusi became king after his brother's murder, the Incas and the Spanish began another round of fighting. During the eight years of warfare that ensued, the Spaniards raped and killed many members of Titu Cusi's family. Finally, Titu Cusi decided to end the war in the hopes of ending the violence. He declared his allegiance to the king of Spain and allowed Spanish priests to bring the Christian religion into the capital at Vilcabamba. Then Titu Cusi died sud-

Tupac Amarú, the last Sapa Inca. He was beheaded by the Spaniards in 1572. *The Art Archive/Museo Historico Nacional Buenos Aires/ Dagli Orti.*

denly. His remaining brother, Tupac Amarú, believed that Titu Cusi had been poisoned. The exile community erupted in anger and destroyed all traces of Christianity at Vilcabamba.

Tupac Amarú became Sapa Inca in 1571. Around the same time Spanish noble Francisco de Toledo (1515–1582) became the viceroy (the governor of a country or province who rules as the representative of a king or sovereign) of Peru. Not long after he took office, Toledo sent messengers to the Inca capital at Vilcabamba with a communication for the Sapa Inca. Tupac Amarú despised the Spaniards and their religion, and he did not want to deal with them at all. Tupac Amarú had the messengers killed. Toledo immediately began a plan to go to war with the exiled kingdom. In 1572 an army of about 250 Spanish soldiers with a large supporting unit of native Andeans entered Vilcabamba. They met with fierce resistance from the Incas but finally penetrated to the Inca capital. By the time the Spaniards arrived, the Incas had burned their city and fled. The Spanish pursued them into the jungle. After days of tracking him, they captured Tupac Amarú, the last Inca king. They brought him back to Cuzco, gave him a brief and unfair trial and tried to convert him to Christianity. Though many Spanish priests and officials pleaded for the last Sapa Inca's life, he was sentenced to death. At a huge gathering of more than ten thousand people, including the mourning Incas, Tupac Amarú was beheaded. The Spanish rounded up other Inca royalty and banished them to faraway places. The Inca empire had ended forever.

After Tupac Amarú was captured and beheaded, the Spanish stuck his head on a pike and placed it in the plaza of Cuzco as a warning to rebels. Then they noticed that the Inca people were visiting the head nightly as if in worship. The Spanish had hoped that the head would instill fear, not inspire reverence. Since it was not having the intended effect, they took the head down and buried it. When the head was buried, the Incas found reason to hope. According to one Andean myth, Tupac Amarú's vanished head is slowly growing its body back. When the body is complete, the Incas will return to rule their land.

The Andean peoples after the Incas

The populations of the native Andean peoples may have been reduced by as much as 75 percent by the civil war and smallpox. Native populations were then decimated by war with the Spanish. Later the Spanish reduced Andean populations even further by forcing native people to work in dangerous silver mines, where many lost their lives. They also denied the Andeans land and the means to survive, condemning them to a slow but certain demise. According to some estimates, by 1780 the population of native people in the Andean region may have been about one-tenth of what it was during the era of Inca dominance. In 1780, the frustration of the native people boiled over. Tupac Amarú II (c. 1742–1781), an Andean leader who claimed to be a grandson of the last Inca king, demanded that the Spanish return the rule of the Andean highlands to the native people. His call rallied tens of thousands of native people and mestizos (people of mixed native and Spanish descent) to join him in an uprising. The Spanish were too strong for them, and thousands of the rebels were killed. Tupac Amarú II was captured and tortured to death. When more rebellions followed, the Spanish tracked down the descendants of the Inca kings, executing some of them and sending others to jail.

Peru declared its independence from the Spanish in 1821, but the policies of the new government only deepened the poverty of the native Andean people. It was not until 1969—almost four hundred years after the fall of the last Inca king—that land reform in Peru offered some hope of justice for the descendants of the Incas. Modern Peru has struggled to create a more fair and multicultural society, but it has been plagued by economic problems, poor governments, and terrorism.

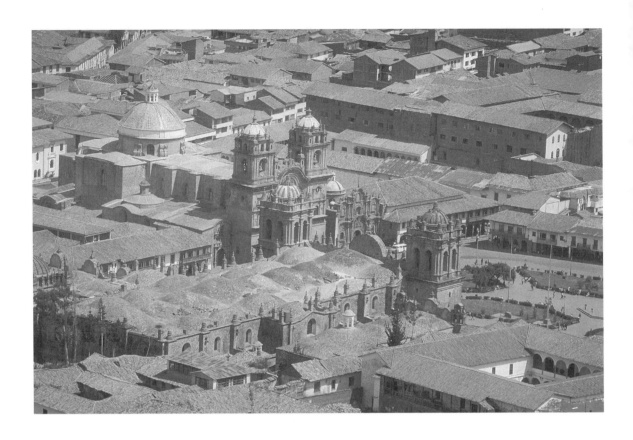

View of present-day Cuzco, with its Spanish-style buildings and rooftops built on top of Inca streets and structures. © *Brian Vikander/Corbis.*

Descendants of the Inca empire today

About half the population of Peru is made up of Quechua-speaking (pronounced KECH-wah) Andean peoples—descendants of the Inca empire. Traditions of the pre-Columbian (existing before Spanish explorer Christopher Columbus arrived in the Americas in 1492) past are obvious in modern Andean culture, particularly in rural areas. Poor highland farmers still operate within the *ayllu* (pronounced EYE-yoo) system, sharing their farmland and working communally in groups of extended families. These groups still follow the principle of *ayni,* or give-and-take, willingly helping others and expecting to be paid back in kind at a later date. In small highland villages, some of the older people have not learned the Spanish language and speak only Quechua. In these remote places, the Inca culture thrives—the food, religion, and music of the ancient Andes remain central to the lives of the people.

In the cities of Peru, however, some of the traditions are disappearing. The sacred buildings of Cuzco symbolize the imposition of Spanish culture on Inca tradition. Though the strong stone walls of the ancient buildings are still clearly visible, newer Spanish-style buildings have been built right on top of them.

Quechua was the language of the Inca state. It is now spoken by nearly eight million people in Peru alone. Between one million and two million people in Ecuador use Quechua, and one million residents of Bolivia also speak the language. Unlike most other native South American languages, Quechua is an official language, recognized by the government of Peru and given the same status as Spanish. Although it does not happen often, it is acceptable for Peruvian senators and congresspeople to give congressional speeches in Quechua.

The most significant crafts produced by modern native Andeans are textiles. Women throughout the Andes can be seen spinning wool almost all day, even while they are sitting at the market or waiting for a bus. Both llama and sheep wool are used. The Andeans are skilled weavers, and their products are increasingly in demand for the tourist and export markets.

A recent surge of interest in the ruins of the ancient Andean civilizations has brought many tourists to the former Inca empire. The tourists bring in badly needed money and create jobs in many impoverished areas. But they also damage the fragile environment and the ancient ruins. The Andean people now face a new challenge: to reap the benefits of the world's interest in their past while protecting the artifacts (items made or used by humans of earlier times) and remains (bones) of their ancient ancestors.

For More Information

Books

Betanzos, Juan de. *Narrative of the Incas*. Originally completed in 1557. Translated by Roland Hamilton. Austin: University of Texas Press, 1996.

Davies, Nigel. *The Ancient Kingdoms of Peru*. London and New York: Penguin, 1997.

Stirling, Stuart. *The Last Conquistador: Mansio Serra de Leguizamón and the Conquest of the Incas.* Phoenix Mill, Thrupp, Stroud, Gloucestershire, UK: Sutton Publishing, 1999.

Time-Life Books. *Incas: Lords of Gold and Glory.* Alexandria, VA: Time-Life Books, 1992.

Web Site

Jacobs, James Q. "Tupac Amarú: The Life, Times, and Execution of the Last Inca." http://www.jqjacobs.net/andes/tupac_amaru.html (accessed on October 12, 2004).

Where to Learn More

Books

Adams, Richard E. W. *Ancient Civilizations of the New World.* Boulder, CO: Westview Press, 1997.

Adovasio, J. M., with Jake Page. *The First Americans: In Pursuit of Archaeology's Greatest Mystery.* New York: Random House, 2002.

Betanzos, Juan de. *Narrative of the Incas.* Translated by Roland Hamilton. Austin: University of Texas Press, 1996.

Burger, Richard L. *Chavín and the Origins of Andean Civilization.* London and New York: Thames and Hudson, 1992.

Clendinnen, Inga. *Aztecs: An Interpretation.* Cambridge, UK: Cambridge University Press, 1991.

Coe, Michael D. *Mexico: From the Olmecs to the Aztecs,* fourth ed. New York: Thames and Hudson, 1994.

Coe, Michael D., and Mark Van Stone. *Reading the Maya Glyphs.* London and New York: Thames and Hudson, 2001.

Coe, Michael, Dean Snow, and Elizabeth Benson. *Atlas of Ancient America.* New York: Facts on File, 1986.

Davies, Nigel. *The Ancient Kingdoms of Peru.* London: Penguin, 1997.

Dewar, Elaine. *Bones: Discovering the First Americans.* New York: Carroll and Graf, 2001.

Díaz, Bernal (del Castillo). *The Conquest of New Spain.* Translated by J. M. Cohen. London and New York: Penguin Books, 1963.

Fagan, Brian. *Kingdoms of Gold, Kingdoms of Jade: The Americas Before Columbus.* London and New York: Thames and Hudson, 1991.

Gallenkamp, Charles. *Maya: The Riddle and Rediscovery of a Lost Civilization,* third ed. New York: Viking, 1985.

Galvin, Irene Flum. *The Ancient Maya.* New York: Benchmark Books, 1997.

Henderson, John S. *The World of the Ancient Maya,* second edition. Ithaca and London: Cornell University Press, 1997.

Hull, Robert. *The Aztecs.* Austin, TX: Steck-Vaughn, 1998.

Incas: Lords of Gold and Glory. Editors of Time-Life Books. Alexandria, VA: Time-Life Books, 1992.

Katz, Friedrich. *The Ancient American Civilizations.* London: Phoenix Press, 2000.

Lanyon, Anna. *Malinche's Conquest.* New South Wales, Australia: Allen & Unwin, 1999.

León-Portilla, Miguel, ed. *The Broken Spears: The Aztec Account of the Conquest of Mexico.* Translated from Nahuatl into Spanish by Angel Maria Garibay K. English translation by Lysander Kemp. Boston: Beacon Press, 1992.

León-Portilla, Miguel. *Fifteen Poets of the Aztec World.* Norman: University of Oklahoma Press, 1992.

The Magnificent Maya. Editors of Time-Life Books. Alexandria, VA: 1993.

Malpass, Michael A. *Daily Life in the Inca Empire.* Westport, CT: Greenwood Press, 1996.

Meyer, Carolyn. *The Mystery of the Ancient Maya,* revised edition. New York: Margaret K. McElderry Books, 1995.

Meyer, Michael C., and William L. Sherman. *The Course of Mexican History,* fifth ed. New York and Oxford: Oxford University Press, 1995.

Morris, Craig, and Adriana Von Hagen. *The Inka Empire: And Its Andean Origins.* New York: Abbeville Press, 1993.

Morris, Craig, and Adriana Von Hagen. *The Cities of the Ancient Andes.* New York: Thames and Hudson, 1998.

Moseley, Michael E. *The Incas and Their Ancestors: The Archaeology of Peru.* London and New York: Thames and Hudson, 1992.

Montgomery, John. *Tikal: An Illustrated History.* New York: Hippocrene Books, 2001.

Newsome, Elizabeth A. *Trees of Paradise and Pillars of the World: The Serial Stela Cycle of "18-Rabbit-God K," King of Copan.* Austin: University of Texas Press, 2001.

Sabloff, Jeremy A. *The Cities of Ancient Mexico: Reconstructing a Lost World,* revised edition. New York and London: Thames and Hudson, 1997.

Schele, Linda, and Mary Miller. *The Blood of Kings: Dynasty and Ritual in Maya Art.* New York: W.W. Norton, 1986.

Schobinger, Juan. *The First Americans.* Grand Rapids, MI: William B. Eerdmans Publishing Company, 1994.

Stirling, Stuart. *The Last Conquistador: Manso Serra de Leguizamón and the Conquest of the Incas.* Phoenix Mill, Stroud, Gloucestershire, UK: Sutton Publishing, 1999.

Thomas, Hugh. *Conquest: Montezuma, Cortés, and the Fall of Old Mexico.* New York: Simon & Schuster, 1993.

Wood, Tim. *The Aztecs.* New York: Viking, 1992.

Periodicals

McClintock, Jack. "The Nasca Lines Solution." *Discover,* December 2000.

Morell, Virginia. "Empires Across the Andes." *National Geographic,* June 2002.

Wade, Nicholas, and John Noble Wilford. "New World Ancestors Lose 12,000 Years." *New York Times,* July 25, 2003.

Wright, Karen. "First Americans (Origins of Man)." *Discover.* February 1999.

Web Sites

"Aztec Books, Documents, and Writing," *Azteca.com.* Available at http://www.azteca.net/aztec/nahuatl/writing.html (accessed December 8, 2004).

Begley, Sharon, and Andrew Murr. "The First Americans." *Newsweek,* April 26, 1999. Available at http://www.abotech.com/Articles/firstamericans.htm (accessed December 8, 2004).

Dillehay, Tom. "Tracking the First Americans." *Nature,* Vol. 425, September 4, 2003. Available at http://www.nature.com (accessed December 8, 2004).

Donnan, Christopher B. "Iconography of the Moche: Unraveling the Mystery of the Warrior–Priest." *National Geographic,* Vol. 174, No. 4, October 1988, pp. 551–55. Available at

http://muweb.millersville.edu/~columbus/data/art/DONNAN01.ART (accessed December 8, 2004).

"Early Archaeology in the Maya Lowlands." University of California. Available at http://id-archserve.ucsb.edu/Anth3/Courseware/History/Maya.html (accessed December 8, 2004).

"Early Maya Murals at San Bartolo, Guatemala." Peabody Museum of Archaeology and Ethnology. Available at http://www.peabody.harvard.edu/SanBartolo.htm (accessed December 8, 2004).

Ebersole, Rene S. "What Lies Beneath: Discovery of a Maya Palace in Guatemala, and Insights into the Maya Civilization around Cancuen." *Current Science,* November 17, 2000. Available at http://www.findarti

cles.com/p/articles/mi_m0BFU/is_6_86/ai_67326281 (accessed December 8, 2004).

Hooker, Richard. "Civilizations in America." *World Civilizations, Washington State University.* Available at http://www.wsu.edu/~dee/CIVAMRCA/MAYAS.HTM (accessed December 8, 2004).

"The Lost Pyramids of Caral." *BBC: Science and Nature: TV and Radio Follow-Up.* January 31, 2002. Available at http://www.bbc.co.uk/science/horizon/2001/caraltrans.shtml (accessed December 8, 2004).

Lovgren, Stefan. "Masks, Other Finds Suggest Early Maya Flourished." *National Geographic News,* May 5, 2004. Available at http://news.nationalgeographic.com/news/2004/05/0504_040505_mayamasks.html (accessed December 8, 2004).

Lovgren, Stefan. "Who Were the First Americans?" *National Geographic,* September 3, 2003. Available at http://www.nationalgeographic.com (accessed December 8, 2004).

Marcus, Joyce. "First Dates: The Maya Calendar and Writing System Were Not the Only Ones in Mesoamerica—or Even the Earliest." *Natural History,* April 1991, pp. 22–25. Available at http://muweb.millersville.edu/~columbus/data/ant/MARCUS01.ANT (accessed December 8, 2004.

Maya Civilization. Canadian Museum of Civilization Corporation. "Maya Calendars"available at http://www.civilization.ca/civil/maya/mmc06eng.html (accessed August 17, 2004). "Maya Writing and Hieroglyphics" available at http://www.civilization.ca/civil/maya/mmc04eng.html (accessed December 8, 2004).

"The Olmec." *Mesoweb: An Exploration of Mesoamerican Cultures.* Available at http://www.mesoweb.com/olmec/ (accessed December 8, 2004.)

Pringle, Heather. "Temples of Doom." *Discover,* March, 1999. Available at http://www.findarticles.com/cf_dls/m1511/3_20/54359911/p6/article.jhtml?term= (accessed December 8, 2004.)

Parsell, D. L. "Oldest Intact Maya Mural Found in Guatemala." *National Geographic News,* March 22, 2002. Available at http://news.nationalgeographic.com/news/2002/03/0312_0314_mayamurals.html (accessed December 8, 2004).

Ross, John F. "First City in the New World? Peru's Caral Suggests Civilization Emerged in the Americas 1,000 Years Earlier Than Experts Believed." *Smithsonian.* August 2002. Available at http://www.smithsonianmag.si.edu/smithsonian/issues02/aug02/caral.html (accessed December 8, 2004.)

Rostworowski, Maria. "The Incas." Available at http://incas.perucultural.org.pe/english/hissurg4.htm (accessed December 8, 2004.)

Schuster, Angela M. H. "New Tomb at Teotihuacan." *Archaeology, Online Features.* December 4, 1998. Available at http://www.archaeology.org/online/features/mexico/ (accessed December 8, 2004).

Williams, Patrick Ryan, Michael E. Moseley, and Donna J. Nash. "Empires of the Andes." *Scientific American: Discovering Archaeology,* March/April 2000. Available at www.aymara.org/biblio/baul.html (accessed December 8, 2004).

Index

A

Aboriginal, *1:* 20
Acamapichtli, *2:* 471, 480, 484
Aclla, 1: 206–7, 207 (ill.), 222, 229
Acllahuaci, 1: 156, 159, 200, 207, 208 (ill.)
Acosta, José de, *1:* 23
Adams, Richard E.W., *2:* 425
Administration, *1:* 180. *See also* Government
Administrative center, *1:* 122
Administrators, *1:* 60, 88, 138, 156; *2:* 372
Adobe, *1:* 88, 96, 106, 138
Adovasio, James M., *1:* 26, 33
Adultery, *1:* 193
Afterlife, *1:* 205; *2:* 375–80
Agriculture. *See also* Irrigation
    Aztec, *2:* 461–62, 496–97, 498 (ill.)
    Caral, *1:* 52
    defined, *1:* 2
    development of, *1:* 4–5, 6
    early Andean, *1:* 35, 43, 44 (ill.), 52
    early Mesoamerican, *2:* 264–65, 266 (ill.)
    Inca, *1:* 194–95, 195 (ill.), 196 (ill.), 202, 216
    kingdom of Chimor, *1:* 148, 149–50
    labor for, *1:* 224–27
    Maya, *2:* 422–25
    Olmec, *2:* 287–88
    raised farming system, *1:* 116–17
    slash-and-burn, *2:* 288, 423–25, 424 (ill.)
    Teotihuacán, *2:* 327
    Tiwanaku, *1:* 116–17
    Toltec, *2:* 450–51
    Wari, *1:* 128, 129 (ill.), 131
Ahaw kings, *2:* 380–85
Ahuitzotl, *2:* 462–63, 474, 485, 532
Ainu, *1:* 29
Akab Szib, *2:* 366
Akapana pyramid, *1:* 110–11
Alcoholic beverages
    chicha, 1: 36, 122, 131, 156, 233
    pulque, 2: 447, 524–25

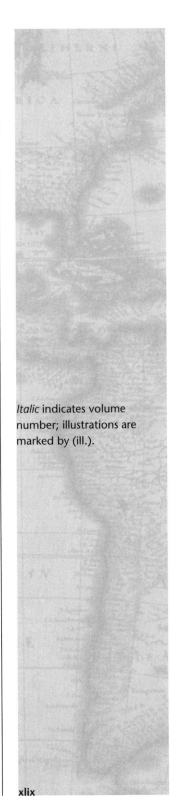

Italic indicates volume number; illustrations are marked by (ill.).

Alcohuans, *2:* 480–81

Aliens, *1:* 83

Alliances, *2:* 416. *See also* Triple Alliance

Almagro, Diego de, *1:* 247–48, 254

Alpaca
  defined, *1:* 36
  description of, *1:* 42, 43
  kingdom of Chimor and, *1:* 149
  modern day, *1:* 259
  Tiwanaku and, *1:* 118

Altar Q, *2:* 364–65, 364 (ill.)

Altars, *2:* 398

Altiplano, *1:* 36, 38, 40, 40 (ill.)

Alva, Walter, *1:* 94–95

Alvarado, Pedro de, *2:* 541

Amaranth, *2:* 524, 525

Amerindians
  ancestors of, *1:* 31
  defined, *1:* 20; *2:* 334, 502, 530
  genetics of, *1:* 31–32
  languages of, *1:* 32–33; *2:* 434
  post-Spanish conquest, *2:* 546–50

Anáhuac. *See* Valley of Mexico

Anasazi, *2:* 453

Ancestor worship
  Inca, *1:* 204
  kingdom of Chimor, *1:* 150–51
  Wari, *1:* 132–33
  Zapotec, *2:* 309

Ancient civilizations, *1:* 8–15. *See also* specific civilizations

Andean region. *See also* Early Andeans
  after the Inca, *1:* 257–59
  description of, *1:* 37–39, 38 (ill.), 39 (ill.), 40 (ill.)
  early civilizations, *1:* 8–12, 8 (ill.), 10 (ill.), 35–57

Animal sacrifices
  Inca, *1:* 205, 205 (ill.)
  Maya, *2:* 379, 380, 383
  Wari, *1:* 132

Animal spirit companions, *2:* 289–90, 377

Animals. *See* Domestic animals

Anonymous History of Trujillo (1604), *1:* 145

Anthropology, *1:* 20–21

Antisuyu, *1:* 158

Apartment buildings, *2:* 321–22, 453

Apos, 1: 187, 223

Aqueducts, *1:* 76, 78–79; *2:* 465

Archaeological excavations, *2:* 262, 334. *See also* specific sites

Archaeology, *1:* 2, 16, 16 (ill.), 20; *2:* 334

Architecture
  Aztec, *2:* 463, 464, 464 (ill.), 523–24
  Cancuen, *2:* 417
  Chan Chan, *1:* 140–42, 140 (ill.), 141 (ill.)
  Chavín, *1:* 61–65
  Chichén Itzá, *2:* 366 (ill.), 387 (ill.)
  Cival, *2:* 349
  Copán, *2:* 335–36, 336 (ill.)
  Cotton pre-Ceramic era, *1:* 45–48
  defined, *1:* 36
  Inca, *1:* 10–11, 159–65, 160 (ill.), 162 (ill.), 211–12, 212 (ill.), 231–33
  kingdom of Chimor, *1:* 139–43, 140 (ill.), 141 (ill.), 151–52, 151 (ill.)
  Maya, *2:* 349, 351–57, 355 (ill.), 359–62, 359 (ill.), 360 (ill.), 364–67, 366 (ill.), 367 (ill.), 398
  Moche, *1:* 89–91, 90 (ill.), 91 (ill.)
  modern Cuzco, *1:* 258 (ill.)
  monumental, *1:* 2–3, 37, 45–48, 48 (ill.), 61
  Nazca, *1:* 76–77
  Olmec, *2:* 282, 283, 284
  Palenque, *2:* 337 (ill.), 359–61, 359 (ill.)
  residential, *1:* 231–33, 231 (ill.); *2:* 321–22, 427–28, 428 (ill.), 464
  Spanish-style, *1:* 258 (ill.), 259
  Teotihuacán, *2:* 318–22, 319 (ill.), 321 (ill.), 323 (ill.), 331
  Tiwanaku, *1:* 108–14, 110 (ill.), 111 (ill.), 112 (ill.), 113
  Toltec, *2:* 441–44, 442 (ill.), 443 (ill.), 455, 455 (ill.)
  Wari, *1:* 124–28, 125 (ill.)
  Zapotec, *2:* 304–6, 304 (ill.)

Arctic, *1:* 20

Armies. *See* Military forces

Arrow Knights, *2:* 493

Art

    Aztec, *2:* 512 (ill.), 513–20, 515 (ill.)

    Chavín, *1:* 70–72, 71 (ill.)

    Inca, *1:* 210–16, 213 (ill.)

    kingdom of Chimor, *1:* 144, 144 (ill.), 147 (ill.), 148–49, 149 (ill.), 151–52, 210

    Maya, *2:* 352, 362, 391, 396–404, 397 (ill.), 399 (ill.)

    Moche, *1:* 87, 99–102, 100 (ill.), 101 (ill.)

    Olmec, *2:* 285–86, 292–93, 293 (ill.)

    Sumerian, *1:* 9

    Teotihuacán, *2:* 329–31, 330 (ill.)

    Tiwanaku, *1:* 118 (ill.), 119–20

    Toltec, *2:* 444, 454–55, 455 (ill.)

    Wari, *1:* 133–34, 134 (ill.)

    Zapotec, *2:* 310, 311 (ill.)

Artifacts, *1:* 2, 20, 94; *2:* 262, 277, 316, 334, 438

Artisans

    Aztec, *2:* 497–98, 513–14

    Cancuen, *2:* 417, 419

    Inca, *1:* 196, 224

    kingdom of Chimor, *1:* 148–49

    Teotihuacán, *2:* 320, 326–27

Asian migrants, *1:* 28–31, 32

Aspero, Peru, *1:* 46–47

Astronomers, *2:* 392

Astronomical observatories

    defined, *1:* 76; *2:* 348

    Maya, *2:* 354, 367, 412

    Nazca, *1:* 81

    Zapotec, *2:* 305–6, 308 (ill.), 312

Astronomy

    defined, *2:* 316

    Inca, *1:* 219–20

    Maya, *2:* 349, 411–13

    Olmec, *2:* 296

Atahuallpa

    death of, *1:* 250–51, 252 (ill.)

    Huáscar and, *1:* 176–77, 246, 246 (ill.)

    Huayna Capac and, *1:* 243

    Pizarro and, *1:* 9–10, 248–51, 251 (ill.)

    rule of, *1:* 171, 182

    wife of, *1:* 168

Atlantes, 2: 438, 443, 450 (ill.), 455

Atlatls, 2: 455, 495

Atole, 2: 524

Audiencias, 1: 141

Authoritarian governments, *1:* 122

Aveni, Anthony, *1:* 84

Avenue of the Dead, *2:* 318–19

Aviary, *2:* 502

Axayácatl, *2:* 485

Axe bearers, *2:* 385

Axes, jade, *2:* 351

Ayacucho Valley, Peru, *1:* 123–24, 128

Ayar Anca, *1:* 170

Ayar Cachi, *1:* 170, 171

Ayar Manco. *See* Manco Capac

Ayar Uchu, *1:* 170

Ayllu

    daily life in, *1:* 225–26

    defined, *1:* 36, 106, 156, 180, 200, 222

    development of, *1:* 55

    Inca, *1:* 171, 185, 203–4, 225–26

    present day, *1:* 258

    Tiwanaku, *1:* 115–16

    worship, *1:* 203–4

Aymara people, *1:* 107, 116, 117

Aymoray, *1:* 207

Ayni, 1: 116, 188, 258

Azángaro, Peru, *1:* 124 (ill.), 126

Azcapotzalco, Mexico, *2:* 471, 481, 484

Aztecs

    agriculture, *2:* 461–62, 496–97, 498 (ill.)

    architecture, *2:* 463, 464, 464 (ill.), 523–24

    art, *2:* 512 (ill.), 513–20, 515 (ill.)

    background of, *2:* 467–70

    class system, *2:* 488–92

    creation myths, *2:* 324–25

    daily life, *2:* 520–27, 521 (ill.)

    descendents of, *2:* 549–50, 549 (ill.)

    development of, *2:* 272

    economy, *2:* 477–79, 481, 483–85, 487, 495–99

    empire building, *2:* 471–73, 480–86, 529–30

    epidemics and, *2:* 542–43

government, *2:* 472, 477–95
history of, *2:* 465–74
Itzcoatl history of, *2:* 471–72
kings and emperors, *2:* 484–85, 488
location of, *2:* 460–61, 460 (ill.), 479 (ill.), 531 (ill.)
medicine, *2:* 526–27
military forces, *2:* 468–69, 471–73, 477–78, 492–95, 494 (ill.), 499
religion, *2:* 502–11
rise of, *2:* 457–75
sciences, *2:* 511–13
Spanish chronicles of, *1:* 16–17; *2:* 468–69
Spanish conquest of, *1:* 12–13; *2:* 501–2, 529–51
Toltec and, *1:* 14–15; *2:* 437–39, 444, 480
writing and language, *2:* 514–20, 515 (ill.)
Aztlán, *2:* 467

B

Bajo, 2: 348, 354
Bajo de Santa Fe, *2:* 354
Ball games
    Aztec, *2:* 463
    Maya, *2:* 355, 367–68, 376–77, 383, 383 (ill.), 433
    Olmec, *2:* 290–92
Balls, rubber, *2:* 281, 292
Balsa wood, *1:* 248
Baptism, *2:* 530, 547
Bar and dot number system
    Aztec, *2:* 512
    Maya, *2:* 404–6
    Olmec, *2:* 294, 295, 296
    Teotihuacán, *2:* 331
    Zapotec, *2:* 307
Barbarians, *2:* 438, 458, 466
Barrios, 1: 142
Basalt, *2:* 277, 280, 282, 287, 292
Bas-relief
    defined, *2:* 392, 438
    Maya, *2:* 398, 399 (ill.)
    Toltec, *2:* 455
Batabs, 2: 385
Batán Grande, Peru, *1:* 139 (ill.), 144

Beans, *2:* 429
Beauty, personal, *2:* 432
Beer. *See Chicha*
Bennett Stela, *1:* 112
Benson, Elizabeth, *1:* 98
Bering Land Bridge, *1:* 23–25, 24 (ill.), 27–28, 32
Beringia, *1:* 23
Berlin, Heinrich, *2:* 394–95
Betanzos, Juan de, *1:* 168–69, 239–40, 244–45
Big Hand, *2:* 449
Bingham, Hiram, *1:* 164
Bioglyphs, *1:* 76, 80–81, 82 (ill.), 84
Birth glyphs, *2:* 395
Birú, *1:* 247
Black Tezcatlipoca, *2:* 503
Bloodletting rituals, *2:* 378–80, 382
Blue Tezcatlipoca. *See* Huitzilopochtli
Boats, seaworthy, *1:* 27–28
Bonampak murals, *2:* 403, 403 (ill.), 404–5
Book of Council, *2:* 376, 404
Bowls. *See* Pottery
Brain surgery, *1:* 218–19
Bridges, *1:* 216
"Broken Spears," *2:* 546
Bronze ingots, *1:* 148–49
Building J, *2:* 305–6, 312
Burger, Richard L., *1:* 62, 65
Burial chambers
    kingdom of Chimor, *1:* 140, 150–51
    Maya, *2:* 360, 400
    Moche, *1:* 93, 95
    Zapotec, *2:* 310
Burial offerings, *2:* 262
Burial practices. *See also* Mummies
    early Mesoamerican, *2:* 268
    Inca, *1:* 239–40
    Maya, *2:* 356–57, 360

C

Cabello de Balboa, Miguel, *1:* 145–46
Cacao bag, *1:* 213 (ill.)

Cacao beans, *2:* 420 (ill.), 431 (ill.)
  chocolate from, *2:* 422, 430–31
  defined, *2:* 416, 478
  as money, *2:* 498
Cactus beverage, *2:* 447, 524–25
Cactus, San Pedro, *1:* 70
Cahuachi, Peru, *1:* 76–77
Caiman imagery, *1:* 69; *2:* 292
Cajamarca, Peru, *1:* 158 (ill.), 174, 249–51
Calakmul, Guatemala, *2:* 357, 385
Calculators. *See Quipu*
Calendar Round system, *2:* 307, 312
Calendars. *See also* Sacred calendars; Solar calendars
  Aztec, *2:* 506, 512–13
  Calendar Round system, *2:* 307, 312
  52-year cycle, *2:* 377–78, 410, 506
  Inca, *1:* 219–20
  Long Count, *2:* 283–84, 294, 410–11
  Maya, *2:* 354, 377–78, 406–11, 409 (ill.)
  Nazca line drawings as, *1:* 82
  Olmec, *2:* 283–84, 294, 296, 306
  Teotihuacán, *2:* 331
  two-calendar systems, *2:* 283–84, 294, 296, 306
  Zapotec, *2:* 306–7, 312
Callanca, 1: 156
Calmecac, 2: 463, 493–94, 523
Calpullec, 2: 491
Calpulli, 2: 478, 491, 495, 498, 502, 517
Camelids, *1:* 36, 42–43. *See also* Alpaca; Llamas
Canals, *1:* 61, 110–11. *See also* Irrigation
  Aztec, *2:* 461–62, 464
  kingdom of Chimor, *1:* 152
  Maya, *2:* 424–25
Canatares mexicanos, 2: 519
Cancuen, Guatemala, *2:* 416–19, 418 (ill.)
Capac Raymi, *1:* 207–8
Capac Yupanqui, *1:* 170 (ill.), 171
Captives. *See* Prisoners of war
Caracol, *2:* 367
Caral, Peru, *1:* 49–54, 51 (ill.)

Caravanserai, *1:* 138
Casma Valley, Peru, *1:* 143, 144
Castedo, Leopold, *2:* 490
Castillo, *1:* 64–65
Cat imagery. *See* Feline imagery
Catherwood, Frederick, *2:* 334–38, 340, 345, 362, 364
Cauac Sky, *2:* 399
Caucasoid features, *1:* 29, 31
Cave paintings, *1:* 42
Caves, *2:* 324, 377
Cempoala, Mexico, *2:* 537
Cenotes, *2:* 348, 365, 368, 416, 424
Central Acropolis, *2:* 355
Ceque, 1: 200
Ceramics. *See* Pottery
Ceremonial centers. *See also* specific sites
  vs. cities, *1:* 48
  defined, *1:* 2, 36, 60, 76, 88; *2:* 262, 277, 300, 316, 348
  early Andean, *1:* 35–36
Cerro Baúl, Peru, *1:* 126–27, 127 (ill.), 135
Cerro Blanco, Peru, *1:* 89–92, 96, 102
Cerro Sechín, Peru, *1:* 56, 56 (ill.)
Cerro Victoria, Peru, *1:* 165
Chac, *2:* 375
Chacmool, 2: 438, 443, 455, 455 (ill.)
Chalcatzingo, Mexico, *2:* 284–85
Chan Bahlum, *2:* 359, 361
Chan Chan, Peru, *1:* 137, 139–42, 151 (ill.)
  architecture, *1:* 140–42, 140 (ill.), 141 (ill.)
  Inca defeat of, *1:* 152–53
  kingdom of Chimor and, *1:* 143, 147
  location of, *1:* 139 (ill.)
Chancas, *1:* 172–73, 179, 190
Charisma, *2:* 372
Charles V, *2:* 538, 539 (ill.)
Chasqui, 1: 180, 192, 193 (ill.)
Chavín culture, *1:* 11, 59–73
  architecture, *1:* 64–65, 64 (ill.), 65 (ill.)
  arts and sciences, *1:* 70–72, 71 (ill.)
  decline of, *1:* 72
  economy, *1:* 67–69
  government, *1:* 67

history, *1:* 65–67
location of, *1:* 60, 62 (ill.)
religion, *1:* 59, 66, 68, 69–70
Chavín de Huántar, Peru, *1:*
    59–69, 62 (ill.), 65 (ill.)
    New Temple, *1:* 64–65, 69–70
    Old Temple, *1:* 61–64, 63 (ill.),
    64 (ill.), 66, 69–70
Chewing gum, *2:* 435
Chicha, 1: 36, 122, 131, 156, 233
Chichén Itzá, Mexico
    architecture, *2:* 366 (ill.), 387
    (ill.)
    ball courts, *2:* 383 (ill.)
    government, *2:* 388
    rise and decline of, *2:* 347,
    365–68, 387–88
    Toltec and, *2:* 444–45
Chichimecs, *2:* 445–46, 456, 466
Chichle trees, *2:* 435
Chiefdoms
    defined, *1:* 88; *2:* 300, 348, 438
    Maya, *2:* 352–53
    Moche, *1:* 93, 96
    Moundbuilders, *2:* 452
Children
    Aztec, *2:* 522–23
    Maya, *2:* 425–30
    of nobles, *1:* 237
    sacrifice of, *1:* 205; *2:* 511
    working class, *1:* 230–31; *2:* 523
Chili peppers, *1:* 233; *2:* 429
Chimalpopoca, *2:* 484
Chimor. *See* Kingdom of Chimor
Chimú. *See* Kingdom of Chimor
China, *1:* 5
Chinampa, 2: 458, 461–62, 465,
    478, 496–97, 497 (ill.)
Chincasuyu, *1:* 158
Chinchorro, *1:* 6, 41
Chinese migrants, *1:* 32
Chocolate, *2:* 422, 430–31, 524
Cholula, Mexico, *2:* 445, 538
Cholulans, *2:* 538
Chosen women, *1:* 206–7, 207
    (ill.), 208 (ill.), 212
Chot, Peru, *1:* 146
Chotuna, Peru, *1:* 146
Christianity. *See also* Missionaries
    Atahuallpa and, *1:* 250
    Aztec and, *2:* 547
    conversion to, *1:* 168; *2:* 547
    Maya and, *2:* 343, 433–34

Chronicle of Peru (Cieza de
    León), *1:* 169
Chroniclers, *1:* 156, 242; *2:* 530.
    See also Spanish chronicles
Chronicles of Cabello de Balboa
    (1581), *1:* 145–46
Chuños, 1: 234
Cieza de León, Pedro, *1:* 169
Cihuacoatl, 2: 489, 526
Cities, *1:* 48, 53
City-states
    Aztec, *2:* 459
    defined, *1:* 2; *2:* 300, 334, 348,
    372, 458
    Maya, *2:* 384–85
    Sumerian, *1:* 9
    Zapotec, *2:* 306
Ciudadela, 1: 139–42, 150,
    151–52; *2:* 319
Cival, Guatemala, *2:* 349–51
Civil war, *1:* 243–47
Civilization, *1:* 4–5, 6, 9. *See also*
    specific civilizations
Class system
    Aztec, *2:* 488–92
    Caral, *1:* 51
    Chavín, *1:* 69
    development of, *1:* 6
    Inca, *1:* 184, 223–25
    Maya, *2:* 384–86, 385 (ill.), 388,
    421
    Mexico, *2:* 548
    Olmec, *2:* 288–89
    Tiwanaku, *1:* 115
    Zapotec, *2:* 307–8
Classic era, *2:* 341, 353–65,
    383–85, 398, 401, 420
Clay, white, *2:* 285
Clendinnen, Inga, *2:* 492, 499
Cliff carvings, *2:* 285
Cliff dwellings, *2:* 453
Cloth. *See* Textiles
Clothing
    Aztec, *2:* 525
    Inca, *1:* 235–36, 238–39, 238
    (ill.)
    Maya, *2:* 429–30
    nobles, *1:* 238–39, 238 (ill.)
    working class, *1:* 235–36
Cloud People. *See* Zapotecs
Cloud Serpent, *2:* 446
Clovis First theory, *1:* 24–25, 27,
    28, 32

Clovis points, *1:* 24–25, 25 (ill.), 28

Coat of armor, *2:* 495

Coatlicue, *2:* 504–5, 507–8, 509 (ill.)

Cobá, *2:* 387

Cobata head, *2:* 283

Cobo, Bernabé, *1:* 168, 202–3, 214

Coca, *1:* 218

Cocijo (Rain God), *2:* 309

Codex
  Aztec, *2:* 469, 516–18
  burning, *2:* 547
  defined, *2:* 334, 392, 458, 502
  Maya, *2:* 343–44, 344 (ill.), 400–1

Coe, Michael D.
  on Aztecs, *2:* 483, 522
  on hunter-gatherers, *1:* 33–34
  on Maya culture, *2:* 392–93, 402
  on Moundbuilders, *2:* 452–53
  on Olmecs, *2:* 288
  on Toltec culture, *2:* 441–42

Colca, 1: 156

Collasuyu, *1:* 158

Colloa, Peru, *1:* 173

Colonies
  defined, *1:* 106, 122; *2:* 316
  Inca, *1:* 189–90
  Teotihuacán, *2:* 325–26
  Wari, *1:* 123, 130, 131–32

Columbus, Christopher, *2:* 419–20, 452

Common people. *See* Working class

Companion spirits, *2:* 289–90, 377

Complex for Astronomical Commemoration, *2:* 354

Conquest slabs, *2:* 305, 305 (ill.), 311–12

Conquistadores, *1:* 156, 242; *2:* 334, 348, 534–35. *See also* Spanish conquest

Controversial, *1:* 20

Copán, Honduras
  Altar Q, *2:* 364–65, 364 (ill.)
  architecture, *2:* 335–36, 336 (ill.)
  rediscovery of, *2:* 335–36, 338
  rise and decline of, *2:* 333, 361–65

  stelae, *2:* 363 (ill.), 399

Copper ingots, *1:* 148–49

Copper metalwork, *1:* 101–2

Copper mines, *1:* 228

Cordillera Occidental, *1:* 38

Cordillera Oriental, *1:* 38

Córdoba, Francisco Fernández de, *2:* 368–69

Coricancha (Temple of the Sun), *1:* 159, 202, 203 (ill.), 204; *2:* 361

Corn. *See* Maize

Corn harvest ceremony, *1:* 207

Cortés, Hernán
  arrival of, *1:* 12; *2:* 534–36
  Charles V and, *2:* 538, 539 (ill.)
  crew of, *2:* 535–36
  Díaz, Bernal on, *2:* 468
  epidemics and, *2:* 542–43
  life of, *2:* 534–35
  Montezuma II and, *2:* 448, 454, 536–43
  route of, *2:* 538 (ill.)

Cota Coca, Peru, *1:* 165

Cotton, *1:* 52, 212

Cotton pre-Ceramic era, *1:* 44–48

Counting boards, *1:* 217

Counting cord devices. *See Quipu*

Coya, 1: 180, 182, 207, 222, 223

Crafts industry. *See also* Artisans
  Aztec, *2:* 497–98
  Inca, *1:* 224
  kingdom of Chimor, *1:* 148–49
  Teotihuacán, *2:* 326–27

Craniometric analyses, *1:* 29

Creation myths
  Aztec, *2:* 324–25, 503, 505–8
  Inca, *1:* 118–19, 167, 170–73, 201–2, 202 (ill.)
  Maya, *2:* 352
  Teotihuacán, *2:* 324–25
  Toltec, *2:* 451

Creator God. *See* Viracocha

Creole, 2: 530, 548

Crime, *1:* 193–94

Cross-eyes, *2:* 432

Cuanuhnahuac, Mexico, *2:* 484

Cuauhtémoc, *2:* 544, 545–46

Cuicuilco, Mexico, *2:* 322

Cuitláhuac, *2:* 543–44

Culhuacán, Mexico, *2:* 467–68

Culhua-Mexicas, *2:* 468

Cults
  Aztec, *2:* 468, 492

Chavín, *1:* 59
defined, *1:* 60
Toltec, *2:* 443, 449–50, 451, 455
Cultural groups, *2:* 277
Culture, *1:* 2, 20, 60, 88. *See also* specific civilizations
Cumbi cloth, *1:* 212
Cuntisuyu, *1:* 158
Curaca, 1: 180, 185, 187, 193, 222
Curare, *1:* 218
Cuzco, Peru
  establishment of, *1:* 8
  Incas and, *1:* 157–58, 159–65, 171, 237
  kingdom of Chimor and, *1:* 152
  location of, *1:* 158 (ill.)
  map of, *1:* 11 (ill.)
  modern architecture, *1:* 258 (ill.)
  Pachacutec and, *1:* 174
  Spanish attack on, *1:* 10, 251–54, 253 (ill.)
Cuzco Valley, Peru, *1:* 124

D

Dance, *1:* 213; *2:* 514
Dani Biaa. See Monte Albán, Mexico
Davies, Nigel, *1:* 143, 151
Day names, *2:* 306–7, 311, 331, 407–8, 513
Days of the Dead, *2:* 549–50, 549 (ill.)
Death glyphs, *2:* 395
Death penalty, *1:* 194
Decipher, *2:* 392, 416
Deforestation, *2:* 435
Deities, *1:* 60, 88; *2:* 502. *See also* Gods
Demarest, Arthur, *2:* 416–19
Democracy, *2:* 479
Dental studies, *1:* 32
Desert culture, *2:* 264–65
Desert line drawings, *1:* 75–76, 79–84, 80 (ill.), 82 (ill.)
Díaz (del Castillo), Bernal, *2:* 468–69, 534, 539
Diehl, Richard, *2:* 288
Dillehay, Tom, *1:* 25–26, 27
Diseases. *See also* Epidemics; Smallpox

influenza, *2:* 369
malaria, *2:* 334
measles, *2:* 369, 542–43
Divine right, *1:* 146–47; *2:* 398
Divorce, *2:* 426, 520
Dogs, *2:* 524
Domestic animals. *See also* Alpaca; Llamas
  early Andean, *1:* 43
  early Mesoamerican, *1:* 5
  Maya, *2:* 425
Donnan, Christopher, *1:* 94, 95, 101
Dot and glyph number systems, *2:* 511–12
Doyle, Arthur Conan, *2:* 354
Drama, *1:* 216
Dresden Codex, *2:* 401, 411
Drinking rituals, *1:* 131
Drought
  defined, *1:* 36, 88
  Moche and, *1:* 102
  Tiwanaku and, *1:* 120
  Wari and, *1:* 135
Drugs, hallucinogenic. *See* Hallucinogenic drugs
Drums, *2:* 514
Dyes, *1:* 212

E

Eagle Knights, *2:* 493
Early American Civilizations, *1:* 1–17. *See also* specific civilizations
Early Andeans, *1:* 8–12, 8 (ill.), 10 (ill.), 35–57, 39 (ill.)
  after Caral, *1:* 54–56
  agriculture, *1:* 35, 43, 44 (ill.), 52
  Cotton pre-Ceramic era, *1:* 44–48
  hunter-gatherers, *1:* 39–41
  Norte Chico discoveries, *1:* 49–54
  warfare and, *1:* 55–56
  year-round settlements, *1:* 41–43
Early Classic era, *2:* 268–69
Early Mesoamericans, *2:* 261–73
  agriculture, *2:* 264–65
  culture, *2:* 269–71

desert culture, *2:* 264–65
first Mesoamericans, *2:* 263–64
glyphs, *2:* 271–72
location of, *2:* 263 (ill.)
pre-Olmec, *2:* 266–69
timeline of, *2:* 268–69
village settlements, *2:* 265–66
Early post-Classic era, *2:* 269
Earplugs, *1:* 184, 208, 237, 239
Earth Goddess, *1:* 202; *2:* 504–5,
    507–8, 509 (ill.)
Earthquakes, *1:* 39, 87, 102; *2:*
    509
East Plaza, *2:* 355
Eclipse, *2:* 412
Economy
    Aztec, *2:* 477–79, 481, 483–85,
        487, 495–99
    Caral, *1:* 51–52
    Chavín, *1:* 67–69
    Inca, *1:* 194–97
    kingdom of Chimor, *1:* 148–50
    Maya, *2:* 415–25
    Moche, *1:* 99
    Teotihuacán, *2:* 325, 326–27,
        419
    Tiwanaku, *1:* 115–18
    Toltec, *2:* 450–51
Ecosystems, *1:* 36, 106
Egalitarian society, *1:* 2, 7; *2:* 530
Egypt, *1:* 5, 6
Ehecatl, *2:* 463, 505 (ill.)
18 Rabbit, *2:* 362, 399
El Manatí, *2:* 280–81
El Mirador, Guatemala, *2:* 351–53
El Niño
    defined, *1:* 36, 88
    early Andeans and, *1:* 39
    Moche and, *1:* 87
    Nazca and, *1:* 85
El Paraíso, Peru, *1:* 47–48, 48 (ill.)
El Tajín, *2:* 445
El Tigre Pyramid, *2:* 351
Elite, *1:* 88, 138; *2:* 262, 277, 300,
    316, 334–35, 372, 392, 416,
    438. *See also* Nobles
Empire, *1:* 2, 106, 122, 138, 156,
    180, 200, 222, 242; *2:* 316,
    458, 478, 502, 530
Encomendero, 2: 548
Encomienda, 2: 530, 535, 548
Entertainment, *2:* 431–33
Epidemics. *See also* Smallpox
    Aztec and, *2:* 542–43, 544

defined, *1:* 242
Incas and, *1:* 176, 244–45, 247,
    257
influenza, *2:* 369
Lacandón Maya and, *2:* 435
Maya and, *2:* 369
measles, *2:* 369, 542–43
Spanish conquest and, *2:*
    542–43
Epi-Olmec script, *2:* 295
Equinox, *2:* 348, 392, 412
Espiritu Pampa, Peru, *1:* 158 (ill.),
    164
Estrada-Belli, Francisco, *2:* 349
Ethnic groups, *1:* 235
Europeans, *1:* 176. *See also* Mis-
    sionaries; Spanish conquest
Evolution, *1:* 20
Excavations, *1:* 2, 20, 36–37; *2:*
    277, 316
Exports, *1:* 138. *See also* Trade

F

Fagan, Brian, *1:* 101, 159; *2:* 290,
    296–97, 343, 455
Famine, *1:* 196; *2:* 473, 509–10
Farfán, Peru, *1:* 139 (ill.), 142, 143
Farmers, *1:* 224–26. *See also* Agri-
    culture; Working class
Farming. *See* Agriculture
Feathered Serpent God. *See* Quet-
    zalcoatl
Feline imagery
    Chavín, *1:* 69–70, 70 (ill.), 71
        (ill.), 72
    defined, *1:* 61
    Moche, *1:* 96–97
Fertile Crescent, *1:* 9
Fertility rites, *1:* 47; *2:* 316
Fertilizers, *2:* 465, 496–97
Festival of the Sun, *1:* 207,
    208–10, 210 (ill.)
Festivals
    Inca, *1:* 207, 221
    Maya, *2:* 432–33
    Wari, *1:* 131, 236
    working class and, *1:* 236
Fifth Sun legend, *2:* 324–25,
    505–7
52-Year cycle, *2:* 377–78, 410,
    506

First Americans, *1:* 19–34
    Bering Land Bridge theory, *1:* 23–25, 24 (ill.), 27–28, 32
    Clovis First theory, *1:* 24–25, 27, 28, 32
    Great Ice Age and, *1:* 22–23
    life of, *1:* 33–34
    Mesoamerican, *2:* 263–64
    Paleoamerican origins, *1:* 28–31
    seaworthy boats for, *1:* 27–28
First New Chronicle and Good Government (Poma de Ayala), *1:* 169
First Step Shark, *2:* 357
Fishing, *1:* 149–50
Flayed One, *2:* 309
Floating gardens, *2:* 461–62, 496–97
Floods, *2:* 288
Florentine Codex, *2:* 469
Flour, *1:* 233–34
Flower wars, *2:* 472, 473, 486
Flu, *2:* 369
Food. *See also* Agriculture; Maize
    Aztec, *2:* 524–25
    Inca, *1:* 233–35
    Maya, *2:* 428–29
Foot plows, *1:* 227
Freedom, individual, *1:* 7
Freidel, David, *2:* 352, 366
Friezes, *1:* 37, 61, 106, 138
Frost, Peter, *1:* 165
Furniture, *2:* 428

G

Galindo, Peru, *1:* 92, 102
Gallinazo, *1:* 96
Gateway God, *1:* 112, 112 (ill.)
Gateway of the Sun, *1:* 112, 112 (ill.)
Genetics, Amerindian, *1:* 31–32
Geoglyphs, *1:* 75–76, 79–84, 80 (ill.)
Geography, sacred, *1:* 70
Glyphs
    Aztec, *2:* 515–16
    birth, *2:* 395
    death, *2:* 395
    deciphering, *2:* 394–96

defined, *2:* 262, 277, 300, 316, 334, 348, 372, 392, 394, 416, 502
    early Mesoamerican, *2:* 271–72
    Hieroglyphic Staircase, *2:* 359–60, 362, 364, 399–400
    Maya, *1:* 16; *2:* 271, 341–45, 342 (ill.), 357, 362–64, 391–96, 396 (ill.)
    in number systems, *2:* 511–12
    Olmec, *2:* 271, 294–96
    on pottery, *2:* 402
    Temple of Inscriptions, *2:* 359–60, 400
    Teotihuacán, *2:* 331
    Zapotec, *2:* 271, 303, 307, 311–12
Goddesses
    Aztec, *2:* 504–5, 507–8, 509 (ill.)
    Inca, *1:* 202
    Maya, *2:* 373
    Teotihuacán, *2:* 327–28
Gods. *See also* Rain Gods; Religion; Sun Gods
    Aztec, *2:* 463, 467, 483, 503–4
    Chavín, *1:* 63–64, 69, 70 (ill.)
    Inca, *1:* 202–3
    kingdom of Chimor, *1:* 150, 151–52
    Maya, *2:* 349–51, 352, 372–75
    Olmec, *2:* 289–90
    sacrifice of, *2:* 324–25, 505–6
    Teotihuacán, *2:* 328 (ill.), 329
    Tiwanaku, *1:* 112–13, 112 (ill.)
    Toltec, *2:* 448
    Zapotec, *2:* 309
Gold, *1:* 247–48, 249–51, 254
Gold artwork
    Chavín, *1:* 71 (ill.)
    kingdom of Chimor, *1:* 147 (ill.)
    Moche, *1:* 101 (ill.)
Gold mines, *1:* 228
Government
    authoritarian, *1:* 122
    Aztec, *2:* 472, 477–95
    Chavín, *1:* 67
    defined, *1:* 2
    development of, *1:* 6–7
    kingdom of Chimor, *1:* 146–48
    Maya, *2:* 371–89, 430–31
    Moche, *1:* 96–99

Nazca, *1:* 79
nomads and, *1:* 1
Spanish, *2:* 548
Tiwanaku, *1:* 114–15
Valley of Mexico, *2:* 466
Zapotec, *2:* 306–9
Grains, *1:* 4, 6, 233–34
Grant holders, *2:* 548
Gray, Martin, *2:* 366
Great Ball Court, *2:* 367, 368
Great Festival, *1:* 207–8
Great Ice Age, *1:* 22–23, 22 (ill.), 42
Great Plaza, *2:* 305, 355, 355 (ill.)
Great Pyramid, *2:* 354
Great Speaker, *2:* 488
Grolier Codex, *2:* 401
Group of the Thousand Columns, *2:* 367
Guanaco, *1:* 37, 42, 43, 106
Guano, *1:* 99
Guidon, Niede, *1:* 27
Guilds, *1:* 149

H

Haab. See Solar calendars
Haas, Jonathan, *1:* 54
Hairstyles, *2:* 430
Hallucinogenic drugs
Chavín and, *1:* 70
defined, *1:* 61, 122; *2:* 277, 372
Maya and, *2:* 378
Olmec and, *2:* 289–90
Wari and, *1:* 132
Hanan, 1: 156
Harpies, *2:* 292
Harqubus, *1:* 242
Harvest Mountain Lord, *2:* 295
Head sculptures, *2:* 276, 280, 281 (ill.), 282, 292
Head shape, *2:* 432
Health. *See* Medicine
Heartland, *2:* 277
Heaven, *2:* 375–80
Herbs, *1:* 218, 219 (ill.); *2:* 527
Hero Twins, *2:* 376–77, 383
Heyerdahl, Thor, *1:* 143
Hierarchy, *1:* 180, 222; *2:* 478, 530. *See also* Class system
Hieroglyphic Staircase, *2:* 359–60, 362, 364, 399–400

Highlands, *2:* 334
Hispaniola, *1:* 244
Historia del Nuevo Mundo (Cobo), *1:* 168
Historical art, *2:* 397
History of the Incas (Sarmiento de Gamboa), *1:* 168
History of the New World (Cobo), *1:* 168
Honey, *2:* 420
Hooker, Richard, *2:* 340
Horses, *1:* 249; *2:* 263–64, 537
Hostages, *1:* 189
House of Phalli, *2:* 366
House of the Deer, *2:* 365
Houses
Aztec, *2:* 464
Inca, *1:* 231–33, 231 (ill.)
Maya, *2:* 427–28, 428 (ill.)
Teotihuacán, *2:* 321–22
Huaca. See also Shrines
Cuzco, *1:* 159–65
defined, *1:* 37, 88, 156
priests and, *1:* 206
worship, *1:* 203–4
Huaca de La Luna, *1:* 89–92, 91 (ill.), 96, 98–99
Huaca de Los Idios, *1:* 46–47
Huaca de Los Sacrificios, *1:* 46–47
Huaca del Sol, *1:* 89–92, 90 (ill.), 96
Huaca Fortaleza, Peru, *1:* 102–3
Huaca Prieta, Peru, *1:* 46
Huaca Rajada, Peru, *1:* 94–95
Huantsán Mountain, Peru, *1:* 70
Huánuco Pampa, Peru, *1:* 158 (ill.), 161–62
Huaqueros, 1: 94
Huari culture. *See* Wari culture
Huarpa people, *1:* 128
Huáscar, *1:* 171, 176, 182, 245–46
Huayna Capac, *1:* 175 (ill.)
death of, *1:* 176, 244–45
mummy of, *1:* 239–40
Pachacutec and, *1:* 173
rule of, *1:* 171, 175–76, 182, 242–45
Huehuetls, 2: 514
Huejotzingo, Mexico, *2:* 474
Huemac, *2:* 449, 455–56
Huey tlatoanis, 2: 472, 484
Huitzilhuitl, *2:* 484
Huitzilopochtli, *2:* 504, 508 (ill.)
conquered people and, *2:* 483

cult of, *2:* 507–8
emergence of, *2:* 467, 504
feast of, *2:* 541
human sacrifice for, *2:* 511
temple for, *2:* 463, 474
Hull, Robert, *2:* 481
Human sacrifices. *See also* Prisoners of war
Aztec, *2:* 463, 472–74, 473 (ill.), 492, 494, 508–11
of children, *2:* 465, 511
defined, *2:* 300
Inca, *1:* 205, 205 (ill.)
mass, *2:* 438, 444, 454, 458, 473–74, 473 (ill.)
Maya, *2:* 368, 379, 379 (ill.), 380, 383
Moche, *1:* 97–99, 98 (ill.)
Olmec, *2:* 291
Tiwanaku, *1:* 111
Toltec, *2:* 444, 449, 454
Wari, *1:* 130, 132
Zapotec, *2:* 303, 311
Humbolt Current, *1:* 39
Hummingbird of the South. *See* Huitzilopochtli
Hun Hunapu, *2:* 376
Hunab Ku, *2:* 373
Hunah-pu, *2:* 376–77
Hungry Coyote. *See* Nezahualcoyotl
Hunter-gatherers
early Andean, *1:* 39–40
early Mesoamerican, *1:* 5; *2:* 264
life style of, *1:* 4, 33–34
Moundbuilders, *2:* 452
Hurin, 1: 157
Hybrid, *2:* 262
Hymns, *1:* 215–16

I

Ice ages, *1:* 22 (ill.), 23, 42
Iconography, *1:* 61, 71–72
Idols, *1:* 200
Illapa (Thunder God), *1:* 202
Imports, *1:* 138. *See also* Trade
Inca chronicles, *1:* 166, 169
Inca Religion and Culture (Cobo), *1:* 214
Inca Roca, *1:* 170 (ill.), 171
Inca Yupanqui. *See* Pachacutec

Incas
agriculture, *1:* 194–95, 195 (ill.), 196 (ill.), 202, 216
architecture, *1:* 10–11, 159–65, 160 (ill.), 162 (ill.), 211–12, 212 (ill.), 231–33
art, *1:* 210–16, 213 (ill.)
burial practices, *1:* 239–40
civil war, *1:* 243–47
class system, *1:* 184, 223–25
conquered lands of, *1:* 184–90
creation myths, *1:* 118–19, 167, 170–73, 201–2, 202 (ill.)
daily life of, *1:* 221–40
defined, *1:* 3, 157, 179–81
descendants of, *1:* 258–59
economy, *1:* 194–97
government, *1:* 179–98
history of, *1:* 165–77
important sites, *1:* 158–65
kingdom of Chimor and, *1:* 145, 152–53, 172, 175
land management by, *1:* 185–86
laws, *1:* 192–94
location of, *1:* 157–58, 158 (ill.), 182 (ill.), 202 (ill.), 243 (ill.)
military forces, *1:* 190–91
rebellion against, *1:* 188–90, 242–43
religion, *1:* 181–82, 189, 199–210
rise of, *1:* 8–11, 155–77
roads, *1:* 191–92, 192 (ill.), 216
rulers, *1:* 170 (ill.), 171, 182–84
science of, *1:* 216–20
smallpox epidemics and, *1:* 176, 244–45, 247, 257
Spanish chronicles on, *1:* 16–17, 165, 166–67, 168–69
Spanish conquest of, *1:* 241–60
Tiwanaku and, *1:* 106, 118–19
Wari and, *1:* 122–23, 135
Incas-by-privilege, *1:* 184, 223, 239
Incidents of Travel in Central American, Chiapas and Yucatán, 2: 337
Indigenous, *1:* 20
Individual freedom, *1:* 7
Indus Valley, *1:* 5
Influenza, *2:* 369
Ingots, *1:* 148–49
Inti Raymi, *1:* 207, 208–10, 210 (ill.)

Inti (Sun God), *1:* 167, 167 (ill.), 182, 201, 202
Irrigation
  Caral, *1:* 52
  development of, *1:* 6
  early Andean, *1:* 54
  Inca, *1:* 196, 226–27
  kingdom of Chimor, *1:* 148
  Maya, *2:* 424–25
  Moche, *1:* 93, 99
  Nazca, *1:* 78–79
  Sumerian, *1:* 9
  Tiwanaku, *1:* 116–17
  Toltec, *2:* 450–51
  Wari, *1:* 128–29
Itzá, *2:* 365
Itzamná, *2:* 373, 374, 374 (ill.)
Itzcoatl, *2:* 471–72, 481, 484, 507, 517–18
Ix Chel, *2:* 373

J

Jade masks, *2:* 360
Jade sculptures
  Aztec, *2:* 514
  Maya, *2:* 351, 417, 418–19, 420
  Olmec, *2:* 282, 283 (ill.), 285, 292–93
Jadeite, *2:* 292
Jaguar Gods, *2:* 284
Jaguar imagery
  Olmec, *2:* 290, 292
  Teotihuacán, *2:* 327–28, 329
  Toltec, *2:* 455
Jaguar Knights, *2:* 493
Jailli, *1:* 215–16
Jails, *2:* 355
Jang-Jang. *See* Chan Chan, Peru
Jequetepeque Valley, Peru, *1:* 142, 143–44
Jewelry. *See also* Metalwork
  Aztec, *2:* 514, 525
  Inca, *1:* 239
  kingdom of Chimor, *1:* 147 (ill.)
  Maya, *2:* 429–30
  Moche, *1:* 101 (ill.)
  Wari, *1:* 134
Judges, *2:* 489, 526
Justeson, John, *2:* 294–95

K

Kalasasaya platform, *1:* 112
Kan Xul, *2:* 361
Karwu, *1:* 68
Katun, *2:* 413
Katz, Friedrich, *1:* 196
Kaufman, Terrence, *2:* 294–95
Kennewick Man, *1:* 30–31, 31 (ill.)
Khipu. See Quipu
Kin groups. *See Ayllu*
King 3 Ajaw, *2:* 296
Kingdom of Chimor, *1:* 94, 137–53
  agriculture, *1:* 148, 149–50
  architecture, *1:* 139–43, 140 (ill.), 141 (ill.), 151–53, 151 (ill.)
  art and sciences, *1:* 144, 144 (ill.), 147 (ill.), 148–49, 149 (ill.), 151–52
  decline of, *1:* 152–53
  economy, *1:* 148–50
  government, *1:* 146–48
  history, *1:* 143–44
  Incas and, *1:* 145, 152–53, 172, 175
  location of, *1:* 138–39, 139 (ill.)
  metalwork, *1:* 210
  religion, *1:* 150–51
  Spanish chronicles of, *1:* 144–46
Kings. *See* Rulers
Kinich Ahaw, *2:* 374–75
Knights, *2:* 493
Knorozov, Yuri Valentinovich, *2:* 394
Kolata, Alan, *1:* 111, 114, 117
Kosok, Paul, *1:* 81, 82
Kukulcán, *2:* 373, 448
Kukulcán Pyramid, *2:* 367, 367 (ill.)

L

La Danta Pyramid, *2:* 351
La Mojarra stela, *2:* 294, 295
La primer nueva corónica y buen gobierno (Poma de Ayala), *1:* 169

La Venta, Mexico, *2:* 276, 281–82, 285–86, 287, 292
Labor obligations
    drinking rituals and, *1:* 131
    festivals and, *1:* 131, 236
    Inca, *1:* 186 (ill.), 187–88, 191, 194, 226
    Tiwanaku, *1:* 116
    of women, *1:* 228, 230
    working class, *1:* 116, 227–28
Lacandón Maya, *2:* 435
Laguna de los Cerros, *2:* 287
Lake Texcoco, *1:* 14–15, 14 (ill.); *2:* 465
Lake Titicaca, *1:* 107–8, 108 (ill.), 109 (ill.), 114, 172, 201
Lambayeque Valley, Peru, *1:* 92, 102, 142–43, 145–46, 152
Land distribution, *1:* 225–26
Landa, Diego de, *2:* 342–44, 394, 401, 406–7
Languages
    Amerindian, *1:* 32–33
    Aztec, *2:* 514
    Mayan, *2:* 338–39
    Mixe-Zoquean, *2:* 293
    Nahuatl, *2:* 458, 478, 502, 514–15, 549
    Olmec, *2:* 293
    Otomanguean, *2:* 310
    Proto-Mayan, *2:* 338–39
    Quechua, *1:* 157, 200, 214–15, 242, 259
    Yucatec, *2:* 344
    Zapotec, *2:* 303, 310–12
Lanyon, Anna, *2:* 534
Lanzón, *1:* 63, 64 (ill.), 69
Lapa de Boquet, Brazil, *1:* 26
Late Classic era, *2:* 269
Late post-Classic era, *2:* 269
Late pre-Classic era, *2:* 268
Laws, *1:* 6–7; *2:* 481–82, 526
Legends, *1:* 157
León-Portilla, Miguel, *2:* 519–20, 542–43, 546
Lequizamón, Mansio Serra de, *1:* 255
Levees, *2:* 288
Line drawings, Nazca, *1:* 75–76, 79–84, 80 (ill.), 82 (ill.)
Linguistic evidence, *1:* 32–33
Literature, Inca, *1:* 213–16
Llamas, *1:* 42–43, 43 (ill.)
    Chavín and, *1:* 68–69

defined, *1:* 37, 106
Inca and, *1:* 194, 212
modern day, *1:* 259
Tiwanaku and, *1:* 117–18
Lloque Yupanqui, *1:* 170 (ill.), 171
Logogram, *2:* 392, 394–95, 396
Logosyllabic, *2:* 392
Loma del Zapote, *2:* 279
Long Count, *2:* 283–84, 294, 410–11
Looters, *1:* 94
Lords. *See* Nobles
Lords of Death, *2:* 376
Los Toldos, Argentina, *1:* 26
Lost World complex, *2:* 354
Lower class. *See* Working class
Lowlands, *2:* 334
Luque, Hernando de, *1:* 247–48
Lurín Valley, Peru, *1:* 68
Luzia, *1:* 29, 32 (ill.)

M

Machu Picchu, Peru, *1:* 158 (ill.), 162–64, 162 (ill.), 163 (ill.)
MacNeish, Richard Scotty, *1:* 27, 28–31
Macuahuitl, 2: 495
Madrid Codex, *2:* 401
Mah K'ina K'uk Mo', *2:* 362, 364
Mahogany, *2:* 435
Maize
    Aztec and, *2:* 524
    chicha from, *1:* 55, 233
    Inca and, *1:* 232 (ill.), 233
    Maya and, *2:* 422, 423 (ill.), 428–29
    Olmec and, *2:* 287
Maize God, *2:* 352, 375
Malaria, *2:* 334
Malinche, *2:* 536, 538
Malpass, Michael A., *1:* 160, 187, 230
Mama Huaco, *1:* 170
Mama Ipacura, *1:* 170
Mama Ocllo, *1:* 170, 171
Mama Raua, *1:* 170
Mama-Cocha, *1:* 202
Mamaconas, 1: 206, 229
Mama-Quilla, *1:* 202
Mammoths, *1:* 22 (ill.); *2:* 262

Manchán, Peru, *1:* 139 (ill.), 143
Manco Capac, *1:* 167, 167 (ill.), 170–71, 170 (ill.), 201
Manco Inca, *1:* 171, 251–54
Mangrove swamps, *1:* 40–41
Manhood ceremony. *See* Puberty ceremony
Mani, Mexico, *2:* 343
Manly Heart. *See* Tlacaelel
Mano, 2: 429
Marcus, Joyce, *2:* 312
Marketplace, *2:* 320, 327, 463, 498
Marriage
  Aztec, *2:* 520–22
  Inca, *1:* 182, 194, 206, 229–31, 237
  Maya, *2:* 425–26, 427
Masks, *2:* 330 (ill.), 331, 349–51, 360
Mass human sacrifice
  Aztec, *2:* 473–74, 473 (ill.)
  defined, *2:* 438, 458
  Toltec, *2:* 444, 454
Mass production, *1:* 224
Maya, *1:* 13–14; *2:* 333–46
  agriculture, *2:* 422–25
  Ahaw kings, *2:* 380–85
  architecture, *2:* 349, 354–57, 355 (ill.), 359–62, 359 (ill.), 360 (ill.), 364–67, 366 (ill.), 367 (ill.), 398
  art, *2:* 352, 362, 391, 396–404, 397 (ill.), 399 (ill.)
  astronomy, *2:* 349, 411–13
  Aztec and, *2:* 483
  calendars, *2:* 356, 377–78, 406–11
  cities, *2:* 333, 334–38, 347–70, 349 (ill.), 381–82, 425
  class system, *2:* 384–86, 385 (ill.), 388, 421
  Classic era, *2:* 341, 353–65, 383–85, 398, 401, 420
  codex, *2:* 343–44, 344 (ill.), 400–1
  creation myths, *2:* 352
  daily life, *2:* 415–16, 425–30, 434 (ill.)
  dates of, *2:* 339–41
  decline of, *2:* 347–70, 386, 387–89
  description of, *2:* 338–39
  economy, *2:* 415–25

  entertainment, *2:* 431–33
  government, *2:* 371–89, 430–31
  Lacandón, *2:* 435
  languages, *2:* 338–39
  location of, *2:* 339–40, 339 (ill.), 349 (ill.), 393 (ill.), 417 (ill.)
  nobles, *2:* 382, 384–86
  number systems, *2:* 404–6
  population density, *2:* 425
  post-Classic era, *2:* 341, 365–68, 401, 420–21
  pre-Classic era, *2:* 341, 349–53
  rebellion against, *2:* 386, 388
  rediscovery of, *2:* 334–38
  religion, *2:* 371–89
  rise of, *2:* 271–72, 347–70
  Spanish chronicles of, *1:* 16–17
  Spanish conquest of, *1:* 14; *2:* 342, 368–69
  survival of, *2:* 433–35
  universe, *2:* 375–80
  writing systems, *1:* 16; *2:* 271, 341–44, 342 (ill.), 345, 391–96
Mayapán, Mexico, *2:* 333, 365, 368, 388
Mayta Capac, *1:* 170 (ill.), 171
McEwan, Gordon, *1:* 125–26, 133
Meadowcroft Rockshelter, Pennsylvania, *1:* 26, 33
Measles, *2:* 369, 542–43
Meat, *1:* 233; *2:* 425, 524
Medicine
  Aztec, *2:* 526–27
  Inca, *1:* 216, 218–19
Memorization, *1:* 214
Mercenary soldiers, *2:* 458, 469, 471, 478
Merchants, *2:* 490–91
Mérida, Mexico, *2:* 369
Mesoamericans, early. *See* Early Mesoamericans
Mesopotamia, *1:* 5, 6, 9
Mestizo, 1: 242; *2:* 530, 548
Metalwork
  Aztec, *2:* 514
  Chavín, *1:* 71, 71 (ill.)
  Inca, *1:* 210, 228
  kingdom of Chimor, *1:* 144, 144 (ill.), 147 (ill.), 148–49, 149 (ill.), 152, 210
  Moche, *1:* 99–101, 101 (ill.)
  Toltec, *2:* 451
  Wari, *1:* 134

Metate, 2: 429

Mexico, *1:* 244; *2:* 548. *See also* Valley of Mexico

Mexico City, Mexico, *1:* 12; *2:* 546

Meyer, Michael C., *2:* 444, 490

Middle class, *1:* 6, 51

Middle pre-Classic era, *2:* 268

Migrations
  Bering Land Bridge, *1:* 23–25, 24 (ill.), 32
  First Americans, *1:* 19–34
  Paleoamerican, *1:* 28–31
  Paleo-Indian, *1:* 30
  seaworthy boats and, *1:* 27–28

Military forces. *See also* Warfare
  Aztec, *2:* 468–69, 471–73, 477–78, 492–95, 494 (ill.), 499
  development of, *1:* 7
  Inca, *1:* 190–91
  Maya, *2:* 430–31
  mercenary, *2:* 458, 469, 471, 478
  Teotihuacán, *2:* 325, 329–30
  Toltec, *2:* 448–50
  Wari, *1:* 129

Miller, Mary, *2:* 382

Milpa, 2: 416, 423–25

Minchancaman, *1:* 145, 153

Mines, *1:* 228, 257

Missionaries
  Atahuallpa and, *1:* 249–50
  as chroniclers, *1:* 168
  codex and, *2:* 401
  defined, *1:* 157; *2:* 530
  Maya and, *2:* 342–44, 433–34

Mit'a, 1: 186 (ill.), 187–88, 191
  agriculture and, *1:* 194
  ayllu and, *1:* 116, 188
  defined, *1:* 181, 222
  requirements of, *1:* 187–88, 227–28, 230

Mitima, 1: 181, 189, 243

Mixcoatl, *2:* 446

Mixe-Zoquean language, *2:* 293

Mixtec, *2:* 313

Moche culture, *1:* 87–103
  architecture, *1:* 89–92, 90 (ill.), 91 (ill.)
  art and sciences, *1:* 87 (ill.), 99–102, 100 (ill.), 101 (ill.)
  decline of, *1:* 102–3
  economy, *1:* 99

government and religion, *1:* 96–99

history, *1:* 92–96

human sacrifice rituals, *1:* 97–99, 98 (ill.)

important sites, *1:* 89–92

kingdom of Chimor and, *1:* 143

location of, *1:* 88–92, 89 (ill.)

religion, *1:* 96–99

Mochica culture. *See* Moche culture

Moctezuma. *See* Montezuma I

Monarchy, *2:* 480. *See also* Rulers

Mongoloid features, *1:* 28–29

Monogamy, *1:* 194, 222; *2:* 426. *See also* Marriage

Monte Albán, Mexico, *2:* 299, 303–6
  astronomical observatory, *2:* 305–6, 308 (ill.), 312
  decline of, *2:* 312–13
  government and economy, *2:* 306–9
  history of, *2:* 303–6
  location of, *2:* 301, 302 (ill.)
  stone carvings, *2:* 310, 310 (ill.)
  trade with, *2:* 287

Monte Verde, Chile, *1:* 25–26, 27, 39–40

Montejo, Francisco de, *2:* 369

Montezuma I, *2:* 472–73, 485

Montezuma II, *2:* 532 (ill.)
  capture of, *2:* 539–41, 541 (ill.)
  Cortés, Hernán and, *2:* 448, 454, 536–43
  death of, *2:* 542
  rule of, *1:* 15; *2:* 474, 485, 531–33

Montezuma Ikhuicamina. *See* Montezuma I

Monumental architecture, *1:* 2–3, 5–6, 37, 45–48, 48 (ill.), 61

Moon Goddess, *1:* 202; *2:* 373

Moquegua Valley, Peru, *1:* 108, 126

Morris, Craig, *1:* 67

Moseley, Michael, *1:* 128, 185

Motecuhzoma Xocoyótzin. *See* Montezuma II

Moundbuilders, *2:* 452–53

Mummies
  Chincorro, *1:* 41
  defined, *1:* 181, 200

Huayna Capac, *1:* 239–40
Inca, *1:* 183–84, 239–40, 239
(ill.)
kingdom of Chimor, *1:* 150
Sapa Inca, *1:* 204, 239–40
Wari, *1:* 133, 133 (ill.)
Mummification, *1:* 222
Murals, *2:* 329, 352, 403–5, 403
(ill.)
Music, *1:* 213; *2:* 514
Myths, *1:* 200. *See also* Creation
myths

N

Naguals, 2: 289–90
Nahuatl, *2:* 458, 478, 502,
514–15, 549
Naming ceremony, *1:* 230
Nancenpinco, *1:* 145
Narrative of the Incas (Betanzos),
1: 168–69
Native American Graves Protection and Repatriation Act, *1:*
30–31, 80–81
Naylamp, *1:* 145–46
Nazca society, *1:* 66, 75–85
architecture, *1:* 76–77
art, *1:* 83–85, 84 (ill.)
decline of, *1:* 85
desert line drawings, *1:* 75–76,
79–84, 80 (ill.), 82 (ill.)
government, *1:* 79
history, *1:* 78–79
important sites, *1:* 76–78
location of, *1:* 76–78, 77 (ill.),
78 (ill.)
religion, *1:* 79
Nazca Valley, Peru, *1:* 76, 78 (ill.)
Negroid features, *1:* 29
New Fire Ceremony, *2:* 506–7
New Temple (Chavín de Húntar),
1: 64–65, 69–70
New World, *1:* 3
New World camelids. *See*
Camelids
Nezahualcoyotl, *2:* 482 (ill.)
code of laws, *2:* 481–82, 526
poetry of, *2:* 519–20
Triple Alliance and, *2:* 471, 481
Nezahualpilli, *2:* 482
Nichols, Johanna, *1:* 32–33

Ninancuyoci, *1:* 245
Nobles
Aztec, *2:* 489–90, 489 (ill.),
493–94, 499, 520, 523–25
clothing, *1:* 238–39, 238 (ill.)
daily life, *1:* 236–39
Inca, *1:* 192–93, 194, 196,
236–39
Kingdom of Chimor, *1:* 147
Maya, *2:* 382, 384–86
Olmec, *2:* 288–89
personal attendants for, *1:*
228–29
Spanish and, *2:* 547
Teotihuacán, *2:* 322, 326
Nomadic life. *See also* Hunter-
gatherers
defined, *2:* 262, 478, 530
early Andean, *1:* 35
history of, *1:* 1
transition to urban life, *1:* 2–3
Norte Chico, Peru, *1:* 11–12,
49–54
North Acropolis, *2:* 355
Northern Asians, *1:* 28–29, 32
Nueva corónica y buen gobierno
(Poma de Ayala), *1:* 169
Number systems
Aztec, *2:* 511–12
bar and dot, *2:* 294–96, 307,
331, 404–6, 512
development of, *1:* 6
dot and glyph, *2:* 511–12
Maya, *2:* 404–6
Olmec, *2:* 294, 295, 296
Teotihuacán, *2:* 331
vigesimal, *2:* 300, 392, 405–6,
502, 511–12
Zapotec, *2:* 307
Núñez de Balboa, Vasco, *1:* 247
Nunnery, *2:* 366

O

Oaxaca Valley, Mexico, *2:* 267,
299
Observatories. *See* Astronomical
observatories
Obsidian
Cancuen and, *2:* 417, 419
defined, *2:* 262, 316, 416, 438
Maya trade in, *2:* 420

Olmec and, *2:* 285
   Teotihuacán and, *2:* 322, 323,
      327, 331
Obsidian Snake. *See* Itzcoatl
Ocean Gods, *1:* 150, 151–52
Offerings, *2:* 277. *See also* Sacrifices
Old Temple (Chavín de Húantar),
   1: 61–64, 63 (ill.), 64 (ill.),
   66, 69–70
Oldstone, Michael, *2:* 543
Ollantay, 1: 216
Olmec culture, *1:* 13; *2:* 267,
   275–97
   agriculture, *2:* 287–88
   architecture, *2:* 282, 283, 284
   art, *2:* 285–86, 292–93, 293 (ill.)
   economy, *2:* 287–88
   glyphs, *2:* 271
   government, *2:* 288–89
   history of, *2:* 285–86
   important sites, *2:* 279–85
   location of, *2:* 278–79, 279 (ill.)
   religion, *2:* 289–92
   science, *2:* 296–97
   writing and language, *2:* 283–84,
      293–96, 295 (ill.), 296 (ill.)
   Zapotecs and, *2:* 300
Ometeotl, *2:* 503
Oracles, *1:* 65, 68
Oral tradition
   Aztec, *2:* 469, 517
   defined, *1:* 20
   Inca, *1:* 166, 213–16
   prehistory and, *1:* 20, 21
   Valley of Mexico, *2:* 471–72
Orejones, 1: 184
Otomanguean languages, *2:* 310
Outposts, *1:* 122
Oxa, 1: 146

P

Pacal, *2:* 358–61, 360 (ill.), 395,
   400
Pacariqtambo Cave, Peru, *1:* 167,
   170–71, 201
Pacatnamu, Peru, *1:* 139 (ill.),
   143–44
Pachacamac, *1:* 68
Pachacutec, *1:* 170 (ill.), 174 (ill.)
   Machu Picchu and, *1:* 163

rule of, *1:* 159, 171, 173–74,
      179, 182
   Sacsahuaman and, *1:* 160–61
   version of history, *1:* 166–67
Pachacuti. *See* Pachacutec
Pacha-Mama, *1:* 202
Paintings, cave, *1:* 42
Palenque, Mexico, *2:* 333, 337,
   337 (ill.), 358–61, 359 (ill.)
Paleoamericans, *1:* 21, 28–31
Paleo-Indians, *1:* 21, 30
Pampa, 1: 76
Pampa Grande, Peru, *1:* 92, 102–3
Pampa Koani, Bolivia, *1:* 117
Panaca, 1: 183, 242, 245–46
Pantheon, *1:* 61, 181; *2:* 300, 372,
   438, 502. *See also* Gods
Paper, *2:* 400–1
Paracas Peninsula, Peru, *1:* 84
Paris Codex, *2:* 401
Patagonia, *1:* 21
Peasants. *See* Working class
Peat bogs, *1:* 25–26
Pedra Furada, Brazil, *1:* 27
Pendejo Cave, New Mexico, *1:* 27
Peninsulares, 2: 530, 548
Personal attendants, *1:* 228–29
Personal beauty, *2:* 432
Peru, *1:* 11–12, 257. *See also* An-
   dean region
Petén region, *2:* 347–48, 423, 433
Piedra Museo, Argentina, *1:* 26
Piedras Negras, Guatemala, *2:* 395
Pikillacta, Peru, *1:* 124–26, 124
   (ill.), 125 (ill.), 133, 135
Pilgrimages, *2:* 277
Pilgrims, *1:* 61, 76
Piramide Mayor, *1:* 50–51
Pizarro, Francisco, *1:* 8, 10, 247
   (ill.), 248 (ill.)
   Atahuallpa and, *1:* 248–51, 251
      (ill.)
   death of, *1:* 254
   Inca and, *1:* 247–51, 254–57
   Spanish chronicles and, *1:* 168
Pizarro, Hernando, *1:* 249
Place of Reeds. *See* Tula, Mexico
Place of the Temple of Jaguar
   Gods, *2:* 284
Plague. *See* Epidemics
Plateaus, *2:* 262
Plaza of the Seven Temples, *2:*
   355
Pleistocene ice age, *1:* 23

Plows, foot, *1:* 227
Pochteca, 2: 490–91, 496, 517
Poetry, *1:* 215–16; *2:* 518–20
Pok-a-tok, 2: 290, 355, 433
Polygamy, *1:* 222. *See also* Marriage
Poma de Ayala, Felipe Huaman, *1:* 169
Pongmassa, *1:* 146
Popol Vuh, 2: 376, 404
Population density, *1:* 5
Post-Classic era, *2:* 341, 365–68, 401, 420–21
Potatoes, *1:* 234–35, 235 (ill.)
Potrero Nuevo, *2:* 279
Pottery
    Andean Mountain region, *1:* 12
    Chavín, *1:* 71
    early Andean, *1:* 54–55
    early Mesoamerican, *2:* 265–66
    Inca, *1:* 224
    kingdom of Chimor, *1:* 152
    Maya, *2:* 401–2, 402 (ill.), 420
    Moche, *1:* 99–100, 100 (ill.)
    Nazca, *1:* 84–85
    Olmec, *2:* 285
    Teotihuacán, *2:* 330–31
    Wari, *1:* 133, 134 (ill.)
Poverty Point, Louisiana, *2:* 452
Pre-Ceramic era, Cotton, *1:* 44–48
Pre-Classic era, *2:* 268, 341, 349–53
Pre-Clovis sites, *1:* 25–27
Pre-Columbian
    civilizations, *1:* 16–17, 16 (ill.); *2:* 452–53
    defined, *1:* 3, 21, 76, 88, 106, 138, 242; *2:* 392
    remains, *1:* 30–31
Prehistory
    defined, *1:* 3, 21; *2:* 262, 334, 392
    evidence from, *1:* 20–21
    glyphs and, *2:* 271–72
    reading about, *1:* 15–17
Pre-Olmec culture, *2:* 266–69
Priest-rulers
    Maya, *2:* 380–85
    Olmec, *2:* 288–89
    Tiwanaku, *1:* 114–15
    Zapotec, *2:* 308, 309–10
Priests
    Aztec, *2:* 463, 523, 547
    Inca, *1:* 205–6

Maya, *2:* 393
    Olmec, *2:* 289–90, 290 (ill.)
    role of, *1:* 7
Primogeniture, *2:* 372
Prisoners of war
    Aztec sacrifice of, *2:* 472, 473–74, 473 (ill.), 492, 494, 510
    flower wars and, *2:* 472, 473, 486
    Maya sacrifice of, *2:* 379 (ill.), 380, 383
    Toltec sacrifice of, *2:* 449
    Wari sacrifice of, *1:* 130
Propaganda, *1:* 122, 133; *2:* 300
Proskouriakoff, Tatiana, *2:* 395
Proto-Mayan language, *2:* 338–39
Puberty ceremony, *1:* 208, 230, 237; *2:* 426
Public administrators, *1:* 223–24
Public projects, *1:* 5–6, 7
Pueblo Indians, *2:* 453
Pulque, 2: 447, 524–25
Puna, *1:* 38, 40 (ill.)
Pyramid B, *2:* 442, 443
Pyramid C, *2:* 442
Pyramid IV, *2:* 356–57
Pyramid of the Magician, *1:* 15 (ill.)
Pyramid of the Moon, *2:* 318–19, 325
Pyramid of the Sun, *1:* 13; *2:* 318–19, 323 (ill.), 324, 325
Pyramids. *See also* Architecture
    Caral, *1:* 49
    Maya, *2:* 351–52, 356–57, 367, 367 (ill.), 398
    Olmec, *2:* 282
    in Peru, *1:* 11–12
    Teotihuacán, *2:* 318–19
    Toltec, *2:* 441–42
Pyrite, *2:* 419

Q

Quechua language, *1:* 157, 200, 214–15, 242, 259
Quetzal bird, *2:* 420, 438, 514
Quetzalcoatl, *2:* 320 (ill.)
    emergence of, *2:* 503
    Maya and, *2:* 373
    return of, *2:* 532–33, 539

Tenochtitlán and, *2:* 463
Teotihuacán and, *2:* 319–20,
  328–29, 451–52
Toltec and, *2:* 442, 447–48, 448
  (ill.), 451–54
Quichicoy, 1: 230
Quinine, *1:* 218
Quinoa, *1:* 222
Quipu
  defined, *1:* 122, 181, 200
  Inca and, *1:* 186, 217–18, 217
    (ill.)
  Wari and, *1:* 123, 134
Quipu camayocs, 1: 186, 217, 218,
  224
Quiriguá, Guatemala, *2:* 362, 399
Quito, Ecuador, *1:* 175–76, 243

R

Radiocarbon dating, *1:* 21, 37
Raimondi Stone, *1:* 63–64, 69, 70
  (ill.)
Rain forests, *2:* 341 (ill.)
  defined, *2:* 334, 348
  destruction of, *2:* 425
  Maya and, *2:* 340, 353, 354,
    425
Rain Gods
  Aztec, *2:* 463, 504
  Maya, *2:* 375
  Olmec, *2:* 289–90
  Teotihuacán, *2:* 328 (ill.), 329
  Zapotec, *2:* 309
Rainbow Goddess, *2:* 373
Rainwater collection, *2:* 424–25
Raised farming system, *1:* 116–17
Reciprocity principle, *1:* 131, 188
Red House, *2:* 365
Red Tezcatlipoca. *See* Xipe Totec
Reeds, *shicra, 1:* 49–50, 50 (ill.)
Reiche, Maria, *1:* 81–82
Reinhard, Johan, *1:* 82–83
Relación de las cosas de Yucatán
  (Landa), *2:* 344, 406–7
Religion. *See also* Christianity;
  Gods
  Aztec, *2:* 502–11
  Chavín, *1:* 59, 66, 68, 69–70
  development of, *1:* 7
  early Mesoamerican, *2:* 268–69
  Inca, *1:* 181–82, 189, 199–210

kingdom of Chimor, *1:* 150–51
Maya, *2:* 371–89
Moche, *1:* 96–99
Nazca, *1:* 79
Olmec, *2:* 289–92
post-Spanish conquest, *2:*
  549–50
Tiwanaku, *1:* 118–19
Toltec, *2:* 451–52
Wari, *1:* 132–33
Religious art, *2:* 397–98
Religious rites, *2:* 262
Relocation policy, *1:* 189
Remains, *1:* 21, 30–31
Residential architecture
  Aztec, *2:* 464
  Inca, *1:* 231–33, 231 (ill.)
  Maya, *2:* 427–28, 428 (ill.)
  Teotihuacán, *2:* 321–22
Rituals, *1:* 200; *2:* 277, 300, 348,
  372, 392, 502
River levees, *2:* 288
River valleys, *1:* 55–56
Rivera, Oswaldo, *1:* 116, 117
Roads
  Aztec, *2:* 464
  Inca, *1:* 191–92, 192 (ill.), 216
  Maya, *2:* 353, 422
  Teotihuacán, *2:* 318–19
  Wari, *1:* 123
Rock shelters, *2:* 262
*Romances de los señores de Nueva
  España, 2:* 519
Ross, John F., *1:* 49
Rowe, John Howland, *1:* 72
Royal Commentaries of the Incas
  (de la Vega), *1:* 169
Rubber, *2:* 281, 287, 292, 420
Ruler-priests. *See* Priests
Rulers. *See also* Government
  ahaw, 2: 380–85
  Aztec, *2:* 484–85, 488
  divine right of, *1:* 146–47; *2:*
    398
  Inca, *1:* 170 (ill.), 171, 182–84
  kingdom of Chimor, *1:* 146–47,
    150–51
  Maya, *2:* 380–85
  Olmec, *2:* 288–89
  Tiwanaku, *1:* 114–15
  Zapotec, *2:* 308, 309–10
Runasimi. *See* Quechua language
Runners, *1:* 192, 193 (ill.)
Rutichikov ceremony, *1:* 230

S

Sacred calendars, *2:* 306–7
  Aztec, *2:* 506, 512–13
  Maya, *2:* 377, 407–8, 409 (ill.)
  Olmec, *2:* 296, 306
  Teotihuacán, *2:* 331
Sacred geography, *1:* 70
Sacrifices. *See also* Animal sacri-
    fices; Human sacrifices
  defined, *1:* 37, 106, 200; *2:* 372,
    438, 458
  Fifth Sun legend and, *2:* 324–25
  Inca, *1:* 205, 205 (ill.)
  Maya, *2:* 379
Sacrificial stone, *2:* 509, 510 (ill.),
    511
Sacsahuaman, Peru, *1:* 160–61,
    160 (ill.), 175, 253
Sahagún, Bernardino de, *2:* 437,
    468, 469
Salt, *2:* 498
San Bartolo, Guatemala, *2:* 352,
    403–4
San José Mogote, *2:* 302–3, 311
San Lorenzo, Mexico, *2:* 279–81,
    285–86, 287–88, 292
San Lorenzo Tenochtitlán, *2:* 279
San Pedro cactus, *1:* 70
Sapa Inca, *1:* 9, 182–84
  chosen women and, *1:* 207
  defined, *1:* 157, 180, 181
  mummy, *1:* 204, 239–40
  palace of, *1:* 184 (ill.)
  status of, *1:* 223
  wives of, *1:* 182–83
Sarcophagus, *2:* 360, 392, 400
Sarmiento de Gamboa, Pedro, *1:*
    168
Saturno, William, *2:* 352
Sayri Tupa Inca, *1:* 171, 254–55
Schele, Linda, *2:* 366, 382
Schools, *2:* 463, 493–94, 523
Scribes
  Aztec, *2:* 516 (ill.), 517
  defined, *2:* 392, 416, 502
  Maya, *2:* 392–93, 394–95
Script, *2:* 277
Sculptures, *2:* 276, 280, 281 (ill.),
    282, 283 (ill.), 285, 292–93,
    351, 417, 418–19, 420, 514.
    See also Stone carvings
Sea goddess, *1:* 202
Sea worship, *1:* 150

Seaworthy boats, *1:* 27–28
Sedentary, *1:* 3
Semi-nomads, *1:* 40
Semi-subterranean Temple, *1:* 110
    (ill.), 112, 119 (ill.)
Serpent God, *2:* 448
Serpent Wall, *2:* 443, 443 (ill.)
Serpentine, *2:* 292
Sewage systems, *1:* 114, 120, 159;
    2: 465, 496–97
Shady Solís, Ruth, *1:* 49–51, 53
Shaman-kings. *See* Priests
Shamans, *1:* 62, 70; *2:* 372,
    378–80
Shark imagery, *2:* 292
Sheep, *1:* 43
Sherman, William L., *2:* 444, 490
Shicra, *1:* 47, 49–50, 50 (ill.)
Shrine of the Idols, *1:* 46–47
Shrine of the Moon, *1:* 89–92, 91
    (ill.), 96, 98–99
Shrine of the Sacrifices, *1:* 46–47
Shrine of the Sun, *1:* 89–92, 90
    (ill.), 96
Shrines, *1:* 70, 203–4, 206
Silver, *1:* 147 (ill.), 248, 251
Silver mines, *1:* 228, 257
Sinchi Roca, *1:* 170 (ill.), 171
Sipán, Peru, *1:* 94–95, 95 (ill.),
    101, 144
Slab carvings, *2:* 305, 305 (ill.),
    311–12
Slash-and-burn agriculture, *2:*
    288, 423–25, 424 (ill.)
Slaves, *2:* 388, 422, 491–92
Smallpox
  Aztec and, *2:* 542–43, 544
  defined, *2:* 530
  Incas and, *1:* 176, 244–45, 247,
    257
  Maya and, *2:* 369
Smoke Imix (Smoke Jaguar), *2:*
    362
Smoke Shell, *2:* 362, 400
Smoked Mirror, *2:* 447–48, 503
Snake imagery, *2:* 455
Snake Woman, *2:* 489
Social class. *See* Class system
Social rights, *1:* 196
Socialism, *1:* 196
Solar calendars, *2:* 306–7
  Aztec, *2:* 506, 513
  Maya, *2:* 377, 408–10
  Olmec, *2:* 296, 306

Solar cycle calendars, *2:* 377–78, 410, 506
Soldiers. *See* Military forces
Solstice, *2:* 348, 392, 412
Solutrean culture, *1:* 28
Songs, *1:* 215–16; *2:* 518
Soto, Hernando de, *1:* 249
Southeast Asia, *1:* 29
Spanish chronicles
 on Aztecs, *1:* 16–17; *2:* 468–69
 on Incas, *1:* 165, 166–67, 168–69
 on kingdom of Chimor, *1:* 144–46
 on Montezuma II, *2:* 532
Spanish conquest. *See also* Cortés, Hernán; Pizarro, Francisco
 aftermath of, *2:* 546–49
 Aztec and, *1:* 12–13; *2:* 501–2, 529–51
 in Cuzco, *1:* 251–54
 Díaz, Bernal on, *2:* 468–69
 epidemics and, *2:* 542–43
 gold and, *1:* 247–48, 249–51, 254
 Incas and, *1:* 176–77, 241–60
 Machu Picchu and, *1:* 164
 Maya and, *1:* 14; *2:* 342, 368–69
 Mesoamerican peoples and, *2:* 269
 rebellion against, *1:* 251–54, 257
 written accounts of, *1:* 16–17
Spanish missionaries. *See* Missionaries
Spanish-style architecture, *1:* 258 (ill.), 259
Spear points, Clovis, *1:* 24–25, 25 (ill.), 28
Spear throwers, *2:* 495
Spear-thrower Owl, *2:* 326
Specialize, *1:* 3
Speech scroll, *2:* 295–96, 296 (ill.)
Spider Woman, *2:* 327–28
Spirit nature, *2:* 289–90, 372
Spondylus shell, *1:* 134, 150
Squatting position, *1:* 232
Staff God, *1:* 53–54, 63–64, 69, 70 (ill.), 113
Starvation. *See* Famine
Stelae
 defined, *1:* 61, 106; *2:* 277, 334, 348, 372, 392, 416

Maya, *2:* 356 (ill.), 357, 362, 363 (ill.), 381, 398–400
Olmec, *2:* 283, 294, 295
Stela C, *2:* 283, 294, 295
Stephens, John Lloyd, *2:* 334–38, 340, 345, 361–62, 364
Stirling, Matthew, *2:* 276
Stirling, Stuart, *1:* 237
Stirrup spout vessels, *1:* 100
Stone carvings
 Aztec, *2:* 513
 Chavín, *1:* 62, 63, 63 (ill.), 70–71
 Maya, *2:* 398
 Olmec, *2:* 285
 Teotihuacán, *2:* 331
 Tiwanaku, *1:* 119 (ill.), 120
 Toltec, *2:* 455
 Zapotec, *2:* 305, 305 (ill.), 310, 311–12
"Stone in the Center", *1:* 107
Stone masonry, *1:* 119–20, 157, 200, 211–12. *See also* Architecture
Stonemasons, *1:* 106
Storytellers, *1:* 133, 166–67, 214. *See also* Oral tradition
Streets. *See* Roads
Subordinate, *2:* 478
Succession, *1:* 138; *2:* 478
Sumerians, *1:* 9
Sun, Festival of the, *1:* 207, 208–10, 210 (ill.)
Sun Gods
 Aztec, *2:* 483, 508 (ill.)
 Inca, *1:* 167, 167 (ill.), 182, 201, 202
 Maya, *2:* 349–51, 374–75
 Teotihuacán, *2:* 329
 Tiwanaku, *1:* 112–13, 112 (ill.)
Sun Lord Quetzal Macaw, *2:* 362
Supe Valley, Peru, *1:* 11–12, 53
Surplus, *1:* 3, 5–6, 196, 233–34
Suyo, *1:* 157
Suyus, *1:* 158
Syllabograms, *2:* 392, 394–95

T

Tahuantinsuyu, *1:* 157, 158
Taima-Taima, Venezuela, *1:* 26, 64–65

Talud-tablero, 2: 331
Tamales, 2: 429
Tarascans, *2:* 486
Tattoos, *2:* 432, 525
Tawantinsuyu, *1:* 157, 158
Taxes, *2:* 483, 498. *See also* Tribute
Taycanamo, *1:* 145
Taypi Kala, *1:* 107
Tello Obelisk, *1:* 63, 69
Telpochcalli, 2: 463, 523
Temple mounds. *See also* Architecture; Pyramids
   Cahuachi, *1:* 77
   Caral, *1:* 49–51
   Chavín, *1:* 61–65, 63 (ill.), 64 (ill.), 66, 69–70
   Cotton pre-Ceramic era, *1:* 45–46
   El Paraíso site, *1:* 48
Temple of Inscriptions, *2:* 359–60, 400
Temple of Quetzalcoatl, *2:* 319–20, 320 (ill.)
Temple of the Cross, *2:* 361
Temple of the Danzantes, *2:* 305, 305 (ill.), 310, 310 (ill.)
Temple of the Foliated Cross, *2:* 361
Temple of the Sun, *1:* 159, 202, 203 (ill.), 204; *2:* 361
Temple of the Three Lintels, *2:* 366
Temple of the Warriors, *2:* 367
Templo Mayor, *2:* 463
Tenochtitlán, Mexico. *See also* Aztecs
   Cortés, Hernán in, *2:* 538–43, 540 (ill.)
   description of, *1:* 14 (ill.), 15; *2:* 461–65, 462 (ill.), 464 (ill.)
   establishment of, *2:* 461–62, 470–71
   fall of, *2:* 544–46, 545 (ill.)
   location of, *2:* 460, 460 (ill.)
   marketplace, *2:* 320, 327, 498
   Tepanecs and, *2:* 479–80
Teopantecuanitlán, Mexico, *2:* 284
Teotihuacán, Mexico, *2:* 267, 315–32
   architecture, *2:* 318–22, 319 (ill.), 321 (ill.), 323 (ill.), 331
   art and science, *2:* 329–31, 330 (ill.)

   Aztec and, *2:* 463
   decline of, *1:* 13; *2:* 331–32, 445, 465
   development of, *2:* 272, 465
   economy, *2:* 325, 326–27, 419
   government, *2:* 326
   history of, *2:* 322–26
   layout of, *1:* 13 (ill.); *2:* 318–19
   location of, *2:* 317–18, 318 (ill.)
   Olmec and, *2:* 287–88
   Quetzalcoatl and, *2:* 451–52
   religion, *2:* 327–29, 503
   Zapotecs and, *2:* 300
Tepanecs, *2:* 471, 477, 479–80
Terraces
   Aztec, *2:* 496
   defined, *1:* 181
   Inca, *1:* 194, 195 (ill.), 196, 226–27
   Maya, *2:* 424
   Wari, *1:* 128, 129 (ill.)
   Zapotec, *2:* 304
Texcocans, *2:* 481
Texcoco, Lake, *1:* 14–15, 14 (ill.); *2:* 465
Texcoco, Mexico, *2:* 471, 474, 477, 481–83
Textiles
   Chavín, *1:* 71
   Inca, *1:* 212–13, 213 (ill.)
   kingdom of Chimor, *1:* 144, 148, 149, 150
   Moche, *1:* 100, 102
   modern, *1:* 259
   Tiwanaku, *1:* 118, 118 (ill.)
   Wari, *1:* 134
Tezcatlipoca, *2:* 447–48, 451–54, 463, 533
Theorize, *2:* 277
Thompson, J. Eric, *2:* 394
Thomson, Hugh, *1:* 165
Thunder God, *1:* 202
Thunupa, *1:* 113
Tiahuanaco culture. *See* Tiwanaku culture
Tiahuanacu culture. *See* Tiwanaku culture
Tibitó, Colombia, *1:* 26
Tikal, Guatemala
   rise and decline of, *2:* 333, 347, 353–58, 385
   trade center, *2:* 420, 421
   Zapotecs and, *2:* 300

Titicaca, Lake, *1:* 107–8, 108 (ill.), 109 (ill.), 114, 172, 201
Titu Cusi, *1:* 171, 254–56
Tiwanaku, Bolivia, *1:* 108–14, 111 (ill.), 117, 119 (ill.), 174
Tiwanaku culture, *1:* 105–20
  agriculture, *1:* 116–17
  architecture, *1:* 108–14, 110 (ill.), 111 (ill.), 112 (ill.)
  art and sciences, *1:* 118 (ill.), 119–20
  decline of, *1:* 120, 135
  economy, *1:* 115–18
  government, *1:* 114–15
  history, *1:* 114
  location of, *1:* 107–8, 108 (ill.)
  religion, *1:* 54, 118–19
  Wari and, *1:* 105–6, 121, 127–28, 132, 135
Tizoc, *2:* 485
Tlacaelel, *2:* 472, 484
Tlachtli, *2:* 290
Tlacopan, Mexico, *2:* 471, 474, 477, 481
Tlahuicans, *2:* 484–86
Tlaloc, *2:* 328 (ill.), 329, 463, 504
Tlatelolco, Mexico, *2:* 470–71, 482–83
Tlatilco, Mexico, *2:* 267
Tlatoani, *2:* 458, 466, 472, 478, 489
Tlaxcala, Mexico, *2:* 473, 474
Tlaxcalans, *2:* 486, 537–38, 542–43, 546
Toledo, Francisco de, *1:* 256
Tollan. *See* Tula, Mexico
Toltec culture, *1:* 14–15; *2:* 437–56
  agriculture, *2:* 450–51
  architecture, *2:* 441–44, 442 (ill.), 443 (ill.), 455, 455 (ill.)
  art and sciences, *2:* 444, 454–55, 455 (ill.)
  Aztec and, *1:* 14–15; *2:* 437–39, 444, 480, 503
  Chichén Itzá and, *2:* 444–45
  decline of, *2:* 455–56, 465, 466
  economy, *2:* 450–51
  government, *2:* 449–50
  history of, *2:* 445–49, 466
  important sites, *2:* 441–44
  location of, *2:* 440–41, 440 (ill.)
  Maya and, *2:* 366–68
  religion, *2:* 451–52

Tolteca. *See* Toltec culture
Toltec-Chichimecs, *2:* 440, 446
Tombs. *See* Burial chambers
Tonalpohualli, *2:* 512–13
Tooth decoration, *2:* 432
Topiltzin-Quetzalcoatl, *2:* 446, 447–58
Topper, South Carolina, *1:* 26
Totonacs, *2:* 537
Tourism, *1:* 259
Trade
  Aztec, *2:* 490–91, 497–98, 499
  Cancuen, *2:* 418–22
  Caral, *1:* 51–52
  Chavín culture, *1:* 68–69
  early Mesoamerican, *2:* 268
  Inca, *1:* 195, 196
  kingdom of Chimor, *1:* 147–48, 149
  Maya, *2:* 418–22
  Olmec, *2:* 285–86, 287–88
  Teotihuacán, *2:* 322, 326–27
  Tikal, *2:* 420, 421
  Tiwanaku, *1:* 116, 118
  Toltec, *2:* 453
  Wari, *1:* 128, 130–32, 134
Traders, Aztec, *2:* 490–91, 496, 517
Tragedy of the End of Atahuallpa, 1: 216
Trance state, *2:* 289–90, 372, 377, 380
Transformation, *2:* 372
Treason, *1:* 193
Tres Zapotes, Mexico, *2:* 283–84, 286, 292, 294
Trial marriages, *1:* 229
Tribute
  Aztec, *2:* 481, 483–85, 487, 494–96, 499
  Chavín, *1:* 66
  defined, *1:* 61, 138, 157; *2:* 300, 316, 438, 458, 478, 530
  Spanish, *2:* 535
Triple Alliance, *2:* 471, 477, 480–81, 484
Trophy heads, *1:* 76, 106, 111, 122, 130
True History of the Conquest of New Spain (Díaz), *2:* 468–69, 534, 539
Túcume, Peru, *1:* 139 (ill.), 142–43, 144

Tula, Mexico, *2:* 367, 439, 441–44, 442 (ill.), 443 (ill.)
Tulúm, Mexico, *2:* 338
Tumbes, Peru, *1:* 158 (ill.), 248
Tumebamba, Ecuador, *1:* 174–75
Tupac Amarú, *1:* 171, 254, 256–57, 256 (ill.)
Tupac Amarú II, *1:* 257
Tupac Inca Yupanqui, *1:* 170 (ill.), 171, 173, 174–75, 182
Turquoise, *2:* 453
Tuxtla Mountain, *2:* 287
Tuxtla statuette, *2:* 294–95
Two-calendar systems, *2:* 283–84, 294, 296, 306
Tzapotecatle. *See* Zapotecs
Tzeltal, *2:* 434
Tzolkin. See Sacred calendars
Tzompantli, 2: 443–44, 463, 511
Tzotzil, *2:* 434

U

Uaxactún, Guatemala, *2:* 338
Uayeb, *2:* 408
Ulama, 2: 290
Underworld, *2:* 375–80
United States, Pre-Columbian societies, *2:* 452–53
Upper class, *1:* 6, 51. *See also* Nobles
Urban life, *1:* 3–8
Urbanization, *1:* 3
Urco, *1:* 172–73
Urubamba River gorge, *1:* 163–64
U-shaped monumental architecture, *1:* 48, 61
Ushnu, 1: 157, 162
Uxmal, Mexico, *1:* 15 (ill.); *2:* 337, 338, 365, 368, 387

V

Valley of Mexico
cities, *2:* 465
defined, *1:* 3
description of, *1:* 14; *2:* 270 (ill.), 461
early Mesoamerican settlements, *2:* 267–68, 272

history of, *2:* 465–66
oral tradition, *2:* 471–72
Van Stone, Mark, *2:* 393, 402
Vega, Garcilaso de la, *1:* 169
Velázquez, Diego, *2:* 534–35, 540–41
Ventilla, Peru, *1:* 77–78
Venus, *2:* 453, 513
Verdadera historia de la conquista de Nueva España (Díaz), *2:* 468–69, 534, 539
Vicuña, *1:* 37, 42, 43
Vigesimal number systems
Aztec, *2:* 511–12
defined, *2:* 300, 392, 502
Maya, *2:* 405–6
Vilcabamba, Peru, *1:* 164–65, 254
Villac Umu, 1: 181, 200, 205–6, 223
Village settlements, *2:* 265–66, 430–31
Viracocha, *1:* 113, 119, 170 (ill.), 171–73, 201–2, 202 (ill.)
Virgins of the Sun, *1:* 206–7, 207 (ill.), 229
Volcanos, *1:* 39
Von Däniken, Erich, *1:* 83
Von Hagen, Adriana, *1:* 67
Von Hagen, V.W., *1:* 227

W

War Gods, *2:* 483
Warfare. *See also* Military forces
Aztec, *2:* 477–78, 483–86, 492–95, 494 (ill.)
Caral and, *1:* 51–52
civil, *1:* 243–47
early Andean, *1:* 55–56
Maya, *2:* 386
Teotihuacán, *2:* 330
Toltec, *2:* 448–50, 450 (ill.), 454, 456
Wari, *1:* 129–30
Wari City, Peru, *1:* 123, 124, 124 (ill.), 128, 135
Wari culture, *1:* 103, 121–36
agriculture, *1:* 128, 129 (ill.), 131
architecture, *1:* 124–28, 125 (ill.)

art and science, *1:* 133–34, 134 (ill.)
decline of, *1:* 134–35
economy, *1:* 130–32
festivals, *1:* 131, 236
government, *1:* 129–30
history, *1:* 128–29
Inca and, *1:* 122–23, 135
location of, *1:* 123–24, 124 (ill.)
Nazca and, *1:* 85
religion, *1:* 132–33
Tiwanaku and, *1:* 105–6, 121, 127–28, 132, 135
Warrior cults, *2:* 443, 449–50, 451, 455, 468, 492
Warrior gods, *2:* 504
Warrior priests, *1:* 95, 95 (ill.), 97
Warriors. *See* Military forces; Warfare
Water sources
  Aztec, *2:* 465
  kingdom of Chimor, *1:* 152–53
  Maya, *2:* 365
  Moche, *1:* 93
  Nazca line drawings and, *1:* 82–84
  Wari, *1:* 128–29
Weapons, *2:* 495
Weaving, *1:* 102, 212–13, 230, 237, 259. *See also* Textiles
Welfare state, *1:* 181, 196
Were-jaguar, *2:* 290, 292
Wheel, *1:* 6
White clay, *2:* 285
White Tezcatlipoca. *See* Quetzalcoatl
Williams, Patrick Ryan, *1:* 131
Wind God (Ehecatl), *2:* 463, 505 (ill.)
Women
  Aztec, *2:* 520, 522
  chosen, *1:* 206–7, 207 (ill.), 208 (ill.), 212
  labor obligations of, *1:* 228, 230
  Maya, *2:* 427, 428–29
  Sapa Inca and, *1:* 182–83
Wool, *1:* 43, 118, 259
Working class
  Aztec, *2:* 491, 494, 497, 499, 523–25
  Caral, *1:* 51
  children of, *1:* 230–31; *2:* 523
  clothing, *1:* 235–36
  daily life of, *1:* 225–36

development of, *1:* 6, 7
festivals for, *1:* 236
food, *1:* 233–35
houses, *1:* 231–33, 231 (ill.); *2:* 427–28, 428 (ill.)
Inca, *1:* 192–94, 196, 203–4, 221, 225–36
labor obligations of, *1:* 227–28
marriage, *1:* 229–31
Maya, *2:* 386, 421, 433–34
Olmec, *2:* 289
Workshops, *2:* 417
World Tree, *2:* 376–77, 382, 400
Wright Codex, *2:* 402
Writing systems. *See also* Glyphs
  Aztec, *2:* 514–20, 515 (ill.)
  development of, *1:* 6
  Maya, *1:* 16; *2:* 271, 341–44, 342 (ill.), 345, 391–96
  Olmec, *2:* 283–84, 293–96, 295 (ill.), 296 (ill.)
  Sumerian, *1:* 9
  Teotihuacán, *2:* 331
  Zapotec, *2:* 303, 310–12

X

Xbalanque, *2:* 376–77
Xi. *See* Olmec culture
Xibalbá, *2:* 375–80
Xihuitl, *2:* 513
Xipe Totec, *2:* 309, 342
Xochicalco, *2:* 445
Xocoatl, *2:* 422, 430–31
Xoloti, *2:* 451

Y

Yahuar Huaca, *1:* 170 (ill.), 171
Yampellec, *1:* 146
Yanaconas, *1:* 222, 228–29
Yax Cha'aktel Xok, *2:* 357
Yax Eb' Xook, *2:* 357
Yax Pasah, *2:* 364–65
Yaxchilan, *2:* 405
Yucatán peninsula, *2:* 335, 341 (ill.)
Yucatec languages, *2:* 344
Yucatecs, *2:* 434
Yum Kaax, *2:* 375
Yupanque, Angelina, *1:* 168

Z

Zacan, 2: 429
Zapotecs, *2:* 299–313
  architecture, *2:* 304–6, 304 (ill.)
  art, *2:* 310, 311 (ill.)
  decline of, *2:* 312–13
  glyphs, *2:* 271
  government and economy, *2:* 306–9
  history of, *1:* 13; *2:* 267, 301–6
  location of, *2:* 301, 302 (ill.)
  Olmec and, *2:* 300
  religion, *2:* 309–10
  science, *2:* 312
  writing and language, *2:* 303, 310–12
Zero, *2:* 406
Ziegler, Gary, *1:* 165
Ziggurat, *1:* 3, 9